The Juvenile Skeleton in Forensic Abuse Investigations

Ann H. Ross · Suzanne M. Abel
Editors

The Juvenile Skeleton in Forensic Abuse Investigations

Humana Press

Editors
Ann H. Ross
Department of Sociology & Anthropology
North Carolina State University
10 Current Drive
Raleigh, North Carolina, USA
ann_ross@ncsu.edu

Suzanne M. Abel
Charleston County Coroner's Office
4050 Bridgeview Drive
Perimeter Center, Suite 500
North Charleston, South Carolina, USA
sabel@charlestoncounty.org

ISBN 978-1-61779-254-0 e-ISBN 978-1-61779-255-7
DOI 10.1007/978-1-61779-255-7
Springer New York Dordrecht Heidelberg London

Library of Congress Control Number: 2011931471

Printed on acid-free paper

Humana Press is part of Springer Science+Business Media (www.springer.com)

To Alex and Evelyn

Contents

Contributors

Suzanne M. Abel Charleston County Coroner's Office, 4050 Bridgeview Drive, Perimeter Center, Suite 500, North Charleston, SC, USA, sabel@charlestoncounty.org

Hugo F.V. Cardoso Museu Nacional de Historia Natural & Centro de Biologia Ambiental, Universidade de Lisboa, Lisbon, Portugal; Faculdade de Medicina, Universidade do Porto, Porto, Portugal, hfcardoso@fc.ul.pt; hcardoso@med.up.pt

Leszek Chrostowski Department of Pathology and Cell Biology, University of South Florida, Tampa, FL, USA; Hillsborough County Medical Examiner Department, Tampa, FL, USA, Chrostowskil@HillsboroughCounty.ORG

Sarah L. Cunningham Department of Anthropology, Binghamton University, Binghamton, NY, USA, Sarah.lynn.cunningham@gmail.com

Cynthia Heldrich Roper Saint Francis Physician Partners, Charleston, SC, USA, cmheldrich@comcast.net

Ashley L. Humphries Department of Sociology and Anthropology, North Carolina State University, Raleigh, NC, USA, alhumphri@gmail.com

Erin H. Kimmerle Department of Anthropology, University of South Florida, Tampa, FL, USA, Kimmerle@usf.edu

Scott A. Kirkland Department of Sociology and Anthropology, North Carolina State University, Raleigh, NC, USA, s.a.kirkland@gmail.com

Teresa Magalhães Faculdade de Medicina & Instituto de Ciências Biomédicas Abel Salazar, Universidade do Porto, Porto, Portugal; Instituto Nacional de Medicina Legal – Delegação do Norte, Porto, Portugal; Centro de Ciências Forenses, Coimbra, Portugal, tmaga@med.up.pt

Kristin M. Montaperto Department of Anthropology, National Museum of Natural History, Smithsonian Institution, Washington, DC, USA, montapek@si.edu

Bobbi Jo O'Neal Charleston County Coroner's Office, North Charleston, SC, USA, boneal@charlestoncounty.org

Krista L. Ragan The North Carolina, Child Fatality Prevention Team/NC OCME, Chapel Hill, NC, USA, kragan@ocme.unc.edu; kris.ragan@gmail.com

Ann H. Ross Department of Sociology and Anthropology, North Carolina State University, Raleigh, NC, USA, ann_ross@ncsu.edu

Jennifer Schindell Linn and Benton County Medical Examiner's Office, Corvallis, OR, USA; Oregon State University, Corvallis, OR, USA, jschindell@le.linn.or.us

Rebecca Sutphin Department of Sociology and Anthropology, North Carolina State University, Raleigh, NC, USA, rysutphi@ncsu.edu

Douglas H. Ubelaker Department of Anthropology, National Museum of Natural History, Smithsonian Institution, Washington, DC, USA, ubelaked@si.edu

Chapter 1
Introduction

Ann H. Ross and Suzanne M. Abel

1.1 Homicides and Abductions of Children

According to the US Department of Health and Human Services, the Administration for Children and Families, in 2005, there were an estimated 1,460 fatalities due to child maltreatment [1]. Of these, 42.2% were as a result of neglect only, 24.1% were caused by physical abuse only, and 27.3% were caused by a combination of types. The remainder of deaths included sexual abuse, psychological abuse, medical neglect, and other unknown causes. Children younger than 4 years accounted for 76.6% of all maltreatment fatalities, with 41.9% of these deaths occurring in infants [1]. Child fatality rates per 100,000 children in the United States for years 2000–2005 are presented in Table 1.1. The data show a slight rising trend between 2000 and 2004 [2].

According to the Juvenile Justice Bulletin [3], in 1999, there were approximately 1,800 juvenile victims of homicide in the United States, which is substantially higher than in any other developed country. Data show that the homicide patterns for young children (<5 years of age), middle childhood (6–11 years of age), and teenagers (12–17 years of age) differ significantly and thus should be evaluated independently [3]. According to this report, most homicides of young children are committed by family members and may be significantly undercounted. During the past 30 years, homicide is the only cause of childhood death that has increased in incidence (homicides of infants and children [0–4 years of age] have risen 50% [4]), while other major causes of death such as congenital abnormalities, accidents, and infectious disease have dropped [3]. According to the US Census Bureau [5], homicide is ranked second, third, or (depending on the specific age group) among the top four causes of childhood mortality. Significantly, more children die of homicide in the 0–4 age group than of infectious disease or cancer.

A.H. Ross (✉)
Department of Sociology and Anthropology, North Carolina State University,
Raleigh, NC 27695, USA
e-mail: ann_ross@ncsu.edu

A.H. Ross, S.M. Abel (eds.), *The Juvenile Skeleton in Forensic Abuse Investigations*,
DOI 10.1007/978-1-61779-255-7_1, © Springer Science+Business Media, LLC 2011

Table 1.1 Child fatality rates per 100,000 children, USA, 2000–2005

Reporting year	Number of child fatalities	Rate per 100,000 children	Estimated child fatalities
2000	1,306	1.84	1,330
2001	1,373	1.96	1,420
2002	1,397	1.99	1,450
2003	1,317	1.92	1,400
2004	1,386	2.03	1,490
2005	1,371	1.96	1,460

Adapted from Child Maltreatment (2004, 2005)

According to the NC Child Fatality Prevention Team 2007 report [6], 65 children were victims of homicide, with the majority or 43% being teens (aged 15–17 years), followed by infants (20%), 1–4-year-olds (15%), 10–14-year-olds (15%), and 5–9-year-olds (6%). Ross et al. [7] found that the peak age-at-death categories were 0–3 months (25%) and 2–6 years (19%), which could reflect newborn stress and coincide developmentally with independent stages, respectively. Toddlers were found to be particularly vulnerable to evoking hostile care from their parents during this developmental phase when they show defiance and self-assertiveness in their attempts to seek autonomy [8]. Their results showed that boys were more likely to die of physical abuse than girls, coinciding with conclusions by Sobsey and coworkers [9], who found that more boys were physically abused than girls. A racial bias was also seen in the results. Chi-square tests for independence showed that not only significantly more ($p < 0.0001$) minority children are dying in North Carolina compared to white or European ancestry children, but also significantly more ($p < 0.0001$) minority children are dying as a result of specifically abusive causes [7].

1.2 Disposal and Discovery of Child Remains

In a 1996 FBI study [10], the disposal of the remains was found to be dependent on the age of the victim and the motivation of the perpetrator. Neonates (0–1 months of age) were found to be abducted for replacement reasons or the intent of keeping the child, and in 79% of these cases, the neonate was abducted by a female and was found alive [10, 11]. The remaining 21% were killed for emotional reasons by their parents, of which 67% were disposed of within a 1–5 mile radius and the remaining 33% were disposed of in the residence [10, 11]. In the infant category (1–12 months of age), in 83% of the cases, children were killed for emotional reasons, typically by their biological parents in the residence and disposed of within 5 miles. In the remaining 17% of the cases, the infants were disposed of 5–10 miles from the residence [10, 11]. Toddlers (13–36 months) were primarily killed by a family member (82%) for emotional reasons (90%) and disposed of within 1 mile in 56% of the cases and within 1–5 miles in 22% of the cases. For preschoolers (3–5 years of age), the motivation was divided between emotional based in 54% of the cases, sex based in 30%, and profit based in 16%. In all motivation categories, the victims were disposed of within 100 yards of the offense site in 58% of the cases, within 5–10 miles in 17% of the cases, and within 10–30 miles in 30% of the cases [10, 11]. Generally, it was found that the younger the victim, the closer to the victim's residence the remains were discovered [12].

1.3 Purpose of the Book

These alarming statistics as well as a recent upsurge in media attention to all matters forensic has underscored the need for increased scientific attention and rigor in child abuse cases. The popularity of televised tracking of child abductions and fatalities in the United States has acted to give viewers an *entrée* to the deeper academic, investigative, and collective methodology of those involved in such casework. To address these matters, we have gathered a collection of topics that detail the finer points of investigations surrounding juvenile fatalities under the suspicion of child abuse.

The precise reason why many professionals enter this arena of investigation is, of course, personal and individual. However, at the core of our work is a shared need for simple justice. Victim advocacy and protection of rights of children, both living and deceased, remain a large impetus for those who specialize in child abuse research. This book aims to provide some level of agency, or purposeful voice, for those who cannot stand up and speak for themselves.

1.4 The Holistic Approach

Cases involving child abuse require a multidisciplinary investigative approach. Local law enforcement, death investigators, and crime scene specialists will be the first officials called to the scene. These individuals work closely with the coroner or medical examiner who is the legal authority and whose office acts as a hub to which a large group of consulting specialists will report their individual findings. Pathologists, forensic anthropologists, forensic odontologists, radiologists, and pediatricians work with or for the coroner/medical examiner to provide vital information on the physical status of the victim.

The chapters in this volume reflect this holistic approach as anthropologists and various personnel from medical examiner's and coroner's offices have contributed their individual professional input to juvenile death investigation.

Ragan (Chapter 2) opens with a concise historical timeline of child abuse and then introduces the complexity of determining an accurate incidence of child abuse and neglect. Humphries (Chapter 3) follows with an overview of juvenile skeletal anatomy and growth and development. Ubelaker and Montaperto (Chapter 4) discuss how biomechanical growth and remodeling processes in the juvenile skeleton differ from that found in the adult. They also discuss how knowledge of such features can help reveal the nature and subsequent interpretation of juvenile trauma as well as the timing of fracture events. Continuing the discussion of trauma, Heldrich (Chapter 5) provides a clinical perspective in her discussion of the physical expression of birth trauma in the newborn. She also gives a list of differential diagnoses and conditions that lead to bone fragility. Abel (Chapter 6) underscores the importance of distinguishing between accidental and nonaccidental skeletal trauma, not only for the identification of individuals but also for the possible circumstances surrounding the death event. Schindell and O'Neal (Chapter 7) provide an applied approach to basic scene investigation procedures and discuss the application of these procedures in some of the unique situations commonly encountered in child death investigations, including shaken baby syndrome. Kimmerle and Chrostowski (Chapter 8) discuss the various medicolegal issues of battered baby syndrome through a case presentation. They also present some of the general trends among such cases that illustrate the difficulty in employing this syndrome as a diagnosis. Cardoso and Magalhães (Chapter 9) provide a detailed discussion on evidence of neglect from the assessment of growth differentials in immature human skeletal and dental structures. The authors offer two general approaches for the detection of growth failure from observations in bone and teeth. Ross (Chapter 10) presents a case study illustrating the utility of several biological indicators including bone mineral density in the medicolegal investigation of fatal starvation, a severe form of neglect. She underscores the importance of using multiple lines of evidence such as complete social, medical, and investigative history in order to rule on a cause and manner of death. Sutphin and Ross (Chapter 11) report on the estimation of stature for a juvenile Chilean population. Juvenile stature estimation can be particularly useful in the forensic setting, which may have applications for use as a proxy for nutritional health and possible neglect. Cunningham, Kirkland, and Ross (Chapter 12) provide the results of a short-term study utilizing pig carcasses as juvenile human proxies in order to study osteological decompositional changes occurring within a year in the central Piedmont region of North Carolina. Such taphonomical alterations in intrinsic and extrinsic bone architecture assist the investigator in determining postmortem interval for outdoor depositions of juvenile remains and have implications for the southeastern United States.

References

1. Administration for Children and Families, US Department of Health and Human Services. 2005. Child Maltreatment Annual Report. Available in: http://www.acf.hhs.gov/programs/cb/pubs/cm05/index.htm (accessed February 21, 2010).
2. Administration for Children and Families, US Department of Health and Human Services. 2004. Child Maltreatment Annual Report. Available in: http://www.acf.hhs.gov/programs/cb/pubs/cm04/index.htm (accessed February 21, 2010).
3. Office of Juvenile Justice and Delinquency Prevention, US Department of Justice. 2001. Juvenile Justice Bulletin. Available in: http://www.ncjrs.gov/html/ojjdp/jjbul2001_7_3/contents.html (accessed February 20, 2010).

4. Finkelhor D. 1997. The victimization of children and youth: Developmental victimology. In: Davis RC, Lurigio AJ, Skogan WG, editors. Victims of crime (2nd edition). Thousand Oaks, CA: Sage, pp 86–107.
5. U.S. National Center for Health Statistics, US Census Bureau. 2006. Deaths and death rates by leading causes of death and age Available at: http://www.census.gov/compendia/statab/2010/tables/10s0117.pdf (accessed on February 27, 2010).
6. NC Child Fatality Prevention Team. 2007. A summary and analysis of child deaths investigated by the Office of the Chief Medical Examiner and reviewed by the Child Fatality Prevention Team. Available in: http://www.ocme.unc.edu/nccfpp/index.shtml (accessed February 20, 2010).
7. Ross A, Abel S, Radisch D. 2009. Pattern of injury in child fatalities resulting from child abuse. Forensic Sci Int 188: 99–102.
8. Belsky J. 1993. Etiology of child maltreatment: Developmental ecological analysis. Psychol Bull 114: 413–434.
9. Sobsey D, Randall W, Parrila RK. 1997. Gender differences in abused children with and without disabilities. Child Abuse Neglect 21: 707–720.
10. Boudreaux MC, Lord W, Dutra RL. 1999. Child abduction: Age-based analysis of offender, victim, and offense characteristics in 550 cases of alleged child disappearances. J Forensic Sci 44: 539–553.
11. Morton RJ, Lord WD. 2002. Detection and recovery of abducted and murdered children: Behavioral and taphonomic influences. In: Haglund WD, Sorg MH, editors. Advances in forensic taphonomy: Method, theory, and archaeological perspectives. Boca Raton, FL: CRC Press, pp 151–171.
12. Hanfland KA, Keppel RD, Weis JD. 1997. Case management for missing children homicide investigation. Olympia, WA: Attorney General of Washington.

Chapter 2
Fatal Child Maltreatment: The Challenges of Identifying the Causes and Incidence of Deaths from Abuse and Neglect

Krista L. Ragan

Abstract To many, it is almost unfathomable that a parent is capable of intentionally injuring or murdering their own child. However, history has shown us that abuse and murder of an offspring was acceptable under various conditions in many societies from ancient times through the 20th century. While the past is dotted with social and legal responses to child abuse, widespread interest and study of the topic did not truly begin until the early 1960s. Since that time, much effort has been devoted to determine what causes child abuse and neglect. While a good deal has been learned over the past 50 years, child maltreatment is still an ambiguous field of study. Even with our improved dedication to identifying and understanding the problem of child abuse and neglect, our knowledge of the issue is hampered by the complexity of the problem not only as it occurs but also in our ability to adequately measure the true incidence of child maltreatment.

My relationship with Mom drastically changed from discipline to punishment that grew out of control. It became so bad at times, I had no strength to crawl away – even if it meant saving my life.
Dave Pelzer, A Child Called It [1]

2.1 A Brief History of Child Maltreatment

Child maltreatment in its various forms is well documented throughout history as are child deaths, which were not unexpected due to the prevalence of illness, disease, and accidents. However, as far back as ancient times the first test for a newborn after surviving the trauma of childbirth was not disease, rather surviving their parents or the rules of society. Many cultures thought of infanticide as an acceptable means of keeping a family or society healthy or as a means of controlling the population [2–4]. Infanticide also occurred when the parents decided they did not want the child and they had the right to destroy their own property (as children were property at

K.L. Ragan (✉)
The North Carolina, Child Fatality Prevention Team/NC OCME, Chapel Hill, NC 27599-7580, USA
e-mail: kragan@ocme.unc.edu; kris.ragan@gmail.com

A.H. Ross, S.M. Abel (eds.), *The Juvenile Skeleton in Forensic Abuse Investigations*,
DOI 10.1007/978-1-61779-255-7_2,

that time), when the child was illegitimate, or when the infant failed to pass a test of hardiness [2, 3]. Of note, today, the term infanticide is applied only to infants under the age of 1 year [5], but prior to the 20th century, infanticide applied to children between the ages of birth and 7 years [2, 3].

In the Middle Ages, children were considered liabilities due to widespread poverty [4]. In the 16th and 17th centuries, it appears that children became valued for exploitive purposes. Children were sent to work in factories and mills, and sent into the streets as beggars and prostitutes to provide for their families. [2, 4]. The concept of neglect came into existence in the 18th century in England, mostly as the result of widespread alcohol abuse by parents and others [2].

During the time of the Industrial Revolution, child labor, poverty, and the working class grew [4, 6] as did child maltreatment. Children were still considered property of the parents, and the expectations of children included obedience, respect, and good behavior. It was felt that beatings were necessary to ensure that a child was morally sound, and severe physical punishment, short of death, was acceptable under the law [2]. At the same time, more emphasis was placed on education, and corporal punishment was utilized in schools [4]. It wasn't until the 19th century that change began to occur. Child labor laws were initiated; the family group, coming from communal living in the 17th century, was now an established societal unit; and concerns about the welfare of children increased as literary portrayals by several authors widened the spotlight on the treatment of children [2].

The recognition of the need to protect children was rather piecemeal over time, but has seen rapid growth over the last century and a half [6]. Though there was some attention paid by the courts and even a physician researching child abuse fatalities [3], one of the most recognized cases that led to change occurred in 1874 in New York City [2, 3, 6]. A woman, overhearing the screams of a child being abused, searched for assistance, only to find nothing could be done. The woman turned to an unlikely source, The New York Society for the Prevention of Cruelty to Animals. Arguing that if the child was being denied justice as a human, then the child should at least have the right of an animal not to be abused [2], and advocacy for child protection in the United States was born.

Change continued, as medical knowledge advanced rapidly and social and political action improved living conditions, education, and work opportunities. Child mortality rates declined considerably as a result. The fields of psychology and social sciences began to flourish, and with them the understanding of psychological and emotional development grew as well. These advances led to the recognition that the well-being of children was vital to the future [2]. Subsequently, the abuse and exploitation of children became less accepted socially, and work toward understanding and preventing child abuse began.

It was the seminal article entitled "The Battered-Child Syndrome" authored by Kempe, Silverman, Steele, Droegemueller, & Silver and published in the *Journal of the American Medical Association* in 1962 that has been credited as having the most significant impact on child abuse in professional settings and increasing public awareness of child abuse [3–5]. The article addressed child abuse through medical and psychiatric models [3]. The National Committee for Prevention of Child

Abuse reported that national polls in the mid-1970s showed that only 10% of the general population considered child abuse a serious problem, but 90% of the population started considering it a serious problem by the 1980s [7]. Today, hundreds of advocacy organizations exist across the world to advance children's rights. The United Nations Children's Fund (UNICEF) created the Convention on the Rights of the Child, a legally binding international agreement that specifically addresses in Article 19 the rights of the child to be kept safe from violence and abuse while in the custody of a parent or caregiver [8]. Research and investigation into child abuse and neglect are routinely conducted in a variety of fields including but not limited to psychology, medicine, sociology, and anthropology. And in many countries and almost every state in the United States, child death review teams have been created, charged with reviewing actual child death cases, mainly those due to abuse and/or neglect, and to identify how to prevent similar deaths in the future.

2.2 Child Maltreatment

2.2.1 Incidence

Child maltreatment is recognized as a complex global problem. The estimates of the incidence of maltreatment vary. The World Health Organization (WHO) reports that approximately 31,000 children under the age of 15 years are victims of homicide every year, and international studies have found that 25–50% of children reported being physically abused [9]. In the United States, the National Child Abuse and Neglect Data System (NCANDS) estimated that 772,000 million children were victims of maltreatment in 2008 [10] and that approximately 1,740 children died as a result of child maltreatment that year [11]. However, these numbers do not accurately reflect the actual incidence of child maltreatment, and the number of children who die from child abuse and neglect, in the United States and worldwide, is unknown [9, 12]. Many factors are cited in creating the challenges of understanding, classifying, and measuring child maltreatment, including the definition of child maltreatment [3–6, 9, 12, 13], the country reporting the maltreatment [9], the types of maltreatment being studied, and the types and quality of the research [5, 9, 12].

2.2.2 Definitions

One of the greatest difficulties in studying the causes of child abuse and neglect is a lack of a strong and consistent definition of what actually constitutes the broadest and most recent terminology, child maltreatment. Much of the literature expounds upon this hindrance [3–5, 9, 12, 13]. Bartol proffered that terms and concepts are often broad and ambiguous with inconsistent application in the field of family violence (which includes child abuse) [5]. Steele's appraisal of child maltreatment concludes that human behavior involves traumatic interactions between a child and a parent, caregiver, or stranger [14].

Even global organizations and governments have not agreed upon a common definition. The WHO [9] defines child (under the age of 18 years) maltreatment as

> all types of physical and/or emotional ill-treatment, sexual abuse, neglect, negligence and commercial or other exploitation, which results in actual or potential harm to the child's health, survival, development or dignity in the context of a relationship of responsibility, trust or power. Exposure to intimate partner violence is also sometimes included as a form of child maltreatment.

In the United States, the Child Abuse Prevention and Treatment Act (as amended in 2003) defines the minimum standard of child maltreatment as

> Any recent act or failure to act on the part of a parent or caretaker which results in death, serious physical or emotional harm, sexual abuse or exploitation; or, an act or failure to act which presents an imminent risk of serious harm.

Furthermore, the above definition is only the minimum set forth by the federal government; each state is able to create its own definition of child abuse and neglect based on these minimum standards [15].

2.2.3 Fatal Child Maltreatment

Some may expect that a death from child maltreatment should be rather obvious. The mention of "Child Abuse Homicide" brings to mind injuries such as head trauma and rib fractures, but the deaths that fall into this category are much broader. Researchers cite similar issues in fatal and nonfatal child maltreatment but add that the process of correctly identifying fatal child maltreatment suffers from variations in death investigations, differences among child death review processes, and limited coding options for child deaths through the International Classification of Disease (ICD) codes [12]. Scott et al. [16] also suggest that death certificate data underestimate the number of abuse-related deaths from 55 to 90%, depending on the study [16].

The issues of classification of fatal child maltreatment are broad. Some assert that the numbers of maltreatment fatalities are underestimated because the deaths are incorrectly attributed to falls, drowning, or other causes [9]. Other issues with identifying the role of maltreatment in a death may be that fatal child maltreatment may be a result of chronic abuse over time or may involve a single impulsive or planned incident [12]. It can be a direct result of a caregiver's action, or a result of the caregiver's failure to act. The neglect may be chronic or acute. Neglect to the point of a death being certified as a homicide may include starvation but may also include improper supervision so irresponsible that death could be an expected result, such as leaving an infant unattended in a bathtub for 30 min. National data for the United States found that 40% of the child maltreatment deaths were caused by multiple forms of maltreatment with neglect accounting for over 30% and physical abuse for over 20% of the deaths [11].

Returning to the issue of definitions, NCANDS defines "child fatality" as the death of a child caused by an injury resulting from abuse or neglect, or where abuse or neglect was a contributing factor [12]. This in itself is confusing as the word "fatal" can be defined as "causing death" [17] (not specifically by maltreatment) and "child" is generally accepted to mean a human between the ages of birth and 18 years. Therefore, child fatality means the death of a person under the age of 18 years, which includes deaths from disease, drowning, and other means that may or may not be related to child abuse or neglect.

As noted earlier, studies have found that classification of deaths by using ICD codes on death certificates greatly underestimates the number of deaths due to maltreatment [12, 16, 18] because the deaths are incorrectly attributed to things such as drowning or falls, not neglect or abuse. However, it should be noted that the purpose of the death certificate is to record the actual mechanism or disease process that caused the death and the manner in which the death has occurred. The standard manners of death in the field of forensic pathology are accident, homicide, suicide, natural, and undetermined [19]. These classifications are to indicate how the death came about. For instance, in a firearm fatality, the cause of death would be a gunshot wound, however the manner of death could be categorized as accident (a 2-year-old shoots himself in the head), suicide (a teen distraught over sexual abuse shoots herself), or homicide (a father shoots his children so the mother cannot have them after she is granted custody by the court). In the above examples, the role of the pathologist is to determine (1) whether or not it was the gunshot wound that killed the person and (2) whether the death was the result of the decedent's actions (and knowledge of potential injury) or the actions of another person. If you look closely, all cases could be attributed to child maltreatment. The first is a toddler having access to a firearm, the second could be a child who did not receive much needed mental health services, and the third is the parent taking the life of the child. The role of a pathologist or medical examiner is to determine the cause and manner of death, sorting out the role of neglect or the relationship of the person who inflicted an injury generally falls to the other entities involved in the investigation of a death or to a review team who takes a more in-depth examination of the life and death of the child.

For example, in North Carolina, the State Child Fatality Prevention Team (CFPT) reviews all medical examiner cases, which include accidents, homicides, suicides, deaths in undetermined manner, and deaths that were sudden and unexpected. In the course of a review, maltreatment is assigned as a contributing or causal factor in the death. In cases of homicides, the State Team utilizes the term "Homicide by Parent or Caregiver" [20]. The data are included in national child abuse numbers, but the deaths are examined in a way to determine what factors were involved, as deaths may be classified as maltreatment, but preventing an intentional asphyxiation death of a colicky infant is very different than a man who kills his children as a means of inflicting the ultimate pain on his ex-wife.

Data showing the number of deaths from maltreatment in the United States is woefully inadequate, not just because of the lack of a definition but also due to the sources of information. The Every Child Matters Education Fund report on child maltreatment fatalities reported 26 children had died from abuse and neglect in North Carolina between 2001 and 2007 [21]. Examination of the NC CFPT reports for 2005 [20] and 2007 [22] showed that this 8-year total was equivalent to the 3-year *average* of homicides by parent or caregiver for the state. As the NC CFPT reports also indicate over 100 classifications of contributory neglect each year, one could assert that the national data sources underreport the magnitude of fatalities from child maltreatment.

2.2.4 Factors in Child Maltreatment

As difficult as child maltreatment and maltreatment deaths are to define and measure, the determination of what causes abuse and neglect seems more complex. Child maltreatment is an issue that cuts across the fields of medicine, sociology, law, psychology, child development, religion, psychiatry, biology, and anthropology [14]. Researchers maintain that no single factor or set of factors have been identified as causing child maltreatment [23] and that child maltreatment occurs through a number of complex processes in multiple contexts [7, 14, 23–25]. Initial studies were noted to be psychiatric in nature, focusing on parent psychopathology [3, 4, 26]. Zigler and Hall [4] warn that this view has been discouraged by studies that indicate that only a small fraction of abusers are mentally ill and that it is a dangerous theory as it purports that all mentally ill are potential child abusers [4]. More recent research trends toward ecological or social–ecological models. These models conclude that child maltreatment is a result of complex interactions between the child, parents, family, and society [4, 13, 23–26].

The recent economic conditions provide the setting for an example of this model:

> A child is born prematurely into a family with 3 other children. This child has additional needs and the medical bills are mounting. Due to the economy, the father loses his job. He is now at home, bringing in a fraction of his income from unemployment. The unemployment rates are high, and the father, who has been working since he was a teenager, has not been able to find a job in 6 months and is now questioning his worth as an employee and a provider. The family who now has no insurance, turned to a community agency to get the developmental services needed for their infant and Medicaid for the other children. The community agency provides those programs based on funds from the state. The federal government cuts funding to the states, the states cut funding to the communities. The family loses access to the services and assistance needed for their children. Now the father cannot find a job, cannot provide for his family, is at home with a child with special needs who is not getting the necessary services.

This example is used to illustrate the interrelationships of the factors that may affect child maltreatment. Both neglect and physical abuse could be produced under these circumstances, but as others have noted, we must be wary of applying information obtained through research to individual cases. Several caveats were found throughout the literature (aside from the lack of a definition) regarding the available data on child maltreatment. Researchers acknowledge that the variables and characteristics identified in child maltreatment are done so in aggregate and may not be indicative of abuse in individual cases [13, 23]. Additionally, the need for more research is prominent, from longitudinal studies [13, 26], to broader populations [26], to developmental stages in relationship to the types of abuse and neglect [23]. A further caveat includes the role of cultural and societal beliefs in determining the perceptions of what is considered child abuse and what it is not. Therefore, some of the risk factors identified may not be applicable in certain cultures and societies [9, 15].

2.2.5 Child Characteristics

Belsky and Vondra [25] indicate that child characteristics should be considered in conjunction with parental characteristics when examining parenting and the role it may play in child maltreatment [25]. The most solid child characteristic for child maltreatment victimization is the age of the child. Research has shown that children 4 years of age and younger are the most frequent victims of child abuse [9, 11], while the curve swings back up in adolescence [9]. NCANDS data for 2008 showed that children younger than 1 year accounted for 45% of fatalities, while children younger than 4 years accounted for nearly 80% of fatalities [11]. Younger children may be at greater risk for child abuse fatalities for many reasons, including their dependency and vulnerability [11]. Racial and ethnic information has been noted to increase the risk for child maltreatment; however, some studies indicate that when other variables, such as poverty, are controlled for, this correlation diminishes [10]. Others warn that reporting bias is the reason for correlation between race and child maltreatment [4]. Children born as the result of an unwanted pregnancy or children with particular needs, such as excessive crying or physical problems, have also been noted to be at increased risk for abuse [9].

2.2.6 Characteristics of the Parent or Caregiver

The 2008 child death data reported that child maltreatment deaths occurred at the hands of a parent either alone or with another person in 71% of the deaths, and the deaths from physical abuse occurred at the hands of the father or male caregiver, while the mother is responsible in the majority of deaths from neglect [11]. Studies from the 1960s and the 1980s showed that mothers were the perpetrators of abuse in almost half of maltreatment cases, but when an adult male was present in the home, the male was the perpetrator in two-third of the cases [4]. While the report indicates that there is no single profile of a perpetrator of child maltreatment, it does indicate that certain characteristics have been identified through research. These characteristics include that the perpetrator is a young adult in his or her 20s, with a low education level [4, 11], living at or below poverty level, depressed, may have difficulty with stressful situations, or may have experienced violence first-hand [11].

Other studies have centered on the mother and her interactions with the child. Mersky et al. [23] reported that maternal age at the time of child birth was the most reliable predictor of maltreatment [23]. Additional information has indicated that the mother's unwillingness or inability to bond with a newborn or nurture a child may show a potential for abuse [9, 14, 25]. Examining the work of Bowlby and later work by Answorth on attachment, Steele [14] notes that infants will, out of necessity for survival, begin to bond to "whomever fate" has given the child as a primary caregiver [14]. He states that the mother has no such necessity to provide for the child, and instead, her bonding to the child is based on a number of factors including her own social history, the circumstances of the pregnancy, and her relationship with the father of the child. This view is of particular interest in reference to infanticide. A mother's unwillingness or inability to bond with a newborn is evident in the number of "abandoned infants" found, either alive or deceased, throughout the United States each year.

Many studies cite stress as a factor in maltreatment. Stress may stem from circumstances that include criminal behavior [9], financial strain [4, 9], marital or relationship issues [9, 27], and isolation [4, 9, 27]. Stress may increase when a parent has limited knowledge of development or unrealistic expectations. Parents who lack understanding of child development may become frustrated when an infant or a child is developmentally appropriate but the parent is not prepared to deal with the stages of development [4, 9, 27]. Additionally, parents may have unrealistic expectations of an infant or a child and again may become frustrated because the child is not behaving in a manner that is expected [4, 9, 26, 27]. Another identified factor is parental views, such as how much control the infant or child has of the relationship [4, 27]. Compounding these issues may be the caregiver's ability (or inability) to manage anger and deal with frustration and the lack development of coping skills the parent needs in dealing with stressors [4, 27]. Research has also indicated that characteristics of abusers include the inability of the caregiver to understand the complexities of social interactions such as the needs of others [24].

Additional research has been conducted on the roles of pre-existing cognitive schemas (i.e., beliefs about discipline and child interactions) and contextual (external) factors in child maltreatment. Supporting the theories about the complex interactions between the individual, family, and society, Rodriguez and Richardson [27] found that the schemas and contextual factors most likely influence each other when examining the potential of an individual to commit child maltreatment [27]. They also noted that cognitive factors were no better at predicting the potential for child maltreatment than contextual factors.

Examining some of the contextual or environmental factors in abuse, social learning theory looks at the perceptions, thoughts, expectancies, competencies, and values in order to understand why a person behaves in a certain manner. Thus, each person has his or her own version of the world and lives within that realm [5]. Bandura's work in the 1960s and 1970s was the foundation of many additional studies that have found that children who observed a behavior modeled by an adult would repeat that behavior [5].

2.2.7 Abuse and Neglect in Childhood

Whether referred to as "generational repetition," "intergenerational transmission," or the "cycle of violence," the theory that children who are victims of child abuse or neglect may go on to be perpetrators of abuse or neglect has been a leading topic of study and discussion. It has been reported that approximately one-third of abused and neglected children will go on to eventually victimize their own children [28]. Recent studies have identified maltreatment during childhood as an indicator that a person will perpetrate violence later in life [29], while others report that this is actually a result of early maltreatment causing a disruption in brain development [1, 5].

Steele indicated that generational maltreatment can be subtle and varied, but often includes a sense of justification or identification with the abuser [14]. Zigler and Hall [4] indicate, however, that this theory has never been adequately supported and that to the contrary, the evidence is revealing that the "cycle" can be broken [4]. Steele also asserted that a quarter of abusers will be diagnosed as such, but many will develop other kinds of relationship problems or personality disorders. He notes that those who maltreat often have a significant history of neglect, with or without abuse, in his or her childhood, which may lead to long-term emotional and psychological effects leading to issues that result in generational repetition of maltreatment [14].

2.2.8 Community and Societal Factors

Building outward from the child to the parent/caregiver to the immediate social structures, there are additional factors that may contribute to child abuse. In the immediate family structure, the physical, developmental, or mental health problems of a family member may cause additional stress on caregivers or finances [9]. A breakdown in family relationships [9, 27] or violence between other family members can also contribute to the potential for abuse [9]. When the primary caregiver is isolated or is lacking a supportive network, the situation again can become available for child maltreatment [9, 13, 25, 27].

Much of the literature indicates that lack of economic resources be it at the family, community, or societal level is associated with child abuse and neglect [7, 9, 13, 23, 26]. Economic issues at the family level may increase stress and affect staples such as adequate food or housing. At the community, state, and federal levels, access to and support of services for families and children may be restricted in times of a downed economy. Furthermore, inadequate support of education and health policies or inadequate programs to prevent child maltreatment are societal stressors that may contribute to child maltreatment. [9]. Garbarino [7] notes that economic deprivation and poverty increase the risk for maltreatment, that the correlations may be a reflection of social policy, and that child maltreatment is a symptom of a community in trouble, not just a problem of an individual or a family [7].

Larger issues, such as cultural values and religious beliefs, have also been documented as contributing factors in child maltreatment [15]. When gender roles are strictly defined, when the parent–child relationship is restricted, and when there is a lack of social equality, child abuse risk increases [9]. A society that elevates or accepts violence as a routine and necessary part of life will also increase the likelihood of child maltreatment [9]. However, as mentioned earlier, due to the numerous cultures and beliefs worldwide, what one culture believes to be maltreatment may be accepted as normal treatment in another.

2.3 Discussion

Society as a whole has come far in realizing the atrocities of child maltreatment. Behaviors once believed to be acceptable are now subject to social and legal repercussions. Advocacy groups, professionals, and the public have elevated addressing child maltreatment to the forefront of social issues, and research has contributed much to our ability to identify, within whatever definitions are being utilized, child abuse and neglect. The research shows that there is no single cause of child maltreatment, but instead it is multifactorial and occurs through complex processes on a variety of levels. Further research, based on widely accepted definitions and performed through rigorous standards, is necessary to move past associations to finding strong correlations and the causes of child abuse and neglect.

References

1. Pelzer D. A child called it. Deerfield Beach, FL: Health Communications, 1995.
2. Ten Bensel RW, Rheinberger MM, Radbill SX. Children in a world of violence: the roots of child maltreatment. In: Helfer ME, Kempe RS, Krugman, RD, editors. The battered child. 5th rev. ed. Chicago: University of Chicago, 1997; 3–28.
3. http://www.naccchildlaw.org/?page=ChildMaltreatment
4. Zigler E, Hall NW. Physical child abuse in America: past, present and future. In: Cicchetti D, Carlson V, editors. Child maltreatment: theory and research on the causes and consequences of child abuse and neglect. New York, NY: Cambridge, 1997; 38–75.
5. Bartol CR. Criminal behavior: a psychosocial approach. 6th ed. Upper Saddle River, NJ: Prentice Hall, 2002.
6. Giovannoni J. Definitional issues in child maltreatment. In: Cicchetti D, Carlson V, editors. Child maltreatment: theory and research on the causes and consequences of child abuse and neglect. New York, NY: Cambridge, 1997; 3–37.
7. Garbarino J. The role of economic deprivation in the social context of child maltreatment. In: Helfer ME, Kempe RS, Krugman, RD, editors. The battered child. 5th rev. ed. Chicago, IL: University of Chicago, 1997; 49–60.
8. http://www2.ohchr.org/english/law/crc.htm
9. Child maltreatment. 2010 Aug. Fact Sheet No.: 150. World Health Organization. http://www.who.int/mediacentre/factsheets/fs150/en/print.html
10. http://www.acf.hhs.gov/programs/cb/pubs/cm08/chapter3.htm#backnotesix
11. Child abuse and neglect fatalities: statistics and interventions. 2010 Apr. Child Welfare Information Gateway. www.childwelfare.gov/pubs/factsheets/fatality.pdf
12. Child abuse and neglect fatalities: statistics and interventions. 2008 Jun. Child Welfare Information Gateway. www.child.welfare.gov/pubs/factsheets/fatality.cfm
13. Kolko DJ. Child physical abuse. In: Myers JEB, Berliner L, Briere J, Hendrix CT, Jenny C, Reid TA, editors. The APSAC handbook on child maltreatment, 2nd ed. 2002; 21–54.
14. Steele BF. Psychodynamic and biological factors in child maltreatment. In: Helfer ME, Kempe RS, Krugman, RD, editors. The battered child. 5th rev. ed. Chicago: University of Chicago, 1997; 73–103.

15. What is child abuse and neglect? 2008 Apr. Child Welfare Information Gateway. www.childwelfare.gov/pubs/factsheets/whatiscan.cfm
16. Scott D, Tonmyr L, Fraser J, Walker S, McKenzie K. The utility and challenges of using ICD codes in child maltreatment research. A review of existing literature. Child Abuse Negl 2009 Nov; 33 (11): 791–808.
17. http://www.merriam-webster.com/dictionary/fatal
18. Herman-Giddens ME, Brown G, Verbiest S, Carlson PJ, Hooten EG, Howell E, Butts JD. Underascertainment of child abuse mortality in the United States. JAMA 2000; 283: 337–338
19. http://thename.org/index2.php?option=com_docman&task=doc_view&gid=27&Itemid=26
20. The North Carolina Child Fatality Prevention Team. Fatalities of children in North Carolina: 2005 report. 2007. www.ocme.unc.edu/nccfpp/index.shtml
21. Every Child Matters Education Fund. We can do better: child abuse and neglect deaths in America. Washington, DC: Every Child Matters Education Fund, 2009.
22. The North Carolina Child Fatality Prevention Team. Fatalities of children in North Carolina: 2007 Report. 2009.
23. Mersky JP, Berger LM, Reynolds AJ, Gromoske AN. Risk factors for child and adolescent maltreatment: a longitudinal investigation of a cohort of inner-city youth. Child Maltreat 2009; 14: 73–88.
24. Pianta R, Egeland B, Erickson MF. The antecedents of maltreatment: results of the mother-child interaction project. In: Cicchetti D, Carlson V, editors. Child maltreatment: theory and research on the causes and consequences of child abuse and neglect. New York, NY: Cambridge, 1997; 203–253.
25. Belsky J, Vondra J. Lessons from child abuse: the determinants of parenting. In: Cicchetti D, Carlson V, editors. Child maltreatment: theory and research on the causes and consequences of child abuse and neglect. New York, NY: Cambridge, 1997; 153–202.
26. Ammerman RT, Herson M, editors. Children at risk: an evaluation of factors contributing to child abuse and neglect. New York, NY: Plenum, 1990.
27. Rodriguez CM, Richardson MJ. Stress and anger as contextual factors and preexisting cognitive schemas: predicting parental child maltreatment risk. Child Maltreat 2007; 12: 325–337.
28. Widom CS, Maxfield MG. An update on the “cycle of violence”. Washington, DC: National Institute of Justice; 2001 Feb. Report No.: NCJ 184894.
29. Long term consequences of child abuse and neglect. 2008 Apr. Child Welfare Information Gateway. www.childwelfare.gov/pubs/factsheets/long_term_consequences.cfm

[illegible]

Chapter 3
Basic Juvenile Skeletal Anatomy and Growth and Development

Ashley L. Humphries

Abstract Timely and accurate assessment of skeletal remains is integral to the progression of medicolegal death investigations, including cases involving child maltreatment. These cases have legal implications that could potentially send the innocent to prison or set the guilty free if the assessment is not made correctly. The skeleton can provide useful information regarding an individual's health and disease and evidence of trauma. The juvenile skeleton is characterized by nutrition-dependent rapid growth. It differs from the adult skeleton in several ways including anatomy and morphology, physiology, and biomechanics. Since the juvenile skeleton is in a constant state of change, bone morphology will vary depending on the age and phase of development. Integral to investigating child maltreatment is the ability to recognize abnormalities. Since the juvenile skeleton is very different from that of an adult, an investigator who is not well trained in juvenile skeletal anatomy may overlook important evidence or misdiagnose. Therefore, it is essential for researchers investigating the juvenile skeleton to have an understanding of skeletal growth and development and juvenile skeletal anatomy to accurately and efficiently locate and evaluate a set of remains.

3.1 Introduction

In 2008, the U.S. Department of Health and Human Services reported that 772,000 children were victims of maltreatment. Of these, 71% were classified as victims of neglect, 16% as victims of physical abuse, 9% as victims of sexual abuse, and 7% as victims of emotional abuse [1, 2]. In 2008, an estimated 1,740 children died as a result of neglect and abuse [1, 2]. Of these, 80% of the deaths occurred among children younger than 4 years of age, 10% in children between 4 and 7 years, 4% in children between 8 and 11 years, and 2% in children between 16 and 17 [1, 2]. Since the human skeleton is capable of providing information about

A.L. Humphries (✉)
Department of Sociology and Anthropology, North Carolina State University, Raleigh, NC 27695, USA
e-mail: alhumphri@gmail.com

A.H. Ross, S.M. Abel (eds.), *The Juvenile Skeleton in Forensic Abuse Investigations*,
DOI 10.1007/978-1-61779-255-7_3,

what happened to a person during their life, the skeleton can yield crucial information regarding child maltreatment. For example, it can tell us about a child's health, disease, whether trauma occurred to the bone, and the timing of trauma. In order for an investigator to recognize vital information regarding the health and welfare of a child, one must first have a complete understanding of the juvenile skeleton, what is considered normal, and how juvenile remains differ from the adult skeleton.

The human skeleton serves a number of functions including providing shape, support, and protection for vital soft tissue organs. In addition, it allows movement, produces blood cells, and stores vital vitamins and minerals that are important for bodily function. The human skeleton can also provide a wealth of information about the person to whom they belong. It can provide important evidence in medicolegal death investigations including the identification of unknown remains and child abuse. It holds information regarding an individual's biological sex, age-at-death, ancestral origins, health and disease, and evidence of trauma. Forensic investigations involving juvenile remains are very sensitive, especially when child abuse is suspected as misdiagnosis may send innocent caregivers to prison or, conversely, allow the guilty to walk free. Understanding the juvenile skeleton is essential for proper and timely recovery, identification, analyses of remains, and case resolution in child abuse–related investigations. For example, recovery of juvenile remains can prove difficult if those employed to search for the remains cannot recognize the features and bones that make up the juvenile skeleton. They may become confused if confronted with nonhuman remains, or disregard the remains altogether.

Baker et al. [3] have noted that many osteology courses lack training in juvenile skeletal identification. Rang and Wenger [4] stated it perfectly with their book chapter titled "Children Are Not Just Small Adults." Therefore, having been trained in the identification and methods associated only with the adult skeleton will leave an investigator ill-equipped to accurately assess remains belonging to a child. When investigating juvenile remains, it is important to remember that children's bone react to stresses differently than adult bones because the anatomy, biomechanics, and physiology of a child's skeleton are very different from that of an adult [4]. In addition, identification of the various elements may prove difficult for an individual with little knowledge of the juvenile skeleton since it is morphologically different from the adult skeleton and throughout early development is composed of numerically more elements that are held together by dense connective tissues. This chapter will discuss the differences between juvenile and adult skeletons and provide the reader with an overview of human bone growth and development, juvenile anatomy, and bone health. It is intended to supplement the reading found throughout the rest of this book and provides the reader with a basic understanding of the various concepts that will be discussed in later chapters. However, it is beyond the scope of this chapter to provide a complete treatment of human bone growth and development, juvenile and adult osteology, and bone health as each topic has easily comprised entire textbooks. Therefore, a list of supplemental readings is suggested at the end of this chapter.

3.2 Anatomical Terminology

To efficiently describe the human skeleton and share data, the human skeleton is referred to in terms of anatomical direction. First and foremost, the human skeleton is oriented in what is called "standard anatomical position." This position is characterized by the human body facing forward with the arms lying near the side of the body, the palms facing up, the legs extended together, and the toes pointing forward [5] (Fig. 3.1). This ensures that no bones are crossed over one another. For example, the palms are oriented facing up so that the radius and ulna lie parallel to each another.

The body is then divided into three planes of reference. These include the sagittal, coronal, and transverse planes. The sagittal plane divides the body into left and right

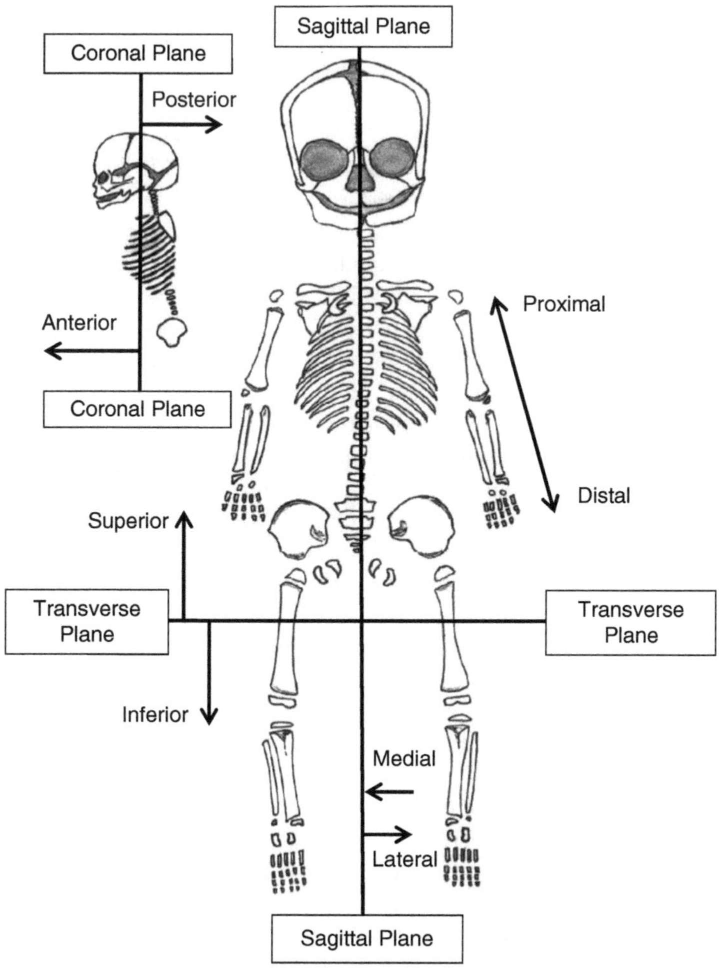

Fig. 3.1 Anatomical orientation and directional terminology (drawing by Humphries)

halves. The sagittal plane runs along the midline of the body and allows us to refer to features and structures that lie medially (toward the center of the body) or laterally (away from the midline of the body). The coronal plane divides the body into front and back halves. The front half of the coronal plane is referred to as anterior and the back half as posterior. Lastly, the transverse plane divides the body into upper and lower halves and passes perpendicular to the sagittal and frontal planes. With reference to the transverse plane, the term "superior" is used to describe features or elements that lie toward the head, while inferior refers to body parts that lie away from the head. The terms proximal and distal are generally used in association with the limb bones. Proximal refers to the portion of bone that is nearest to the axial skeleton, or articulation point. Conversely, distal refers to the portion of bone that is furthest away from the axial skeleton or articulation point. Lastly, the term "cranial" refers to the bones of the skull, and the term "postcranial" refers to all of the bones located below the skull. For an illustration of these descriptions, please see Fig. 3.1.

The figure depicts "standard anatomical position" with the body facing forward, arms extended along the side of the body, palms facing up, legs extended, and toes pointing forward. Also illustrated are the three planes of reference and anatomical directional terminology.

At birth the juvenile skeleton is comprised of roughly 450 ossification centers or elements. Extending from fetal life, these elements continue to mature and grow throughout childhood and fuse together to eventually become the 206 bones found in a typical adult skeleton. These centers include both primary and secondary centers of ossification. The primary centers are the initial sites of ossification, and the majority appear during the embryonic and fetal periods [6]. In some cases, secondary centers of ossification develop, including the proximal and distal ends of the long bones and rib tubercles. These centers appear later, most often after birth [6]. The long limb bones and the tubular bones of the hands and feet form from both primary and secondary centers of ossification. The primary and secondary centers are separated by an organized region of rapid growth that includes the growth plate, epiphyseal plate, and physis, and eventually fuse together to form the whole bone [6]. Many bones such as the cranial bones and the bones of the wrists and ankles form from one or several primary centers of ossification.

Bones are comprised of different types of bones (Fig. 3.2). The smooth, hard, outer portion of bone is known as cortical or compact bone. Sponge-like bone is located within the interior of bone and occurs at the ends of long bones and the vertebral bodies, and between the inner and outer layers of the cranial bones. This type of bone is collectively referred to as cancellous or trabecular bone, and within the cranial vault, it is called the diplöe. Living bone is covered by a layer of vascularized tissue called the periosteum. The inner surface of bones is lined with a cellular membrane call the endosteum. The periosteum and endosteum are osteogenic tissues that contain bone-forming cells and work together to allow bone to grow appositionally. The periosteum is thicker during childhood as the bone-forming cells are numerous and active because of the growing and developing bones [4, 6]. In adulthood, these cells reduce in number but remain active for remodeling and maintenance [4].

Three structures that characterize long bones include the diaphysis, epiphyses, and metaphyses (Fig. 3.2). The diaphysis is considered the shaft and is the portion

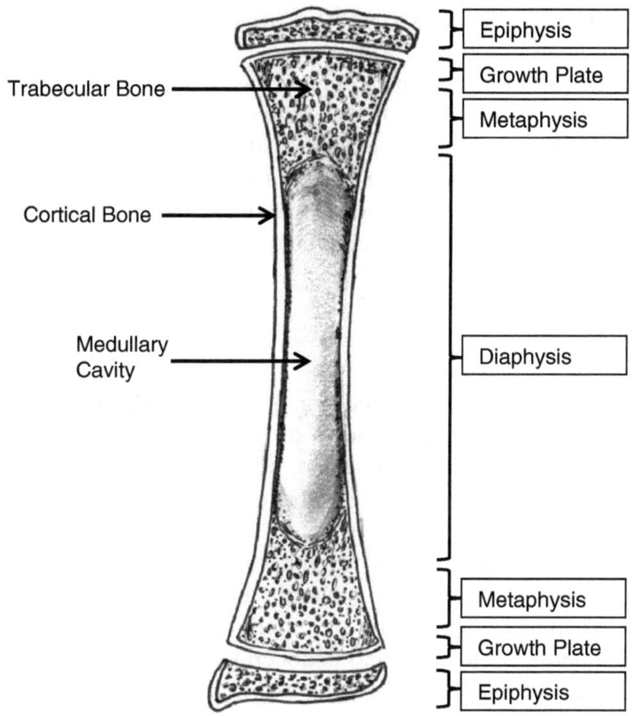

Fig. 3.2 Anatomy of bone (drawing by Humphries)

that comprises the majority of the total length of the long bone. At either end of the diaphysis are the metaphyses. Finally, the epiphyses cap both ends of the diaphysis at the site of the metaphyses. During growth, the diaphysis is considered the primary center of ossification (largely because, in long bones, it is the first structure to appear). The epiphyses that cap either end of the diaphysis are considered secondary centers of ossification, because they form later. Throughout growth, these elements slowly grow together at the site of the growth plate, epiphyseal plate, and physis to form the final element recognized in the adult skeleton [6]. It should be noted that some elements cannot be identified through these three structures (diaphysis, metaphyses, and epiphyses). For example, the bones of the cranial vault form from their own separate primary ossification centers and eventually join the other cranial bones at junctions called sutures.

3.3 Overview of Bone Growth and Development

All bone growth is the result of bone deposition and replacement on a preexisting connective tissue [5]. Osteogenesis, the process of laying down new bone, occurs in two distinct phases in the developing skeleton through intramembranous and endochondral ossification. The bones of the cranial vault, in particular the frontal and parietal bones and the clavicle in the postcrania, are formed by apposition on a primitive mesenchymal tissue, which is an embryonic connective tissue. Most skeletal elements form through endochondral ossification, which is a cartilaginous precursor or model. Essentially, whether bones are formed intramembranously or endochondrally, they are formed on a preexisting "blue print." During the early phase of development, in utero, the skeleton is flexible being composed mostly of a cartilage precursor, which is best for rapid growth and as a rigid frame is unnecessary during this phase of development.

3.3.1 Embryology

At the time of conception, the fertilized egg, or zygote, undergoes a series of mitotic divisions and eventually becomes known as a blastocyst. During this period, the zygote travels down the fallopian tube and, by the end of the first week, has converted into a blastocyst and has begun embedding itself into the uterine lining [7]. By the second week after fertilization, the blastocyst is completely implanted and cell division occurs that gives rise to the embryonic disc that is characterized by the formation of the primitive streak, notochord, and three primary germ layers from which all the structures of the body eventually develop. These three germ layers include the ectoderm, mesoderm, and endoderm. The ectoderm is the outer layer from which the epidermis (hair, nails, and skin), the sensory organs, and the brain and spinal cord arise. The middle layer is the mesoderm, from which the bones, muscles, connective tissues, and circulatory system arise. Lastly, the endoderm is the inner layer from which the epithelial linings of the digestive tract and respiratory passages arise. All major organs and systems of the body form from these three germ layers [7]. Ultimately, the skeletal system forms from the mesoderm.

The establishment of the germ layers begins with a band called the primitive streak. Shortly after the primitive streak appears, cells from within the primitive streak form mesenchyme, a loose network of embryonic connective tissue. Mesenchymal cells leaving the primitive streak eventually migrate to the various sites of osteogenesis where they proliferate and differentiate into various cell types, including fibroblasts, chondroblasts, and osteoblasts [7]. At the beginning of the third week, the notochord, a cellular rod that defines the primitive axis of the embryo and provides support, develops from mesenchymal cells released by the primitive streak. The notochord forms the central axis from which the vertebral column and the neural tube will form.

On both sides of the notochord is a column of mesoderm that becomes divided into cuboidal segments called somites. Somites develop throughout the third week of gestation and are prominent during the fourth and fifth weeks and eventually form the vertebrae, head, and trunk (the bones of the axial skeleton).

Models of the bones are initially formed by condensations of mesenchymal cells. Some bones develop directly from the mesenchyme through intramembranous bone formation, while other bones develop from the transformation of mesenchyme into cartilage bone models that are eventually ossified through the process of endochondral ossification. The mesoderm of the developing embryo condenses and gives rise to the mesenchyme, the embryonic connective tissue that ultimately forms all other connective tissues, including cartilage and eventually bone. These mesenchymal cells migrate to sites of future osteogenesis and differentiate into bone (intramembranously) or into cartilage (endochondrally) and ultimately form the "blue print" or ossification centers from which bone growth commences.

3.3.1.1 Intramembranous Ossification

Bones formed through intramembranous ossification do not begin with a cartilaginous precursor. Bones formed this way include the flat cranial bones, the mandible, and the clavicle. As the mesenchyme condenses, the first sign of ossification is the penetration of a blood vessel. At this time, cells differentiate into osteoblasts (bone-forming cells) and are deposited to form a network of spicules around which collagen fibers are deposited [8, 9]. Calcium salts, phosphates, and other inorganic salts then accumulate around the spicules. These fibers continue to form frameworks of spicules and calcify. As the calcification continues, the framework forms spongy bone. Some osteoblasts become trapped within the matrix and transform into osteocytes (bone cells) and help make up the spongy framework. Meanwhile the remaining osteoblasts stay on the periphery and continue laying new bone, creating layers around vascular channels that become the Haversian systems [6, 8, 9]. Osteoblasts work together with osteoclasts (bone-removing cells) to shape the growing bone tissue through bone deposition and removal.

3.3.1.2 Chondrification

Bones that form from a cartilaginous precursor must first go through chondrification, the process of transforming the mesenchyme bone model into cartilage. Cartilage develops when mesenchyme condenses and the cells proliferate and become rounded. As the cells differentiate, they form two layers, an outer one composed of fibroblasts and an inner one capable of differentiating into cartilage [8]. Together these layers form the perichondrium that covers the surface of the cartilage bone model. Chondroblasts, which are responsible for appositional growth, are found within the inner layer of the perichondrium [6].

Cartilage grows by both interstitial and appositional growth. The cells within the newly developed mass continue to divide and lay down more cartilaginous matrix through the process of interstitial growth. Appositional growth occurs when cells within the perichondrium differentiate and deposit layer after layer of cartilage on the outer surface of the model.

3.3.1.3 Endochondral Ossification

Endochondral ossification is characterized by bone formation that occurs from a preexisting cartilaginous precursor. Initially, the perichondrium of the cartilage model thickens, gives rise to osteoblasts (bone-forming cells), and eventually transforms into the periosteum of the ensuing bone [6]. The osteoblasts initially released by the perichondrium form a bone collar around the midshaft. Next, ossification within the core of the cartilage model begins as the chondrocytes (cartilage cells) swell up and calcium salts are deposited, ultimately forming calcified cartilage [6, 8]. The cartilaginous bone model continues to calcify, is invaded by a system of blood vessels, and then is occupied by osteoblasts and osteoclasts that eventually remodel the mineralized cartilage to form cancellous bone [6]. The osteoblasts deposited on the outer portion of bone form the hard surface known as cortical bone. For an illustration of endochondral ossification, please see Fig. 3.3.

As short bone develops (particularly those that form from a primary center of ossification, i.e., bones of the wrist and ankle), the core of the cartilaginous template ossifies through osteoclast and mineral salt deposition, while at the same time the cartilage continues to grow appositionally [8]. Eventually, the bone formation occurring at the core of the bone will consume the cartilage and form the adult bone.

Endochondral ossification begins on a preexisting cartilage model. The perichondrium produces osteoblasts that form a bone collar and transforms into the periosteum. Cartilage within the center of the cartilage model begins to calcify, becoming the primary center of ossification. Blood vessels then penetrate the bone collar and the secondary centers begin to calcify. Osteoclasts found in the endosteum remove the calcified cartilage to form the medullary cavity as osteoblasts in the periosteum deposit bone on the outside.

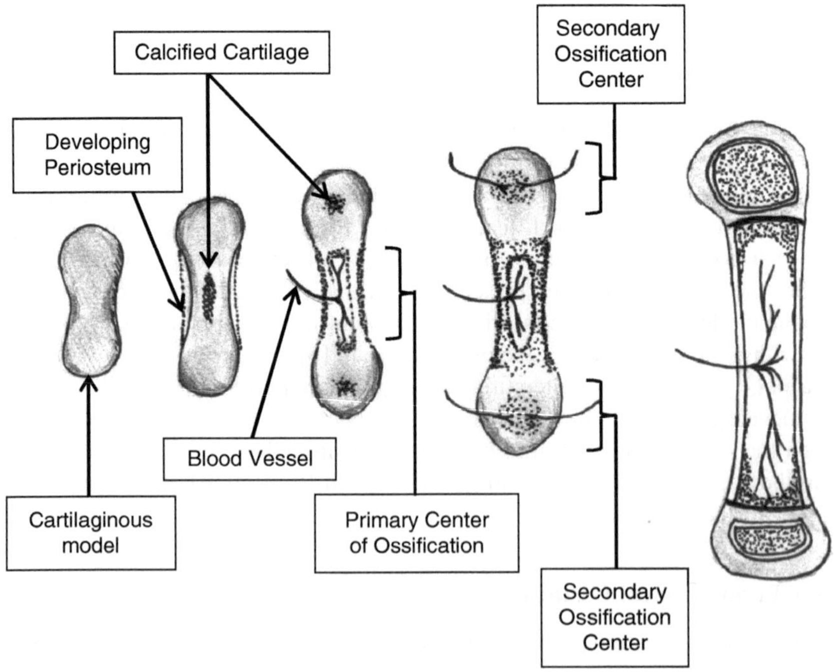

Fig. 3.3 Endochondral ossification (drawing by Humphries)

3.3.1.4 Fusion of Ossification Centers

As mentioned earlier, the initial site of ossification is the primary center. The primary center (diaphysis) does not always extend the entire cartilaginous precursor, and in some regions, separate secondary centers of ossification (epiphyses) will develop. At the site of the periosteum on the diaphysis, osteoblasts cause the shaft to grow in thickness. At the same time, a cavity is formed in the center of the bone by osteoclasts. This cavity eventually becomes the medullary cavity within which blood-forming cells and fat are stored (see Fig. 3.3). The shaft of the bone continues to grow larger in diameter through appositional growth on the outside of the shaft and removal of bone within the center.

At the ends of the diaphysis, the cartilage continues to grow appositionally, while other centers of ossification (secondary) appear at the ends of the future bone. These secondary centers are referred to as epiphyses. A zone of cartilage known at the epiphyseal plate (growth plate) separates the metaphysis of the diaphysis from the epiphysis. This region allows the long bone to increase in length [6]. During childhood the cartilage of the epiphyseal plate continues to grow in thickness, while at the same time ossification proceeds outward from the diaphysis. Eventually, the ossification proceeding from the diaphysis will overcome and consume the cartilage of the epiphyseal plate and form a union between the diaphysis and the epiphysis [6, 8] (see Fig. 3.4). The union or closure of the epiphysis and diaphysis marks the end of growth in length of that bone.

The overall timing of epiphyseal fusion and closure varies in different parts of the skeleton and aids in determining the age of an individual. The reader should consult books such as Baker et al. (2005), Scheuer and Black (2000), and Scheuer et al. (2008) for exact timing.

The growth plate that separates the epiphysis from the diaphysis is a zone of cartilage that grows in thickness throughout childhood. Bone maturing from the direction of the diaphysis eventually consumes the thickening cartilage and forms a union between the diaphysis and the epiphysis. This growth allows long bones to increase in length.

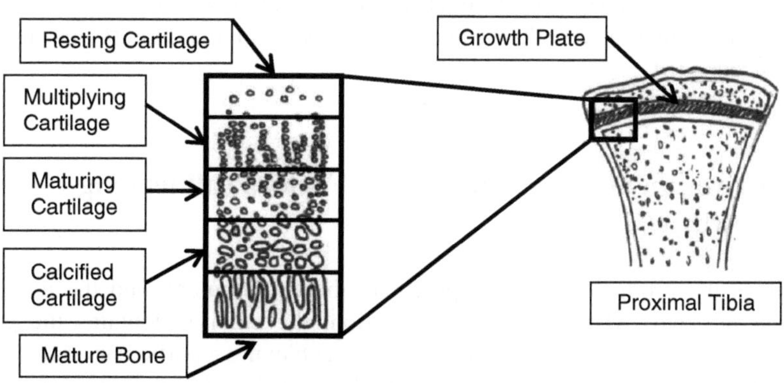

Fig. 3.4 Epiphyseal closure (drawing by Humphries)

3.4 Major Differences Between the Adult and Juvenile Skeleton

Anatomically and morphologically speaking, the juvenile skeleton is very different from the adult skeleton because it is in a constant state of change. At birth, there are about 450 centers of ossification present. These centers eventually ossify and fuse to form the 206 bones that are typically found in the adult human. This process of bone growth and development begins during the fetal life and does not finish roughly until the mid-20s. The juvenile skeleton is different from the adult skeleton in terms of morphology primarily because the young skeleton has not fully fused. At various developmental stages, the juvenile skeleton will have different numbers of elements as the appearance and ossification of the centers change.

The physiology of the juvenile skeleton also differs greatly from that of an adult. This is primarily because the bone is still forming and growing. The juvenile skeleton is characterized by a thick periosteum. The periosteum is the connective tissue covering the outside of bone and aids in bone formation and repair. It bridges the gap between broken segments of bone after a fracture occurs by producing cartilage and/or bone-forming cells. Since the periosteum is responsible for growth and for aiding in the repair of fractures, the juvenile skeleton heals a great deal faster than that of an adult because the actions associated with fracture repair are already present in excessive amounts in the developing skeleton [4].

It is also important to note that the biomechanics are also different. Young bone is more porous and more flexible than adult bone. This is because the Haversian canals occupy a greater portion of the cortex [4]. Because of its construction, a child's bone can withstand a great deal more pressure than an adult bone before breaking. In fact, the bones in a child's forearm can be bent up to 45 degrees before the sound of a fracture is heard [4]. This is due to the greater thickness and strength of the periosteum in the growing juvenile skeleton. In addition, the young bone is composed of more collagen, which allows it to be more flexible and elastic. Additionally, the cartilaginous composition of the growing bone also helps withstand outside pressures as the cartilaginous matrices hold together large volumes of fluid, making it resistant to compression [10]. Once fully developed, the adult skeleton loses its elasticity and turns to a state of remodeling and maintenance where a thick periosteum is no longer needed [8].

3.5 Environmental and Nutritional Factors Influencing Growth

Growth is the product of genetic potential, the environment, and the interaction between the two. At the time of conception, the embryo contains the genetic blueprint that includes a person's potential for achieving a particular adult size and shape; the environment alters this potential [10, 12–14]. As such, a growing child can be adversely affected by diet, socioeconomic resources, and/or poisons in the atmosphere. While poor nutrition may have an adverse effect on growth, one must keep in mind that there are numerous factors that can impair growth that may not necessarily be due to child maltreatment including disease and infection [13].

Proper nutrition is essential for individuals to achieve a normal growth pattern and maximize their potential as adults [11–13]. According to Sinclair and Dangerfield [8], in the first year of life, a baby requires about twice as many calories per unit weight as an adult male engaged in moderately heavy work. Nutritional needs during adolescence may be higher than at any other time during life, and malnourished children may exhibit delayed growth and puberty [13]. However, the growth response will vary depending on the type, intensity, and duration of the nutritional insult [13]. Undernourishment can lead to a cycle in which an undernourished child becomes more susceptible to infection and illness, and once ill, requires more nourishment, and if it is not received, becomes a downward spiral [13]. One of the earliest responses to limited food is growth retardation [13]. When a child is undernourished, the development of the teeth takes precedence over the growth of the bones [8]. Since the teeth are an accurate indicator of age, comparison of the teeth and bone development may yield information regarding the health of a child. A balanced diet that includes vitamins and minerals is essential during childhood to support health bone growth.

A balanced diet includes a variety of foods containing minerals and vitamins including calcium, vitamin D, phosphorus, magnesium, vitamin C, as well as proteins [9]. Calcium is important for several bodily systems, makes up approximately 70% of the composition of bone, and is essential for bone formation [9]. Therefore, consuming foods with calcium is important for the growth and maintenance of bone tissue and for proper functions of the heart, muscles, and nervous system. Bones are the storage vaults from which the body draws calcium. If the body does not have enough calcium for other systems in the body, the body will leach calcium from bone and over time will cause the bones to become thin and weak. Phosphorus works with calcium to strengthen and maintain bone and teeth. In addition, phosphorus aids in the conversion of food into energy [9].

Vitamin D works with calcium and phosphorus. It improves the rate of calcium and phosphorus absorption from the intestine and essentially increases their amounts in the bloodstream, making calcium readily available to perform bodily functions [9]. Therefore, if vitamin D is deficient, so may be calcium. An inadequate supply of calcium in the bloodstream will cause the body to leach out the calcium stored within bone. If vitamin D is deficient, bone will fail to mineralize and, as a result, children may develop rickets. It ultimately causes distorted growth of the epiphyseal plate. If persistent, it will ultimately lead to softened bones that become bent under the weight of the body [8].

Magnesium stimulates the production of calcitonin, a hormone that works with other hormones in the body to raise calcium levels in the bones and prevent calcium from being absorbed into other parts of the body. In addition, magnesium also reduces acid levels in the blood. Bone loss occurs more severely when blood is more acidic [9].

Vitamin C aids in the growth and maintenance of healthy bones, teeth, gums, ligaments, and blood vessels. Vitamin C deficiency causes the intercellular substance of bone to become inadequately formed and can eventually form scurvy [8]. It may cause a decreased growth rate at the epiphyseal plates and deficient bone formation elsewhere.

Protein-energy malnutrition can ultimately lead to conditions known as kwashiorkor and marasmus [13], which are characterized by slowed skeletal growth and maturation. In fact, epiphyseal union may be delayed as much as a year compared with that in properly nourished children [8].

3.6 Summary

This chapter has provided a brief overview of juvenile skeletal anatomy and growth and development. The juvenile skeleton is characterized as a nutrition-dependent and rapidly growing phase. Children's bones are different from adult bones, and those having taken courses only in adult human osteology may have difficulty distinguishing juvenile human remains from nonhuman remains, may have difficulty identifying the various structures and bones of the juvenile skeleton, and may not accurately assess the remains. Since the juvenile skeleton is different from the adult skeleton, it is essential for investigators of child maltreatment to become familiar with juvenile skeletal anatomy and understand what is considered normal variation.

Suggested Reading

Baker BJ, Dupras TL, Tocheri MW. The Osteology of Infants and Children. College Station, TX: Texas A&M University Press, 2005

Scheuer L, Black S, Schaefer MC. Juvenile Osteology: A Laboratory and Field Manual. San Diego, CA: Academic, 2008

Scheuer L, Black S. The Juvenile Skeleton. San Diego, CA: Elsevier Academic Press, 2004

References

1. Center for Disease Control, National Center for Injury Prevention and Control. Child Maltreatment: Facts at a Glance. 2010 http://www.cdc.gov/violencePrevention/childmaltreatment/
2. U.S. Department of Health and Human Services, Administration for Children and Families, Administration on Children, Youth and Families, Children's Bureau. Child Maltreatment. 2008 http://www.acf.hhs.gov/programs/cb/stats_research/index.htm#can
3. Baker BJ, Dupras TL, Tocheri MW. The Osteology of Infants and Children. College Station, TX: Texas A&M University Press, 2005
4. Rang M, Wenger D. Children Are Not Just Small Adults. In: Rang M, Wenger DR, Pring ME, editors. Rang's Children's Fractures, 3rd Ed. Philadelphia, PA: Lippincott Williams & Wilkins, 2005; 1–10

5. White TD. Human Osteology, 2nd Ed. San Diego, CA: Academic, 2000
6. Scheuer L, Black S. Developmental Juvenile Osteology. San Diego, CA: Academic, 2000
7. Moore KL, Persaud TVN. The Developing Human, 5th Ed. Philadelphia, PA: W.B. Saunders Company, 1993
8. Sinclair D, Dangerfield P. Human Growth after Birth, 6th Ed. Oxford: Oxford University Press, 1998
9. Kelly E. The Skeletal System. Westport, CT: Greenwood Press, 2004
10. Hall BK. Bones and Cartilage: Developmental and Evolutionary Skeletal Biology. San Diego, CA: Elsevier Academic Press, 2005
11. Cameron N. Human Growth Curve, Canalization, and Catch-Up Growth. In: Cameron N, editor. Human Growth and Development. Amsterdam: Academic, 2006; 1–20
12. Lejarraga H. Growth in Infancy and Childhood: A Pediatric Approach. In: Cameron N, editor. Human Growth and Development. Amsterdam: Academic, 2006; 21–44
13. Norgan NG. Nutrition and Growth. In: Cameron N, editor. Human Growth and Development. San Diego, CA: Academic, 2006; 139–164
14. Schell LM, Knutson KL. Environmental Effects on Growth. In: Cameron N, editor. Human Growth and Development. San Diego, CA: Academic, 2006; 165–195

Chapter 4
Biomechanical and Remodeling Factors in the Interpretation of Fractures in Juveniles

Douglas H. Ubelaker and Kristin M. Montaperto

Abstract Interpretation of juvenile trauma requires understanding of biomechanical and remodeling factors, as well as the dynamics of the growth process. Although terminology relating especially to biomechanical factors can be complex, use of proper terms is essential to avoid misunderstanding. Analysis can include direct observation, individual history documentation, radiography, microscopy, and bone scintigram study. In addition to the appearance of the trauma, relevant observations include the type and area of bone involved, age of the individual, and possible evidence of repair. Such analysis can elucidate the nature of juvenile trauma and facilitate interpretation of the timing of fracture events.

4.1 Introduction

Bone fractures present key evidence for abuse of juveniles in cases involving skeletonized human remains. Although episodes of abuse, even those resulting in death, may not involve skeletal injury [1], but frequently the skeleton is affected [2–7]. In their study of 32 diagnosed child abuse cases with detailed radiological skeletal survey and bone scintigram in the Royal Children's Hospital in Melbourne, Australia, Mandelstam et al. [8] detected 124 examples of skeletal injury in 30 children. Although skeletal injury in child abuse has been reported to be concentrated in the ribs [4, 5, 8–11], many bones of the skeleton can potentially be involved as well, including the spine [12, 13]. Injury can occur in diaphyseal, metaphyseal, and epiphyseal areas of long bones [2, 14, 15] and has been suggested for the endocranium as well [16]. Interpretation of such cases can be complex since skeletal alterations may be difficult to detect [3, 11, 17, 18] and alterations can result from factors other than abuse [11, 19–22]. Imaging protocols vary considerably relating to suspected child abuse [15, 23–26], and thus reported data are difficult to compare. Taphonomic factors further complicate interpretation [27–29], especially in the very young [30, 31].

D.H. Ubelaker (✉)
Department of Anthropology, National Museum of Natural History, Smithsonian Institution, Washington, DC 20560, USA
e-mail: ubelaked@si.edu

A.H. Ross, S.M. Abel (eds.), *The Juvenile Skeleton in Forensic Abuse Investigations*, DOI 10.1007/978-1-61779-255-7_4, © Springer Science+Business Media, LLC 2011

Fatal injuries are key to abuse investigation but also important are nonfatal injuries that may document history of abuse [32]. Nonfatal bone fractures can be recognized as such through observations on bone remodeling, the skeletal evidence for healing [3–5, 17, 31, 33–35]. Although the evidence for remodeling can be obvious in injuries sustained long before death, detection can be challenging in fractures sustained shortly before death.

Proper detection and interpretation of skeletal evidence for abuse or lack thereof requires a complex methodology of radiography, gross examination and even microscopy, as well as experienced understanding of basic principles of bone growth and remodeling, taphonomy, pathology, and biomechanics. This chapter examines factors of biomechanics and bone remodeling in such interpretation, summarizing what is known from the scientific literature.

4.2 Biomechanics Terminology

Specialized terminology is utilized in the discussion of the biomechanics involved in fracture formation [36–41]. Stress refers to magnitude of the load applied to the affected bone surface area. The nature of the stress applied can be compression, tension, torsion, or shearing. Tensile strength represents the response of the bone to the applied stress. The tensile strength of a bone refers to the stress level at which deformation occurs. Strain describes the bone response to the applied stress. With relatively low stress, the bone response will be elastic without permanent change in shape. The yield stress refers to the stress amount required to cause plastic deformation. Yield stress exceeds the limit that will produce elastic response. With plastic deformation, realignment occurs at the atomic and molecular levels. Fatigue in biomechanical terminology refers to multiple applications of stress at elastic response levels to the point that bone alterations occur. Fracture occurs at the failure point, when the stress levels are too high for the bone to accommodate [36].

As noted by Cunha and Pinheiro [42], bone vulnerability to trauma relates to the bone's ability to absorb energy. The kinetic energy of the applied stress relates to the formula $1\backslash 2mv^2$ with m representing mass and v being velocity.

The stiffness (modulus of elasticity or Young's modulus) [36, 43–45] reflects the extent of resistance of the bone to stress. The "modulus" is greater in bone with greater resistance. The magnitude of the modulus in bone is directly related to the type of bone, bone structure, and the amount of mineral content.

The term "Poisson's ratio" refers to the coordinated deformation response to bone [36]. Within a single bone, a deformation response to stress at one location may produce a corollary and complementary response at other areas. This concept is important in fracture interpretation since a single stress episode can produce different alterations in distinct areas of the same bone. Although these alterations may present different characteristics, they may all be understood with proper consideration of the biomechanical factors reflected in Poisson's ratio.

4.3 The Nature of Bone

Much of the complexity of fracture interpretation reflects the heterogeneous nature of bone. Bone structure varies considerably at different parts of the skeleton, at different sites within a single bone, and at different areas within a single site. Bone structure also changes with advancing age, especially in the juvenile skeleton. Thus bone response to stress load reflects the specific area impacted, its anatomical structure and architecture. External morphology represents an important variable, but cross-sectional anatomical features and the general bone structure are important as well.

Bone has the capacity to respond in different ways (anisotropic) depending on the area of bone impacted and the nature of the stress applied. In bone composition, collagen fibers provide tensile strength while hydroxyapatite crystals contribute compressive strength [37, 46–48]. Key factors in bone composition relative to fracture biomechanics are the layers of compact bone and the cancellous bone, diplöe, or trabecular bone. Variation in thickness and composition of these structures throughout the skeleton influences fracture biomechanics. Juvenile bones generally present more elastic properties than do their more mature counterparts [31, 33, 49–53]. Since fractures occur in areas of least resistance, bone morphology and structure present key factors. Foramina, sutures, preexisting fractures, and areas of skeletal buttressing all can influence fracture formation and location.

In juveniles, bone morphology and structure change dramatically with growth and development. Normal juvenile bone development involves constant remodeling and shifts in length, width, thickness, and shape. In general, juvenile bone is less dense, more porous, and more vascular than adult bone [33, 49, 54]. Juvenile bone has a lower modulus of elasticity, lower mineral content, and lower bending strength. The increased bone porosity in juveniles decreases the probability of sustaining comminuted fractures. Bone load deformation curves in juveniles display a longer plastic phase than seen in adults [33, 50, 52, 54]. The more porous nature of juvenile bone has a greater tendency to limit fracture propagation and thus may contribute to a higher frequency of greenstick fractures. In addition, pediatric bone can absorb more energy without fracturing than adult bone [53]. However, pediatric bone fractures with less force than adult bone [50, 53], which can result in plastic deformation, compression, and greenstick fractures [53].

4.4 Biomechanical Factors in Fracture Interpretation

An understanding of biomechanical factors operating on skeletal anatomical structure facilitates interpretation of bone fractures [40, 41, 55–59], especially when addressing juvenile fractures [31, 50, 60–63]. As noted above, the nature of the stress load can reflect a variety of different types of applied forces. As the term implies, compression forces represent those operating to compress bone. When bending occurs in a long bone, compression occurs on the concave side of the bend [36, 41]. When compression produces fractures, they tend to be multiple and complex [64].

Tension forces operate to pull apart bone. In the bone-bending example discussed above, tension forces operate on the convex side of the bone [41]. When fractures form under tension, they tend to be linear.

Torsion, rotation, and shear forces also can operate on bone. In long bones these forces can produce a twisting effect along the diaphysis, causing spiral fractures [49].

When a bone is impacted with stress loads and bending occurs, both compression and tension forces operate. Bone tissues at the site of impact and concave side (if bending occurs) are subject to compression. In contrast, tissues on the opposite convex side are subject to tension. Specific bone responses to these forces or stress loads can be variable depending not only on the nature and magnitude of the stress but also on the properties of the impacted bone. In juveniles, compression fractures can be expressed as greenstick fractures [31, 49, 51] and bowing in the long bones [31, 49, 52, 65] can result from longitudinal stress. Stuart-Macadam et al. [52] found the highest occurrence of bowing deformities in the juvenile forearm when a hand is outstretched for a fall. This type of compression fracture is less likely in adults, and when it happens it typically results from an industrial accident [52].

When bending occurs in a long bone, compression on the concave side can lead to bone splintering or multiple fractures. As noted above, tension on the convex side of the bone more often produces linear fractures. When the tension and compression fractures connect, a triangular-shaped section of bone can be separated. Such occurrences are termed butterfly fractures because of the distinctive shape of the separated bone segment. Although butterfly fractures are frequently associated with antemortem/perimortem injury, they also can result from postmortem factors [64].

Although this chapter and book focus on skeletal fractures, soft tissue injury usually is involved as well and should be kept in mind in the interpretation of skeletal features [17]. Complications include arterial injuries, compartment syndromes (swelling and increased pressure within a closed anatomical space), fat embolism, hypercalcemia of immobilization, ectopic bone formation, cast syndrome, traction-induced hypertension, spontaneous deep-vein thrombosis, malunion, synostosis (cross-union), late angulation, injury to triradiate cartilage, limb overgrowth, growth disturbances, nonunion, refracture, ligamentous instability, nerve injury, and reflex sympathetic dystrophy [66].

4.5 Stages of Repair

The initial process of repair has been classified as the inflammation stage [33, 41, 67, 68]. The repair process following fracture begins with formation of a hematoma at the fracture site. Blood accumulates from disrupted vessels associated with the fracture site. The extent of blood flow varies with the location of the fracture site and the type of bone and soft tissue involved. These vessels can be located in the medullary cavity, periosteum, and/or overlying muscle tissue [69]. Blood flow and fracture site also influence the probability of bone necrosis (death) [41].

The periosteum is the tissue covering adjacent external bone surfaces and generates bone through the intramembraneous ossification system in normal bone growth. In the area of the growth plate, this tissue is referred to as the pericondrium. With injury and subperiosteal hemorrhage, the periosteum becomes elevated and separates from its normal contact with the bone cortex [6, 51]. The more firmly attached pericondrium in long bones is less likely to elevate, resulting in more hemorrhage and blood clot along the diaphysis and less in the epiphyseal area, obviously dependent on the location and severity of the trauma.

The blood clot or hematoma offers strands of fibrin that some have suggested may provide a framework for cellular proliferation [69]. Coagulation requires 6–8 h [70], and osteoclasts begin their important work of removing damaged or necrotic bone [17]. The release of factors IL-1, IL-6, and PDGF stimulate cell formation involved in removing tissue debris [67, 71, 72]. This is followed by cell differentiation into fibroblasts, chondrocytes, and osteoblasts. The fibroblast growth factor (FGF) stimulates fibroblast proliferation. The factor IGF-II encourages osteoblast collagen synthesis [72].

The proliferation and varied cell formation leads to formation of a primary cellular callus. Heppenstall [68] refers to this development as the stage of soft callus. Callus formation is important in contributing to the immobilization of the fractured segments. Within a few days following fracture, vascularization of the callus begins. Nitric oxide and endothelial cell–stimulating angiogenesis factor promote local vasodilatation and the formation of new blood vessels [71, 72]. Formation of a fibrous union occurs usually by the third week.

The factor TGF-β stimulates osteoblasts to produce collagen and mesenchymal cells to form type II collagen and proteoglycans needed for cartilage production. The initial hematoma is replaced by bridging callus during the reparative phase of healing. Endosteal osteoblasts generate woven bone in the medullary cavity. Periosteally located osteoblasts produce sub-periosteal callus. Calcification progresses through mineral deposition within the callus [67, 72]. Heppenstall [68] refers to the gradual conversion of the callus to fiber bone as the stage of hard callus. In adults, this stage begins at 3–4 weeks and is usually completed (fragments firmly united with new bone) in 3–4 months in major long bones [68]. In juveniles this time is reduced significantly [17, 33, 49, 51, 67].

The remodeling process then slowly produces mature bone and attempts to achieve functional anatomical structure. Much of the original woven bone is replaced and subsequently remodeled. Remodeling of cancellous bone involves thickening of the trabeculae. Gradually, the marrow cavity becomes repopulated with normal marrow cells [72]. This process occurs faster in juveniles than in adults but can be complicated by factors other than age [67] such as the type of fracture, area of the anatomy involved, the extent of bone involved in fracture, extent of immobilization, presence of infection, other health issues, and nutrition. If the broken bone segments are properly aligned, the repair/remodeling process may remove most indications that the fracture occurred, especially in juvenile bone but in adult bone as well, given enough time [72].

Pseudoarthrosis can result when a fibrous pseudojoint forms at the fractured bone ends. Although uncommon in juveniles, pseudoarthrosis involves rounded, remodeled fractured bone ends with sclerosis of the medullary cavity. Factors favorable to pseudoarthrosis formation include mobility, deficient blood supply, relatively great separation of fractured segments, and excessive presence of soft tissue at the fracture site [73].

Additional associated conditions with fracture repair include misalignment, bone shortening, associated infection, bone necrosis, nerve damage, and alteration of articulation patterns. All of these conditions may impact the timing of repair, the external morphology, and function [70].

As noted above, fracture repair in juveniles proceeds more rapidly than in adults. Reasons for this include a stronger and more active periosteum in juveniles [17, 49, 67]. Even in severe fractures of juveniles, frequently an intact periosteal hinge is preserved for utilization in closed reduction of the fracture [74]. Salter and Harris [75] observed this through their research with the epiphyses of immature rabbits. The periosteum and endosteum are also more osteogenic than in adults, promoting faster healing.

4.6 Timing of Fracture Episodes

Interpretation of bone fractures must consider if the observed condition results from postmortem, perimortem, or antemortem activity. Evidence of bone remodeling represents the key factor in the recognition of antemortem fractures. Estimation of the timing of antemortem fracture episodes depends on what is known about the timing of the repair process. In skeletonized cases involving perimortem fractures, it also can be important to estimate the minimum time needed for evidence of repair to be recognized.

The literature presents some variation in the interpretation of the timing of stages of bone repair when addressing adults [36, 76, 77] and juveniles [26]. Maples [77] suggests that the earliest indication of bone remodeling involves subtle rounding of the fractured bone margins with a microscopic polished appearance. Maples [77] suggested that a minimum of 7 days after the time of fracture is required for such remodeling to become apparent. In their study of modern documented collections, Mann and Murphy [76] suggest that at least 2 weeks' time after the fracture is required for recognition of remodeling. Initial alterations consist of indications of bone resorption on the periosteal surface adjacent to the fracture site. Such bone resorption may reflect damage to the periosteum in the area of the fracture [36].

Some radiographic changes can be observed at the fractured bone ends as early as 10 days following the fracture [78]. Spicules of woven bone may appear histologically within the callus as early as 5 days after fracture [79]; however, they likely would not be recognized or recovered in skeletonized cases [36]. Kleinman [6] notes that radiographically within 5–14 days following fracture, a thin layer of subperiosteal new bone can be detected. Radiographic changes are particularly important in juveniles where the timing of a fracture can aid in cases of abuse. Since juvenile fractures present themselves differently and repair at a more rapid rate, these changes can be difficult to observe without radiographs [26].

Age represents an important variable in the timing of bone repair. For example, union for a femur fracture with primary callus formation may require 3 months in an adult but only 2 months in a 15-year-old and 1 month in an infant [69, 80, 81]. Repair also progresses more rapidly in spiral fractures with wide opening of the marrow cavity than in horizontal long bone fractures with more limited medullary cavity exposure. The rate of callus formation relates directly with the magnitude of the available blood supply [69].

The rate of repair also varies with the amount of displacement of the fractured margins. Union progresses more rapidly when the fractured margins are closely aligned than when they are significantly separated. Close alignment also facilitates immobilization, another important variable in bone repair. Mobility at the fracture site encourages production of fibroblasts and chondroblasts, which is counterproductive to bone formation. In the extreme, such mobility and production of fibrocartilaginous tissue can lead to non-union and pseudoarthrosis [69].

O'Connor and Cohen [17] provide useful information on the dating of fractures and fracture repair in juveniles. Table 4.1 summarizes their research on the timing of radiographic changes related to fracture repair. They suggest that resolution of soft tissues can occur as early as 2 days after fracture and as late as 21 days. Periosteal new bone formation can be detected as early as 4 days and as late as 21 days. Loss of fracture line definition and soft callus formation can occur as early as 10 days and as late as 21 days. Hard callus formation ranges from 14 to 90 days. Bone remodeling in juveniles ranges from 3 months to 2 years or up to epiphyseal closure. Variation is produced by age of the juvenile (the younger displaying more rapid repair) and the location and type of injury. O'Connor and Cohen indicate that a "... fracture with a large amount of periosteal new bone or callus is more than 14 days old" ([17] p. 112). They also note that corner fractures or bucket-handle metaphyseal fractures may persist for longer periods of time without periosteal new bone formation and can be dated only by the loss of definition of the margins.

Table 4.1 Radiographic changes in juvenile fractures over time

Stage of bone repair	Length of time
Resolution of soft tissues	2–21 days
Periosteal new bone	4–21 days
Decrease in fracture line	10–21 days
Soft callus	10–21 days
Hard callus	14–90 days
Remodeling	3 months–2 years

Modified from O'Connor and Cohen [17]

Brogdon considers metaphyseal fractures in the juvenile to be "virtually pathognomonic" for abuse ([82] p. 292). Usually seen in the knee, ankle, and distal humerus metaphyses, these fractures traverse the extremity of the metaphysis separating a boney disc between the primary spongiosa and the zone of provisional calcification. This disc may present as a transverse fracture line, a corner fracture, or a bucket-handle fracture depending on location and orientation in radiography. As noted above, metaphyseal injuries are less likely to be associated with periosteal reactive bone than with injuries to the diaphysis.

Maat [83] compiled information from the literature relating to the timing of fracture repair in adults. Although this volume focuses on juveniles, the information on adults synthesized by Maat provides useful comparative perspective. This adult sequence generally is as follows. Hemorrhage and torn periosteum initiate the sequence characterized as hematoma in the fracture cleft with coagulation and loose fibrin mesh. Cell debris phagocytosis occurs in 2–5 days with the appearance of macrophages, the absence of osteocytes near the fracture cleft, empty lacunae, and fibroblast invasion at the margin of the blood clot with granulation tissue callus. Newly formed cartilage and osteoid appear after 3–5 days with the appearance of chondroblasts and osteoblasts, fibrocartilaginous soft callus, and osteoid. The loss of fracture line definition occurs after 4–7 days with the appearance of Howship's lacunae and beveling and smoothing of the fracture margins. Well-developed new bone spicules and cartilage can be noted after 7 days with new bone spicules dispersed throughout the soft tissue callus and the initiation of endosteal and periosteal osteogenesis. Osteoid mineralization begins after 10–12 days. Woven bone appears after 12–20 days marked by the aggregation of spicules into the woven bone from the periphery to the center of the fracture cleft and clinically stable fusiform union. Clearly visible external callus is evident radiologically after 15 days. Woven bone remodels into longitudinally oriented lamellar bone with fields of calcified cartilage and extension of longitudinally oriented osteon cutting and closing cones to the fracture cleft. Union by bridging of cortical bone and attainment of maximum size of the callus occur after 3–4 weeks. Periosteal new bone becomes firmly incorporated in the cortex after 6 weeks. Firm bony union and the beginning of contour smoothening occur after 2–3 months. Adequate immobilization and reconstruction are accomplished after one to 2 years. Maat [83] also notes that pseudoarthrosis can form after 6–9 months with inadequate immobilization. Comparison of this information with that presented above for juveniles supports Maat's [83] suggestion that the timing information summarized for adults may be substantially less in children.

In the long term, the remodeling process attempts to restore function and normal anatomical structure to fractured bones. With time, much of the evidence of some fractures may become obliterated by this process. This is particularly true in juvenile remains that reflect not only the repair process but rapid growth as well. The remodeling factors in the growth of juvenile bones may involve destruction of the area of fracture and new bone formation.

Box 1

Case Example by Ann H. Ross

Mother claimed that 19-month-old died after falling off the couch and hitting his head on the coffee table. The body was concealed for several weeks in the closet prior to discovery. The toddler was found in an advanced state of decomposition with partial skeletonization stuffed in trash bags with bleach-soaked sheets to cover the smell inside a plastic bin.

Skeletal examination revealed two healed rib fractures of the lateral right 11th rib and at the costochondral junction of the left 7th rib (Figs. 4.1 and 4.2). Because fractures heal at an accelerated rate in all stages of healing in infants and young children these fractures are consistent with timing between

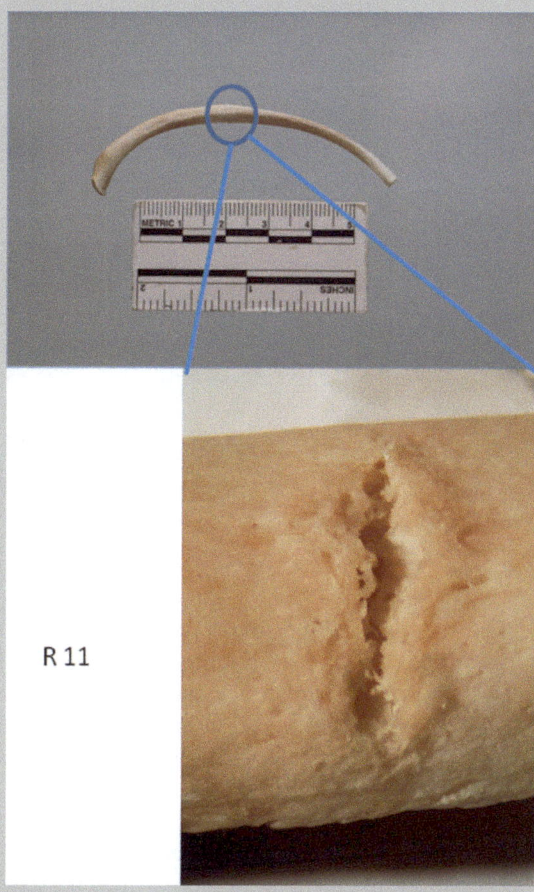

Fig. 4.1 Right 11th rib illustrating almost complete fracture consolidation consistent with healing between 4 weeks and 3 months (photographs by Gary Knight)

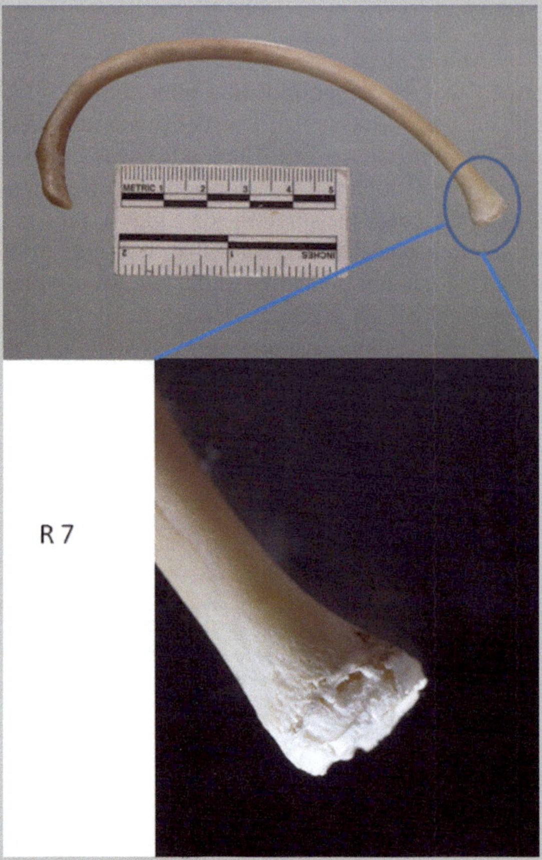

Fig. 4.2 Right 7th rib fracture to the costochondral junction consistent with healing between 4 weeks and 3 months. Fractures to this area are similar to metaphyseal fractures (photographs by Gary Knight)

4 weeks and 3 months. A more recent fracture was also evident on the lateral aspect of the left 10th rib consistent with timing between 7 and 14 days based on the observable periosteal new bone adjacent to the fracture site and the sharp fracture margin (Fig. 4.3). Because these fractures represent different stages of healing they suggest at least two separate episodes of trauma and probably three separate impacts. Lateral rib fractures and fractures at the costochondral junction have been associated with anteroposterior compression and major visceral and abdominal trauma, respectively.

Based on these findings, the medical examiner ruled the cause of death as undetermined homicidal violence. The mother received a first-degree murder charge with no possibility of parole.

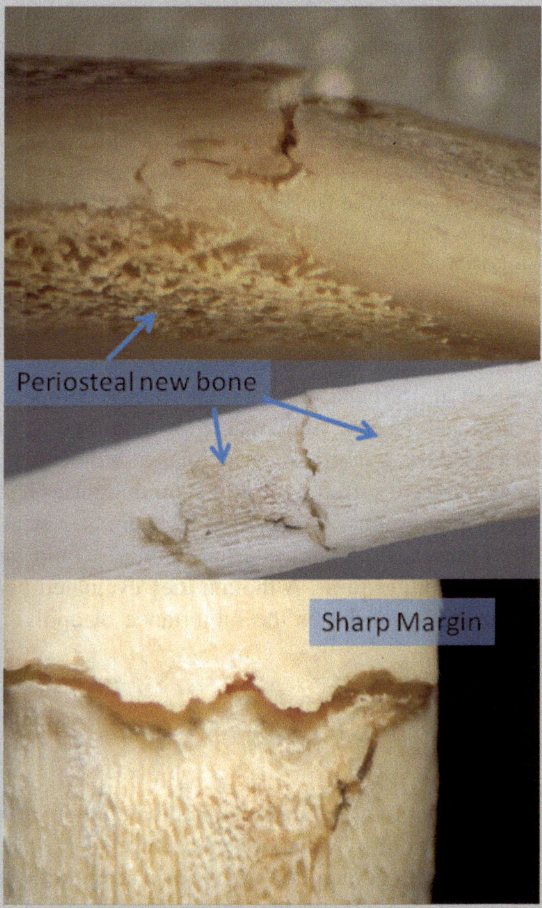

Fig. 4.3 Left 10th rib fracture consistent with healing between 7 and 10 days illustrating periosteal new bone and sharp fracture margin (photographs by Gary Knight)

4.7 Recent Research

As summarized above, much has been learned about bone fracture biomechanics and the repair process through forensic case work, clinical experience, and research. The following paragraphs represent recent published research reports demonstrating that continued innovative research on these issues leads to greater understanding of the complex processes involved.

In their experimental study of the fracture process in young pigs aged 2–28 days, Baumer et al. [84] explored factors of age as well as surface characteristics of the impacting object. They found that the energy required to initiate a fracture increased with increasing age. Age also was reflected in the impact of different surface characteristics. More fracture damage resulted from impact with a compliant surface in the very young. With increasing age, more damage resulted from impact with a rigid surface. They also found that in 70 of the 76 porcine experiments, fracture initiated at the suture edge of the bone rather than at the impact site itself. These research results coupled with others [85, 86] suggest that fracture patterns can reveal considerable information about the forces/objects that led to their formation.

Baumer et al. [87] reported on clinical cases of cranial crush injuries in children as well as modeling experimentation. The experimentation demonstrated how the injuries sustained in the clinical cases can be explained by biomechanics of stress and crushing forces. Fracture patterns generally followed predicted paths in consideration of both stress and anatomical structure.

Arregui-Dalmases et al. [55] analyzed and interpreted compression forces operating on the adult chest using a case study where an individual was killed after being run over by an overloaded truck. Utilizing principles of biomechanics, they assessed whether the victim would have suffered life-threatening injuries if the truck had been properly loaded to its maximum weight. Arregui-Dalmases et al. [55] concluded that life-threatening injuries (bone and internal trauma) would have still occurred at the truck's maximum weight limit. Although they evaluated compression forces on adults, their research demonstrates the importance of applying biomechanical principles to trauma studies.

4.8 Summary

Although biomechanical and remodeling factors influencing juvenile trauma involve complex terminology and multiple components, they are pivotal to proper interpretation. Investigation and documentation may involve not only direct observation and individual history, but also radiography, microscopy, and bone scintigram study. Interpretation should consider not only the appearance of the fracture but also the type and area of bone involved and any and all evidence of repair. Ultimately, interpretation must reflect an understanding of the principles of biomechanics and fracture repair. Although much is known about these principles documented in the scientific literature, additional research and understanding are needed, especially in the timing and nature of repair in juveniles in relation to specific fracture issues.

References

1. Saternus K-S, Kernbach-Wighton G, Oehmichen M. The Shaking Trauma in Infants – Kinetic Chains. Forensic Sci Int 2000;109:203–213.
2. Beals RK, Tufts E. Fractured Femur in Infancy: The Role of Child Abuse. J Pediatr Orthop 1983;3:583–586.
3. Carty HML. Fractures Caused by Child Abuse. J Bone Joint Surg [Br] 1993;75-B:849–857.
4. Kerley ER. Forensic Anthropology and Crimes Involving Children. J Forensic Sci 1976; 21:333–339.

5. Kerley ER. The Identification of Battered-Infant Skeletons. J Forensic Sci 1978;23:163–168.
6. Kleinman PK. Skeletal Trauma: General Considerations. In: Kleinman PK, editor. Diagnostic Imaging of Child Abuse. Baltimore, MD: Williams & Wilkins, 1987;5–28.
7. Schwend RM, Blakemore LC, Lowe L. The Orthopaedic Recognition of Child Maltreatment. In: Beaty JH, Kasser JR, editors. Rockwood and Wilkins' Fractures in Children. 7th ed. Philadelphia, PA: Wolters Kluwer/Lippincott Williams & Wilkins, 2010;192–222.
8. Mandelstam SA, Cook D, Fitzgerald M, Ditchfield MR. Complementary Use of Radiological Skeletal Survey and Bone Scintigraphy in Detection of Bony Injuries in Suspected Child Abuse. Arch Dis Child 2003;88:387–390.
9. Bulloch B, Schubert CJ, Brophy PD, Johnson N, Reed MH, Shapiro RA. Cause and Clinical Characteristics of Rib Fractures in Infants. Pediatrics 2000;105:48–52.
10. Strouse PJ, Owings CL. Fractures of the First Rib in Child Abuse. Radiology 1995;197: 763–765.
11. Worlock P, Stower M, Barbor P. Patterns of Fractures in Accidental and Non-accidental Injury in Children: A Comparative Study. Br Med J 1986;293:100–102.
12. Cullen JC. Spinal Lesions in Battered Babies. J Bone Joint Surg 1975;57-B(3):364–366.
13. Kleinman PK, Marks SC Jr, Richmond JM, Blackbourne BD. Inflicted Skeletal Injury: A Postmortem Radiologic-Histopathologic Study in 31 Infants. AJR Am J Roentgenol 1995;165:647–650.
14. Ogden JA. Injury to the Growth Mechanisms of the Immature Skeleton. Skeletal Radiol 1981;6:237–253.
15. Wellington P, Bennet GC. Fractures of the Femur in Childhood. Injury 1987;18:103–104.
16. Blondiaux G, Blondiaux J, Secousse F, Cotten A, Danze P-M, Flipo R-M. Rickets and Child Abuse: The Case of a Two Year Old Girl from the 4th Century in Lisieux (Normandy). Int J Osteoarchaeol 2002;12:209–215.
17. O'Connor JF, Cohen J. Dating Fractures. In: Kleinman PK, editor. Diagnostic Imaging of Child Abuse. Baltimore, MD: Williams & Wilkins, 1987;103–113.
18. Walker PL, Cook DC, Lambert PM. Skeletal Evidence for Child Abuse: A Physical Anthropological Perspective. J Forensic Sci 1997;42:196–207.
19. Geddes JF, Whitwell HL. Inflicted Head Injury in Infants. Forensic Sci Int 2004;146:83–88.
20. Grant P, Mata MB, Tidwell M. Femur Fracture in Infants: A Possible Accidental Etiology. Pediatrics 2001;108:1009–1012.
21. Lewis ME. The Bioarchaeology of Children: Perspectives from Biological and Forensic Anthropology. Cambridge: Cambridge University Press, 2007.
22. Torwalt CR, Balachandra AT, Youngson C, de Nanassy J. Spontaneous Fractures in the Differential Diagnosis of Fractures in Children. J Forensic Sci 2002;47:1340–1344.
23. Cattaneo C, Marinelli E, Di Giancamillo A, Di Giancamillo M, Travetti O, Vigano L, Poppa P, Porta D, Gentilomo A, Grandi M. Sensitivity of Autopsy and Radiological Examination in Detecting Bone Fractures in an Animal Model: Implications for the Assessment of Fatal Child Physical Abuse. Forensic Sci Int 2006;164:131–137.
24. Kleinman PK. Diagnostic Imaging in Infant Abuse. Am J Roentgenol 1990;155:703–712.
25. Kleinman PL, Kleinman PK, Savageau JA. Suspected Infant Abuse: Radiographic Skeletal Survey Practices in Pediatric Health Care Facilities. Radiology 2004;233:477–485.
26. Prosser I, Maguire S, Harrison SK, Mann M, Sibert JR, Kemp AM. How Old Is This Fracture? Radiologic Dating of Fractures in Children: A Systematic Review. Am J Roentgenol 2005;184:1282–1286.
27. Calce SE, Rogers TL. Taphonomic Changes to Blunt Force Trauma: A Preliminary Study. J Forensic Sci 2007;52:519–527.
28. Wheatley BP. Perimortem or Postmortem Bone Fractures? An Experimental Study of Fracture Patterns in Deer Femora. J Forensic Sci 2008;53:69–72.

29. Wieberg DAM, Wescott DJ. Estimating the Timing of Long Bone Fractures: Correlation Between the Postmortem Interval, Bone Moisture Content, and Blunt Force Trauma Fracture Characteristics. J Forensic Sci 2008;53:1028–1034.
30. Crist TAJ, Washburn A, Park H, Hood I, Hickey MA. Cranial Bone Displacement as a Taphonomic Process in Potential Child Abuse Cases. In: Haglund WD, Sorg MH, editors. Forensic Taphonomy: The Postmortem Fate of Human Remains. Boca Raton, FL: CRC Press, 2006;319–336.
31. Glencross B, Stuart-Macadam P. Childhood Trauma in the Archaeological Record. Int J Osteoarchaeol 2000;10:198–209.
32. West SG, Hatters Friedman S, Resnick PJ. Fathers Who Kill Their Children: An Analysis of the Literature. J Forensic Sci 2009;54:463–468.
33. Chapman S. The Radiological Dating of Injuries. Arch Dis Child 1992;67:1063–1065.
34. Ortner DJ. Identification of Pathological Conditions in Human Skeletal Remains. 2nd ed. San Diego, CA: Academic, 2003.
35. Sauer NJ. The Timing of Injuries and Manner of Death: Distinguishing Among Antemortem, Perimortem and Postmortem Trauma. In: Reichs KJ, editor. Forensic Osteology: Advances in the Identification of Human Remains. 2nd ed. Springfield, MA: Charles C. Thomas, 1998;321–332.
36. Galloway A, editor. Broken Bones: Anthropological Analysis of Blunt Force Trauma. Springfield, MA: Charles C. Thomas, 1999.
37. Huiskes R, van Rietbergen B. Biomechanics of Bone. In: Mow VC, Huiskes R, editors. Basic Orthopaedic Biomechanics & Mechano-Biology. 3rd ed. Philadelphia, PA: Lippincott Williams & Wilkins, 2005;123–179.
38. Miller J. An Introduction to the Forensic Examination of Toolmarks. AFTE J 2001;33: 233–248.
39 Prendergast PJ, Van der Helm FCT, Duda GN. Analysis of Muscle and Joint Loads. In: Mow VC, Huiskes R, editors. Basic Orthopaedic Biomechanics & Mechano-Biology. 3rd ed. Philadelphia, PA: Lippincott Williams & Wilkins, 2005;29–89.
40. Schmitt K-U, Niederer PF, Muser MH, Walz F. Trauma Biomechanics: Accidental Injury in Traffic and Sports. 3rd ed. Heidelberg: Springer, 2010.
41. Whiting WC, Zernicke RF. Biomechanics of Musculoskeletal Injury. 2nd ed. Champaign, IL: Human Kinetics, 2008.
42. Cunha E, Pinheiro J. Antemortem Trauma. In: Blau S, Ubelaker DH, editors. Handbook of Forensic Anthropology and Archaeology. Walnut Creek, CA: Left Coast Press, Inc., 2009;246–262.
43. Currey JD. The Mechanical Adaptations of Bones. Princeton, NJ: Princeton University Press, 1984.
44. Harkess JW, Ramsey WC. Principles of Fractures and Dislocations. In: Rockwood CA, Green DP, Bucholz RW, editors. Fractures in Adults. Philadelphia, PA JB Lippincott, 1991;1–180.
45. Reilly DT, Burstein AH. The Mechanical Properties of Cortical Bone. J Bone Joint Surg 1974;56:1001–1022.
46. Berryman HE, Haun SJ. Applying Forensic Techniques to Interpret Cranial Fracture Patterns in Archaeological Specimens. Int J Osteoarchaeol 1996;6:2–9.
47. Frankel VH, Nordin M. Basic Biomechanics of the Skeletal System. Philadelphia, PA: Lea and Febiger, 1980.
48. Loe L. Perimortem Trauma. In: Blau S, Ubelaker DH, editors. Handbook of Forensic Anthropology and Archaeology. Walnut Creek, CA: Left Coast Press, Inc., 2009;263–283.
49. Bilo RAC, Robben SGF, van Rijn RR. Forensic Aspects of Paediatric Fractures: Differentiating Accidental Trauma from Child Abuse. Heidelberg: Springer, 2010.
50. Currey JD, Butler G. The Mechanical Properties of Bone Tissue in Children. J Bone Joint Surg 1975;57-A:810–814.
51. Hamblen DL, Simpson AHRW. Adam's Outline of Fractures: Including Joint Injuries. 12th ed. Edinburgh: Churchill Livingstone/Elsevier, 2007.

52. Stuart-Macadam P, Glencross B, Kricun M. Traumatic Bowing Deformities in Tubular Bones. Int J Osteoarchaeol 1998;8:252–262.
53. Wilber JH, Thompson GH, Son-Hing J. The Multiply Injured Child. In: Green NE, Swiontkowski MF, editors. Skeletal Trauma in Children. 4th ed. Philadelphia, PA: Saunders, 2009;57–83.
54. Jones E. Skeletal Growth and Development as Related to Trauma. In: Green NE, Swiontkowski MF, editors. Skeletal Trauma in Children. Vol. 3. Philadelphia, PA: W.B. Saunders, 1994;1–13.
55. Arregui-Dalmases C, Teijeira R, Forman J. Injury Biomechanics as a Necessary Tool in the Field of Forensic Science: A Pedestrian Run-over Case Study. Forensic Sci Int 2010;198: e5–e9.
56. Daegling DJ, Warren MW, Hotzman JL, Self CJ. Structural Analysis of Human Rib Fractures and Implications for Forensic Interpretation. J Forensic Sci 2008;53:1301–1307.
57. Langley NR. An Anthropological Analysis of Gunshot Wounds to the Chest. J Forensic Sci 2007;52:532–537.
58. Love JC, Symes SA. Understanding Rib Fracture Patterns: Incomplete and Buckle Fractures. J Forensic Sci 2004;49:1153–1158.
59. Pierce MC, Bertocci GE, Vogeley E, Moreland MS. Evaluating Long Bone Fractures in Children: A Biomechanical Approach with Illustrative Cases. Child Abuse Negl 2004;28:505–524.
60. Bandak FA. Shaken Baby Syndrome: A Biomechanics Analysis of Injury Mechanisms. Forensic Sci Int 2005;151:71–79.
61. Cory CZ, Jones MD, James DS, Leadbeatter S, Nokes LDM. The potential and Limitations of Utilising Head Impact Injury Models to Assess the Likelihood of Significant Head Injury in Infants after a Fall. Forensic Sci Int 2001;123:89–106.
62. Jones MD, James DS, Cory CZ, Leadbeatter S, Nokes LDM. Subdural Haemorrhage Sustained in a Baby-Rocker? A BioMechanical Approach to Causation. Forensic Sci Int 2003;131:14–21.
63. Moen CT, Pelker RR. Biomechanical and Histological Correlations in Growth Plate Failure. J Pediatr Orthop 1984;4:180–184.
64. Ubelaker DH, Adams BJ. Differentiation of Perimortem and Postmortem Trauma Using Taphonomic Indicators. J Forensic Sci 1995;40:509–512.
65. Borden S. Traumatic Bowing of the Forearm in Children. J Bone Joint Surg 1974;56-A: 611–616.
66. Hensinger RN. Complications of Fractures in Children. In: Green NE, Swiontkowski MF, editors. Skeletal Trauma in Children. 3rd ed. Philadelphia, PA: W.B. Saunders, 1994;99–125.
67. Frick SL, Jones ET. Skeletal Growth, Development, and Healing as Related to Pediatric Trauma. In: Green NE, Swiontkowski MF, editors. Skeletal Trauma in Children. 4th ed. Philadelphia, PA: Saunders, 2009;1–18.
68. Heppenstall RB. Fracture Healing. In: Heppenstall RB, editor. Fracture Treatment and Healing. Philadelphia, PA: W.B. Saunders, 1980;35–64.
69. Steinbock RT. Paleopathological Diagnosis and Interpretation: Bone Diseases in Ancient Human Populations. Springfield, MA: Charles C. Thomas, 1976.
70. Aufderheide AC, Rodríguez-Martín C. The Cambridge Encyclopedia of Human Paleopathology. Cambridge: Cambridge University Press, 1998.
71. Keel M, Trentz O. Pathophysiology of Polytrauma. Injury 2005;36:691–709.
72. Waldron T. Palaeopathology. Cambridge: Cambridge University Press, 2009.
73. Watson-Jones R. Reparación de Fracturas (Fracture repair). In: Wilson JN, editor. Fracturas y Heridas Articulares, de Watson-Jones (Watson-Jones – Fractures and Joint Injuries). Vol. 1. Barcelona: Salvat, 1980;11–47.
74. Salter RB. Birth and Pediatric Fractures. In: Heppenstall RB. Fracture Treatment and Healing. Philadelphia, PA: W.B. Saunders, 1980;189–234.

75. Salter RB, Harris WR. Injuries Involving the Epiphyseal Plate. J Bone Joint Surg 1963;45-A:587–622.
76. Mann RW, Murphy SP. Regional Atlas of Bone Disease. Springfield, MA: Charles C. Thomas, 1990.
77. Maples WR. Trauma Analysis by the Forensic Anthropologist. In: Reichs KJ, editor. Forensic Osteology: Advances in the Identification of Human Remains. Springfield, MA: Charles C. Thomas, 1986;218–228.
78. Rogers LF. Radiology of Skeletal Trauma. 2nd ed. New York, NY: Churchill Livingstone, 1992.
79. Ashhurst DE. Macromolecular Synthesis and Mechanical Stability during Fracture Repair. In: Hall BK, editor. Bone. Vol. 5. Boca Raton, FL: CRC Press, 1992;61–121.
80. DePalma AF. The Management of Fractures and Dislocations. Philadelphia, PA: W.B. Saunders, 1970.
81. Watson-Jones R. Fractures and Joint Injuries. Vol. 1. Baltimore, MD: Williams and Wilkins, 1952.
82. Brogdon BG. Forensic Radiology. Boca Raton, FL: CRC Press, 1998.
83. Maat GJR. Case study 5.3: Dating of Fractures in Human Dry Bone Tissue–The Berisha Case. In: Kimmerle EH, Baraybar JP, editors. Skeletal Trauma: Identification of Injuries Resulting from Human Rights Abuse and Armed Conflict. Boca Raton, FL: CRC Press, 2008;245–254.
84. Baumer TG, Passalacqua NV, Powell BJ, Newberry WN, Fenton TW, Haut RC. Age-Dependent Fracture Characteristics of Rigid and Compliant Surface Impacts on the Infant Skull–A Porcine Model. J Forensic Sci 2010;55:993–997.
85. Lynn KS, Fairgrieve SI. Macroscopic Analysis of Axe and Hatchet Trauma in Fleshed and Defleshed Mammalian Long Bones. J Forensic Sci 2009;54:786–792.
86. Lynn KS, Fairgrieve SI. Microscopic Indicators of Axe and Hatchet Trauma in Fleshed and Defleshed Mammalian Long Bones. J Forensic Sci 2009;54:793–797.
87. Baumer TG, Nashelsky M, Hurst CV, Passalacqua NV, Fenton TW, Haut RC. Characteristics and Prediction of Cranial Crush Injuries in Children. J Forensic Sci 2010;55:1416–1421.

Chapter 5
Birth Trauma

Cynthia Heldrich

Abstract It is important to differentiate injuries that can occur in the newborn and infant population from intentional injury because fractures resulting from abuse primarily occur in the infant and toddler age group. Worlock and colleagues showed that 80% of fractures caused by abuse were in children less than 18 months old. On the other hand, 85% of fractures in children older than 5 were due to nonintentional trauma (BMJ 337:a1518, 2008). While these percentages are measures of different types of injuries sustained in different age groups, they emphasize the need in differentiating intentional injury from nonintentional injury in the infant and toddler age group.

5.1 Introduction

Injury can occur during a difficult delivery with or without the involvement of instrumentation. Significant birth injury has been declining, and is more of a problem in underdeveloped countries but still accounts for between 6 and 8 injuries per 1000 live births. There are several risk factors for birth injury. These include infants larger than 4500 g, prematurity, forceps delivery, vacuum extraction, abnormal fetal presentation, prolonged labor, and precipitous delivery [1, 2].

5.2 Trauma Involving the Soft Tissues of the Newborn Head

The mechanics of the birth process is a blend of potentially traumatizing compressions, contractions, torques, and traction. When the process is complicated by abnormal fetal size, maturity, or presentation, this may lead to increased incidence and severity of damage to the soft tissues of the head and even a skull fracture [3]. These are not typically seen with intentional injury of the newborn since they occur at delivery.

C. Heldrich (✉)
Roper Saint Francis Physician Partners, Charleston, SC 29414, USA
e-mail: cmheldrich@comcast.net

A.H. Ross, S.M. Abel (eds.), *The Juvenile Skeleton in Forensic Abuse Investigations*, DOI 10.1007/978-1-61779-255-7_5, © Springer Science+Business Media, LLC 2011

5.2.1 Cephalohematoma

Cephalohematoma is a subperiosteal collection of blood caused by rupture of vessels beneath the periosteum [1]. It occurs in approximately 2.5% of normal newborn deliveries and is typically associated with forceps and breech deliveries [2]. Vacuum extraction often produces these types of hematomas, particularly when the cup has to be reapplied after an unexpected release. Skull fractures are found in 5% of children that have been delivered by vacuum extraction [4].

Cephalohematoma do not cross suture lines and most commonly occur on the parietal and occipital bones. Subperiosteal bleeding may be slow and may not be apparent immediately after birth, but may occur within the first few days of life. Skull fractures may be present in up to 5% of these nonabusive hematomas. They are the linear, nondepressed variety and usually go undiagnosed unless problems arise while the infant is in the newborn nursery [2].

5.2.2 Subgaleal Hematoma

A subgaleal hemorrhage occurs between the galea aponeurosis of the scalp and the periosteum. Ninety percent of these hematomas are caused by the use of vacuum extraction during delivery of the newborn, but a forceps delivery can cause it too.

Subgaleal hemorrhages are associated with head trauma (such as intracranial hemorrhages) or skull fractures 40% of the time [1]. These hemorrhages present with a boggy mass that develops over the scalp most commonly in the occipital area of the skull. The mass can cross suture lines, in contrast to the cephalohematoma. It develops insidiously over 12–72 h after delivery. In severe cases, shock may develop in the infant [1]. These traumas are not primarily indicative of intentional injury.

5.3 Cranial Injuries of the Newborn

Cranial injuries that can occur as a result of birth trauma include both linear and depressed skull fractures. Various studies have shown that in children under 3 years of age, skull fractures are the most common fracture type in both abused and nonabused children. The most common site of the fracture is the parietal area of the skull in both intentional and nonintentional injuries [3].

5.3.1 Linear Skull Fractures

Linear skull fractures are associated with compression of the skull from the application of forceps or from the skull pushing against the maternal symphysis or ischial spines [1].

5.3.2 *Depressed Skull Fractures*

Depressed skull fractures usually occur secondary to compression associated with a forceps delivery, but have been described as occurring in utero. These are typically the "ping-pong ball" type due to the inward buckling of the neonatal calvarium [2]. These rounded deformations occur due to the malleability and elasticity of the immature neonatal skull [4].

A complete newborn history of delivery and nursery stay is critical in determining when the fracture may have occurred. When this is not available, confusion can result.

5.4 Postcranial Fractures

5.4.1 *Clavicular Fractures*

Birth trauma has to be considered as a possible etiology when a fracture is diagnosed in an infant a few weeks old. Clavicular fractures are the most common fracture seen with birth trauma [2]. The reported incidence ranges from 0.3 to 2.9% of newborns. The fracture is not diagnosed at discharge in up to 40% of these injuries. Shoulder dystocia, large for gestational age, and prolonged second stage of labor are risk factors associated with clavicle fracture. Most of these fractures occur in normal newborns during an uncomplicated delivery, the reason why so many go undiagnosed in the hospital [2].

There are complete and incomplete clavicular fractures associated with birth trauma. Many do not cause the newborn any discomfort, especially if the fracture is the incomplete variety. The most common presentation is decreased movement on the affected side. Physical examination may reveal crepitus, a palpable bony prominence, or discoloration over the injury. The fracture is usually found in the mid-shaft region of the clavicle because it is due to compression secondary to a shoulder dystocia. Clavicular fractures can be associated with brachial plexus injuries when traction on the shoulder or arm is needed to deliver the newborn [2]. Fractures of the clavicle occur more often with vaginal deliveries than with Cesarean sections. It is possible to differentiate a clavicle fracture due to birth trauma from clavicle fractures from other causes by dating the fracture with a radiograph. If a callous formation is not seen within 11–14 days after birth, the fracture did not occur during the delivery [4].

5.4.2 *Rib Fractures*

Rib fractures due to birth trauma are rare. Most rib fractures in infants are thought to be due to abuse unless proven otherwise. Rib fractures are the third most common type of injury seen in abused children of all ages. They are rarely associated with external evidence of trauma.

During abuse, most fractures result from compression in the anterior–posterior plane of the chest due to shaking [5]. The fracture that results from anterior–posterior compression may result in stress over the ventral cortex and a fracture on the posterior rib where the rib tubercle articulates with the transverse process. Direct trauma of sufficient force that can be seen during abuse may produce a fracture at the site of the injury.

Various studies have yielded conflicting information on the location of the fractures that can occur due to intentional or nonintentional trauma. According to these studies, fractures on the rib could be either anterior or lateral if abuse was present. Posterior rib fractures were more significantly associated with abuse, as well as multiple rib fractures. Rib fractures in abused children tend to be found in children less than 1 year old. In birth trauma, rib fractures are found posteriorly near the costovertebral junction and are rare unless associated with diseases that produce bone fragility [2, 5].

The mechanical forces associated with cardiopulmonary resuscitation do not result in rib fractures in the newborn unless there are complicating conditions such as severe prematurity or conditions associated with bone fragility such as rickets and osteogenesis imperfecta [5, 6].

Accidental rib fractures are unusual in infants but may occur with massive trauma. In contrast to non-accidental rib fractures, they tend to be associated with older infants and to occur more laterally on the rib shaft [6].

Differentiation between non-accidental trauma and accidental trauma is largely dependent on gathering information from the birth record as well as how the injury occurred. Bone scans are more sensitive than radiography in diagnosing a rib fracture [6].

5.4.3 Fractures of the Extremities

Fractures of long bones such as the humerus and femur are uncommon in newborns and infants. The incidences of these particular types of fractures are only 0.13 and 0.05 per 1000 live births [2].

Fractures of long bones are usually easy to diagnose. They typically present with decreased movement of the affected extremity, swelling at the site, pain when the extremity is manipulated, and crepitus. The obstetrician may have heard a snap at the time of delivery [2]. Occasionally, the fracture is not diagnosed during the newborn hospitalization, and this may make determination of abuse more difficult.

Diagnosis of fractures of long bone is usually made with conventional radiography. This is not true with epiphyseal fractures because the epiphyses are non-ossified at birth. Ultrasonography can establish the diagnosis. Radiographs will show callus formation in 7–10 days, and this may help with defining the time of the injury as well [2].

5.4.3.1 Humeral Fractures

Humeral fractures are the most commonly fractured long bone resulting from birth trauma. These fractures are usually located in the diaphysis of the bone, and are associated with breech presentation, Cesarean delivery, and low birth weight [2, 7].

During a vaginal delivery, humeral fractures can be due to hyperextension or rotation of the arm during passage through the birth canal. These fractures are usually transverse. Large infants are at increased risk for this, as well as infants during a breech presentation (regardless of the size of the infant) [4].

Proximal humeral epiphyseal injury is rare in newborns and may not be diagnosed until several days of age. This injury can occur during the birth process or with child abuse. These fractures present in the same manner with decreased movement of the arm and irritability of the infant when the arm is moved [7].

Spiral fractures that are identified in the humerus are closely associated with intentional trauma and are one of the most common fractures seen in children younger than 15 months of age. Supracondylar fractures are more commonly seen in nonintentional injuries [3].

5.4.3.2 Fractures of the Femur

Femoral fractures due to birth trauma are rare in uncomplicated vaginal deliveries. Spiral fractures of the proximal femur have been reported during breech deliveries, twin deliveries, forceps births, premature births, and Cesarean sections [4]. However, one study found that spiral fractures of the femur was the most common abusive injury seen in children under 15 months of age [3]. Fractures are less common in Cesarean deliveries [8].

Breech deliveries may result in an epiphyseal fracture instead of the more common transverse diaphyseal location due to traction on the extremity. The epiphysis is the specialized area of bone that is linked to the diaphysis by the metaphysis. It is the part of the bone that allows for growth and is therefore more fragile.

Femoral fractures can be seen in association with neuromuscular diseases that prevent or limit movement of the extremity by the fetus while in utero. The bone involved is weakened due to the inactivity, making fractures more likely to occur during any type of delivery [7].

5.5 Causes of Bone Fragility

Congenital and/or metabolic diseases can be responsible for producing bone fragility. The two most frequently recognized disease processes that result in fractures in the newborn period are osteogenesis imperfecta (OI) and metabolic bone disease of prematurity [9]. Both of these diseases present with osteopenia that is seen on a radiograph of the involved bone. Osteopenia is defined as insufficiency of bone mass that results from a reduced production of bone, or an increased breakdown of bone, or both. This increases the susceptibility of fracture of the involved bones. The above-mentioned diseases are caused by a decreased production of bone.

The differentiation between child abuse and non-accidental trauma relies on clinical history and examination supplemented by radiological studies such as plain films and ultrasonography. Dating of fractures by an experienced pediatric radiologist as well as the pattern of the fractures can suggest the causes and mechanisms of certain injuries.

Premature infants tend to present with diaphyseal fractures of long bones and ribs not associated with intentional injury. Metaphyseal fractures can be pathognomonic for intentional trauma when seen in children younger than 2 years of age that have normal bone structure, but are rare in both OI and metabolic bone disease of prematurity. Metaphyseal fractures can be very subtle and often are not associated with tissue swelling or bruising. They can be difficult to see on conventional radiography. They are often called corner or bucket handle fractures, and are the result of twisting or shearing forces.

The occurrence of multiple fractures in children increases the suspicion of child abuse, but can be seen in infants and children with OI. In the case of OI, bone deformities are usually present [9].

5.5.1 Osteogenesis Imperfecta

OI is one of the most common skeletal dysplasias. In the United States, it is estimated to occur in 1 out of 20,000 live births. This may be an inaccurate estimation since the milder types I and IV may be underdiagnosed. It is a congenital defect in the formation of connective tissue in the skeleton and may manifest with findings such as blue sclera, triangular facies, macrocephaly, hearing loss, defective dentition, barrel chest, scoliosis, limb deformities, fractures, joint laxity, and growth retardation.

The defect is present in all the tissues in which type I collagen is an important constituent. These tissues include bone, ligaments, teeth, and sclera. The basic defect is either in the amount of collagen or a reduction in the quality of type I collagen. In 90% of cases of OI, the defect is caused by a mutation in the type I collagen genes COLIA1 and COLIA2, which encode type I collagen -1 and -2 protein chains, respectively.

There are four types of OI. Types I and IV may result in fractures that could be confused with child abuse. Types II and III are so severe that they are not likely to be considered a cause of abuse, so they will be discussed briefly.

Type I OI is an inherited autosomal dominant disease. Ten percent of newborns with OI type I may present with fractures. They do not typically have long bone deformities unless fractures have occurred. The sclera may be blue or white. Teeth may be abnormal, but this is not helpful in the newborn period to distinguish OI from abuse. Fractures can occur anytime, but happen frequently in the newborn period, as previously mentioned. Bowing of the lower limbs can occur. Radiographs reveal osteopenia and normal callus formation at the site of the fracture.

Type II OI is a lethal syndrome. The result is a stillborn infant.

Type III OI presents with severe bone fragility and multiple fractures leading to progressive bone deformities. It has an autosomal recessive inheritance pattern.

Type IV is not as well defined as the other types. Patients may have normal height, and the sclera may not be discolored. Dentition may be normal as well. Like type I, fractures begin in infancy and can occur in utero. Type IV does not have impaired hearing, which is characteristic of type I. Bowing of the lower limbs may be the only manifestation of the syndrome if it is type IV [9–11].

Types I and IV can be mistaken for child abuse. The fractures associated with OI are usually seen in the diaphyseal region of the long bones. However, up to 15% of the fractures may be in the metaphyseal area of the bone [7].

Differentiation will require a detailed family history and a thorough clinical examination, as well as radiography. Due to the defect in the type I collagen protein, the overall bone mass is reduced within the skeletal envelope. Bone biopsies may need to be performed to aid in diagnosing OI. The biopsies reveal a thinner and more porous cortex. Tubular bones are more narrow, leading to an increased risk of fracture when compared to normal bones. Type I OI will show milder abnormalities and the abnormalities in type IV will be more severe.

A molecular diagnosis of the bone disease may be necessary. There are three ways to diagnose this in the laboratory. Biochemical analysis of collagen species and mutational analysis of RNA require skin fibroblasts from a skin biopsy. This may be unacceptable in an infant. The third way is with mutational DNA and is less traumatic [9] (Table 5.1).

Table 5.1 Summary of the types of osteogenesis imperfecta [12]

Type	Characteristics	Genetics	Types of bony involvement
I	Sclera – white or blue, abnormal dentition, impaired hearing	Autosomal dominant	Fractures in newborn, bowing of lower limbs, osteopenia with normal callus formation at fracture site
II	Lethal syndrome	Autosomal dominant	–
III	Severe bone fragility	Autosomal recessive caused by parental mosaicism	Fractures associated with progressive bony deformities
IV	Not as well defined	Autosomal dominant	Fractures in infancy or in utero, bowing of lower limbs; fractures and deformities can be severe

5.5.2 Metabolic Bone Disease of Prematurity

Metabolic bone disease of prematurity (also known as osteopenia of prematurity and preterm rickets) is seen in infants born before 28 weeks of gestation. The fractures that occur because of this disease are in infants (with a corrected gestational age) after 10 weeks of life and no later than 6 months.

Rib fractures are the most common fractures diagnosed in preterm infants, but this may be because preterm infants tend to have a lot of chest radiographs done to evaluate lung maturity and to follow their progress while on the ventilator.

Fractures in the diaphysis of long bones can also occur. The incidence of all types of fractures associated with this disease is not known because the fractures may not be identified because infants are not ambulating and are often critically ill because of their prematurity [9].

Other risk factors for this disease are cholestatic jaundice, bronchopulmonary dysplasia, prolonged intravenous nutrition, and diurectic treatment with furosemide (greater than 2 weeks) that is used to treat bronchopulmonary dysplasia. These risk factors are responsible for decreasing bone mass and compromising the integrity of the bones. Intravenous nutrition is unable to provide the necessary ingredients needed to supply the mineral substrates for bone formation and mineralization.

Metabolic bone disease of prematurity is a self-limiting condition. As the preterm infant begins to eat a calcium-fortified formula and move around more, the bones strengthen and become less fragile. Usually by the age of 2 years, the preterm infant's bone mass and strength have caught up with children born at term gestation [9, 12].

The newborn history and hospital course should be all that is needed to differentiate between child abuse and preterm rickets.

5.6 Uncommon Diseases That May Produce Fractures in Infants and Toddlers

There are several other rare diseases of bone in infants and children that can cause fractures and may be confused with child abuse. However, these are not commonly seen and have other distinguishing characteristics besides fractures.

5.6.1 Menkes' Syndrome

Menkes' syndrome or kinky hair syndrome is associated with inadequate absorption of copper. Metaphyseal fractures and periosteal reactions of bone can be seen in Menkes' syndrome as well as intentional trauma of infants and children.

A periosteal reaction is the formation of new bone in response to injury or other stimuli to the bone. Chronic irritation of the bone can be seen in certain medical conditions such as hypertrophic osteopathy or in response to a healing fracture, chronic stress injury, subperiosteal hematoma, osteomyelitis, or cancer. Periosteal reactions take about 3 weeks to develop. Wormian bones in the skull and reduced serum levels of copper and ceruloplasmin will confirm this diagnosis [7, 12].

5.6.2 Cole–Carpenter Syndrome

Cole–Carpenter syndrome presents with ocular proptosis, hydrocephalus, and osteopenia. This is an extremely rare syndrome, and fractures can be a component of this disease [9, 12].

5.6.3 Bruck Syndrome

Infants with Bruck syndrome are born with joint contractures and bone fragility. This is an extremely rare syndrome, and fractures can be a component of this disease [9, 12].

5.6.4 Idiopathic Juvenile Osteoporosis

Congenital idiopathic juvenile osteoporosis (IJO) has a heterozygotic defect in the gene *LRP5.* Infants with IJO can present with vertebral crush fractures and metaphyseal fractures of long bones. Vertebral crush fractures are caused by osteoporosis and may occur with very minimal force during twisting or even standing [9].

5.6.5 Osteoporosis Pseudoglioma

Osteoporosis pseudoglioma syndrome results from homozygotic genetic mutations. It is very rare, and the infants have a progressively deforming bone disease similar in nature to OI type III. The deformities of the bones are so severe that it is unlikely to be confused with child abuse [9].

5.6.6 McCune–Albright Syndrome

McCune–Albright syndrome is a condition that causes fibrous dysplasia of the skeletal system that weakens the structure of the bone, patchy cutaneous pigmentation, and certain types of endocrine dysfunction. The endocrine dysfunction may result in precocious puberty (the most common), hyperthyroidism, and Cushing syndrome. The bony lesions can result in pathologic fractures [9, 12].

5.6.7 Osteopetrosis

Osteopetrosis is characterized by increased density of bone. Inheritance is usually autosomal recessive, but the inheritance pattern may be autosomal dominant in some people. Fractures are not usually seen in this disease. Hyperostosis is seen radiographically [9, 12].

5.6.8 Caffey's Disease

Caffey's disease is also called infantile cortical hyperostosis. It is seen in children younger than 6 months of age. Cortical thickening is usually seen in the mandible, clavicle, and ulna. It is more commonly confused with osteomyelitis because of a similar periosteal reaction in the involved bone [7, 9, 12].

5.6.9 Infantile Severe Hypophosphatasia

In infantile severe hypophosphatasia, biochemical studies will aid in diagnosis. Infants will have very low serum alkaline phosphatase activity, and there will be elevated urinary levels of phosphoethanolamine. Sometimes the diagnosis can be made in utero. The skull may lack calcification of the frontal, parietal, and occipital bones. Infants with severe cases die in infancy, but those with milder types can present with fractures during this time period [9, 12].

5.6.10 Familial Hypophosphatasia

Familial hypophosphatasia (also known as vitamin D–resistant rickets) was first described in 1937 by Albright, Butler, and Bloomberg. It is usually transmitted as an x-linked dominant trait where males are more severely affected. Children are normal at birth and grow normally until about 6 months of age. At that time, growth retardation develops, phosphate levels fall, and alkaline phosphatase activity becomes elevated. Serum calcium levels remain normal.

Fractures can result because the structural integrity of the bone has been altered. Several typical findings of rickets are seen on radiographs such as cupping of the metaphyseal ends of long bones including the proximal and distal tibia, femur, radius, and ulna. In contrast to vitamin D–deficient rickets, the head and chest are minimally involved. Other radiological findings associated with vitamin D–deficient rickets are fraying of the metaphysis, widening of the physis, and "Looser's zones" (sharply defined, symmetric, transverse stress fractures of long bones) [12].

5.6.11 Scurvy

Scurvy usually presents after 6 months of age and is due to vitamin C deficiency. There may be presence of subperiosteal hemorrhage, thin cortices, and osteopenia. Metaphyseal fractures can occur, but bone mineralization has been impaired, differentiating scurvy from child abuse [7].

5.6.12 *Vitamin A Intoxication*

Vitamin A intoxication rarely produces fractures. There may be widening of the cranial sutures and a thick undulating periosteal reaction of long bones. Vitamin A levels can confirm the diagnosis [7].

5.6.13 *Congenital Insensitivity to Pain*

Congenital insensitivity to pain has an unspecified inheritance pattern. It is seen in males more often than in females and presents in early infancy. Children are completely normal except for pain and temperature insensitivity. Children with this condition do not perspire and develop high fever when exposed to warm environmental temperatures. They can present with multiple fractures and epiphyseal separations in various stages of healing. Clinical history and a detailed neurosensory examination will determine the diagnosis [12] (Table 5.2).

Table 5.2 Disorders that may mimic child abuse

Disease/pathology	Typical age affected	Bones involved and type of fracture	Authors
Osteogeneis imperfecta	Newborn, infant, and toddler	Skull linear, diaphyseal long bone, rarely metaphyseal fractures	[10, 11]
Metabolic bone disease of prematurity	Premature infant > 10 weeks and < 6 months	Diaphyseal long bone and ribs	[9, 12]
Menkes' syndrome	Infant and children	Metaphyseal fractures and periosteal reactions	[7, 12]
Cole–Carpenter syndrome	Infant and children	Long bone fractures	[9, 12]
Bruck syndrome	Infant and children	Long bone fractures	[9, 12]
Idiopathic juvenile osteoporosis	Infants	Vertebral crush fractures and metaphyseal fractures of long bone	[9, 12]
Osteoporosis pseudoglioma	Infants	Multiple fractures and bone deformities	[9, 12]
McCune–Albright syndrome	Infants and children	Pathologic fractures of long bone	[9, 12]
Osteoporosis	Children	Fractures not usually seen	[9, 12]
Caffey's disease	Infants < 6 months	Fractures not usually seen	[9, 12]
Infantile severe hypophosphatasia	Infants	Skull and fractures of long bone	[9, 12]
Familial hypophosphatasia	Infants > 6 months and children	Long bone fractures	[12]
Vitamin A intoxication	Infants and children	Periosteal reaction of bone without fractures	[7]
Congenital insensitivity to pain	Infants and children	Multiple fractures and epiphyseal separations	[12]

5.7 Conclusion

Differentiating nonintentional trauma from intentional trauma is always difficult especially in the infant and young child. There are many injuries that can occur around the time of delivery and many conditions that can cause fragile bones in this age group that increase the risk of sustaining a fracture. Unless there are multiple fractures and other evidence of trauma in a setting compatible with an accident, care must be taken to discover the cause, timing, and mechanisms involved that produced the injury. A complete and comprehensive history and physical examination paying close attention to signs of trauma must be performed. Various laboratory testing and radiological procedures can further delineate who or what is responsible for the injuries sustained.

References

1. Laroia N. Birth Trauma. eMedicine, March, 2010. Retrieved November 14, 2010, from http://emedicine.medscape.com/article/980112-print
2. Uring MR. Management of birth injuries. Pediat Clin N Am 2004;51:1169–1186.
3. Kemp AM, Dunstan F, Harrison S, Morris S, Mann M, Rolfe K, Datta S, Thomas DP, Sibert JR, Maguire S. Patterns of skeletal fractures in child abuse: systematic review. BMJ 2008;337:a1518.
4. Bilo R, Robben S, van Rijn R. Accidental trauma. In: Bilo R, Robben S, van Rijn R. Forensic aspects of paediatric fractures: differentiating accidental trauma from child abuse. New York, NY: Springer, 2009;107–129.
5. Bulloch B, Schubert C, Brophy P, Johnson N, Reed M, Shapiro R. Cause and clinical characteristics of rib fractures in infants. Pediatrics 2000;105(4):e48.
6. Cadzon SP, Armstrong KL. Rib fractures in infants: red alert! J Paediatr Child Health 2000;36(4):322–326.
7. Green N, Swiontkowski M. Skeletal trauma in children, 4th edition. Philadelphia, PA: Saunders Elsevier, 2008.
8. Guo JB, Zhang Y, Yang YM. Fracture separation of the proximal humeral epiphyses in neonate: a case report and literature review. Chin J Traumatol 2010;13(1):62–64.
9. Bishop N, Sprigg A, Dalton A. Unexplained fractures in infancy: looking for fragile bones. Arch Dis Child 2007;92(3):251–256.
10. Plotkin H. Osteogenesis imperfect. eMedicine, March, 2010. Retrieved November 14, 2010, from http://emedicine.medscape.com/article/947588-print
11. Ramachndran M, Jones DHA. Osteogenesis imperfecta. eMedicine, September, 2010. Retrieved November 14, 2010, from http://emedicine.medscape.com/article/1256726-print
12. Behrman R, Kliegman R, Jenson H. Nelson textbook of pediatrics, 17th edition. Philadelphia, PA: Saunders, 2004.

Chapter 6
Non-accidental Skeletal Trauma

Suzanne M. Abel

Abstract Personnel who analyze the biological evidence of fatal child abuse such as forensic anthropologists and pathologists are called upon to assess skeletal trauma and distinguish between injuries stemming from accidental and non-accidental origins. Such analyses assist law enforcement personnel in the identification of individuals and the possible circumstances surrounding death. This chapter offers the reader an essential review of the important literature concerning skeletal evidence of child abuse. It focuses on injuries originating from physically abusive scenarios and also discusses the basic differences between intentional and accidental causes of skeletal trauma.

6.1 Introduction

As part of the multidisciplinary team of personnel investigating child fatalities, forensic anthropologists and pathologists are charged with differentiating injuries stemming from accidental and non-accidental origins. Physicians and dentists may also be called upon to provide their expertise in cases of child abuse in their daily practices and must also be aware of the basic differences between trauma sustained from abuse or accident. Indeed, these practitioners are subject to risk of civil suits and other litigation if abuse is not reported to the appropriate authorities. Most state laws impose criminal penalties, which may include revocation of licenses, for failure to report suspected cases of child abuse. This, along with the expectations of all investigative personnel in the adversarial courtroom setting, presents a daunting challenge [1].

In order to address such clinical and legal demands, this chapter offers the reader an essential review of the important literature concerning skeletal evidence of child abuse that tends to cluster in the infant-to-toddler time span. It focuses on injuries originating from physically abusive scenarios and also discusses the basic differences between intentional and accidental causes of skeletal trauma. Differential diagnoses for trauma sustained in the neonate should consult Heldrich (Chapter 5,

S.M. Abel (✉)
Charleston County Coroner's Office, 4050 Bridgeview Drive, Perimeter Center, Suite 500, North Charleston, SC 29405, USA
e-mail: sabel@charlestoncounty.org

A.H. Ross, S.M. Abel (eds.), *The Juvenile Skeleton in Forensic Abuse Investigations*,
DOI 10.1007/978-1-61779-255-7_6,

this volume) for information on birth trauma. Readers interested in soft tissue injuries resulting from abuse are directed to consult the medical pathology literature.

6.2 Factors to Consider When Diagnosing Skeletal Trauma

One must consider the specific type of fracture (spiral, transverse, oblique, etc.), the age and level of motor development of the child, the reported manner of trauma from the caregiver/witness, and, if possible, the child's description of the events. For example, rib fractures and/or spiral fractures of any long bones should be viewed as suspicious for child abuse in non-ambulatory children. This is especially the case when the description of the event would not plausibly produce the presenting trauma (i.e., spiral femoral fracture in an infant that is accidentally dropped).

Socioeconomic variables such as household income and composition are significantly correlated with trauma frequencies and are discussed by Ragan (Chapter 2, this volume).

6.3 Common Features of Non-accidental Trauma

No single fracture or bony reaction is diagnostic for physical abuse, yet there are certain patterns to trauma that may be suggestive of non-accidental scenarios. The most commonly cited are listed in Table 6.1 [2–8].

The most well-known trauma pattern associated with juveniles, especially infants and young toddlers, is shaken baby syndrome. Originally described by Caffey as "whiplash shaken infant syndrome" [9], it is known today as "shaken baby syndrome" and appears as a cluster of specific soft and hard tissue trauma noted in many infants despite the lack of any other external injury or history of trauma from the caregiver. In such cases, the infant is held by the chest and shaken back and forth while the unsupported head and limbs are left to freely swing about. This may result in subdural, subarachnoid, and retinal hemorrhages. If the child is held by the extremities and shaken, traction-type metaphyseal fractures and subperiosteal hemorrhage can result from the traction and shearing forces (Fig. 6.1).

It is important to note that many cases of physical abuse leave no skeletal evidence [10]. Additionally, while multiple fractures are often touted as pathognomonic for child abuse, approximately half of all child abuse victims are found to have only a single fracture [4].

6.4 Axial Skeleton

6.4.1 Cranial Vault

Head trauma due to abuse is the leading cause of traumatic infant death from injury [11]. Kleinman et al. [12] found 42% of infants in a retrospective study presented

Table 6.1 Skeletal trauma suggestive of child abuse, assuming child is non-ambulatory

Element	Location	Type/description	Mechanism
Cranium	Parietal, frontal, occipital	Simple linear, wide, complex, depressed, diastatic, growing, and/or multiple fractures that cross suture lines	Direct impact
Vertebra	Spinous process	Avulsion	Hyperflexion, hyperextension
	Centrum	Wedge fracture dislocation/subluxation	Compression, hyperflexion, hyperextension
Sternum	Any portion	Transverse	Direct force
1st ribs	1st ribs, lateral	Transverse	Acute axial load
Other Ribs	Any location, but especially posterior (head, costotransverse process) and axillary	Frequently multiple and bilateral	Shaken baby syndrome and direct impact[a]
Clavicle	Lateral	Transverse	Sudden traction on the arm
Scapula	Blade, acromial process	Transverse	Direct force, severe twisting/shaking
Long bones	Metaphysis	Corner/bucket-handle avulsion fracture	Traction injury from shaken baby syndrome[a]
Humerus	Diaphysis	Any fracture except supracondylar, and periosteal reaction in children under the age of three	Gripping and twisting, direct impact
Hands	Metacarpals, phalanges	Torus	Squeezing, forced hyperextension, trampling
Femur	Diaphysis	Any type (but especially spiral), periosteal reaction in children under the age of three	Gripping and twisting, direct impact
Tibia/fibula	Metaphysis	Any fracture or periosteal reaction in children under 1 year of age	Gripping and twisting, direct impact

[a]High specificity for abuse

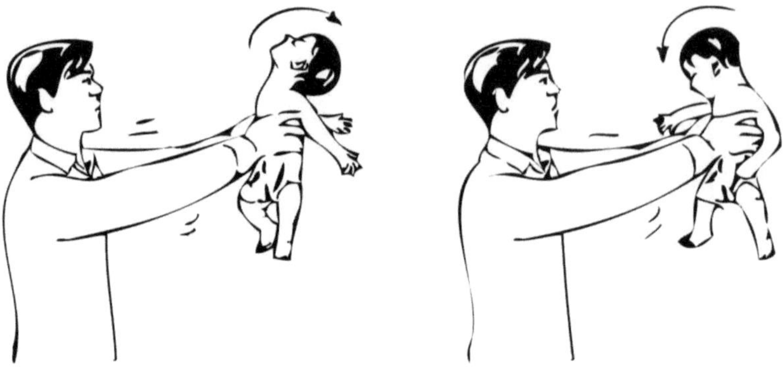

Fig. 6.1 Illustration depicting the movements that result in shaken baby syndrome. (adapted from http://kidsandteensblog.info/shaken-baby-syndrome-sbs-beware)

with skull fractures due to abuse, while Merten et al. [13] report that 50% of all children with complete skeletal surveys under 1 year of age displayed cranial trauma. Hymel et al. [5] report that abusive head trauma accounts for nearly two-thirds of all infant homicides.

The incidence of intentionally inflicted traumatic brain injury is higher in male children, in children aged 1 year and younger, in minority groups, and in those from lower socioeconomic strata [11].

The thin bones that make up the calvarium of young children (especially the parietal bones) lack the more solid adult diploid structure and so may be more vulnerable to fracture. However, the same open-sutured malleability that allows molding of the head during vaginal delivery also results in increased resistance to fractures [14]. In falls of a short distance, young children with open sutures and thin, more malleable crania will generally sustain fractures less often than older children with more tightly closed sutures and a thicker, less malleable crania [15].

The appearance and complexity of cranial fractures is due to different forces and impacts. Types of fractures include simple linear (impact with a large, flat object), concentric (high-energy impact with a solid object), complex (significant violence, multiple blunt force impacts), depressed (impact with an object of small mass and high velocity), diastatic (intrasutural), growing (progressive diastasis of a fracture), and the more rare contracoup (fracture remote from impact site). These fractures occur with widely ranging frequencies based on the age and activity level of the child.

Fatal injury from accidental falls during childhood is very rare. Although possible, it is very unlikely that a short fall in the home will produce complex cranial fractures or retinal/subdural hemorrhage [11]. Indeed, the most common cranial trauma seen in such accidental falls are simple linear fractures, with a very low risk of intracranial sequelae [3].

There are no specific features of skull fractures that are diagnostic of child abuse. Fractures resulting from abuse can be simple linear, complex, bilateral, multiple, or depressed [3]. Multiple or bilateral fractures, or those that crossed suture lines, however, are significantly associated with child abuse [6]. Knight [16] describes bilateral horizontal fractures extending posteriorly from the coronal suture as a common finding in child abuse. These injuries may originate from direct blows to the top of the head or dropping a child on the head.

6.4.2 Facial Elements, Mandible, and Teeth

Galloway [17] notes that, in the mind of the perpetrator, a victim's identity is psychologically linked to the head and face. This may make these areas a focal point of intentional injury. In a study of children less than 2 years of age who were the victims of abuse, Naidoo [18] found the soft tissues of the face to be the most frequently injured (41%) part of the body, with the cheek being the most common site for the injury. Fractures to the midface in the pediatric age group, however, may be a relatively rare occurrence because the mandible and cranium provide protection and absorb most of the traumatic impact to the elastic bones. Blunt force trauma to the eye may result in a blowout fracture of the delicate orbital floor as well as the medial side of the maxilla and neighboring zygomatic bone, but these tend to be rare in children under the age of 8 years [19]. Mandibular fractures are rare in infants and young children and are more likely to originate from high-impact accidental scenarios [20].

Dental trauma is common in children and may result from sports, accidents, and abuse. It is very difficult, however, to distinguish between accidental and non-accidental origins. Fractured, avulsed, and discolored teeth (pulpal necrosis from previous trauma), caries, and/or periodontal disease may or may not indicate some level of child abuse or neglect [21–23]. In these cases it will be important to take into consideration the child's access to preventive dental care as well as the appropriateness of the caregiver's history of how any dental injuries occurred.

6.4.3 Vertebrae

Vertebral trauma is rare in children. However, vertebral trauma may be asymptomatic and therefore may go unrecognized. They are often found incidentally on a skeletal survey without obvious clinical findings [4]. When present, they tend to result from high-energy incidents such as motor vehicle accidents, falls from heights, and sports-related injuries [15]. Such trauma is mostly seen in older children. The most common injuries are compression fractures of the body of the vertebrae, fractures to spinous processes, dislocations, and subluxations.

"Hangman's fractures," or traumatic spondylolisthesis of the second cervical vertebra, were observed historically in case of judicial hangings, where the drop of the body was far enough to generate adequate weight to forcibly produce bilateral fractures separating the neural arch after the sudden stop. In more contemporary times, such fractures occur mainly in sports or motor vehicle accidents and result from hyperextension of the head in relation to the cervical spine. "Hangman's fractures" are rarely observed in suicidal hangings because the orchestrated drop is usually too short to produce the necessary force to generate the fracture [15]. Fatalities from such hangings are usually due to asphyxia more so than traumatic vertebral dislocations.

Avulsion fractures of the spinous processes seen in the lower cervical and upper thoracic spine may be caused by non-accidental hyperflexion. Spinal fracture resulting from severe hyperflexion, however, is rare in the thoracolumbar region [24] and is less frequent in cases of child abuse [25]. In a study of vertebral trauma stemming from known abuse, Cullen [26] found various compression fractures, dislocations, subluxations, and reduced heights of the vertebral bodies throughout the thoracic vertebrae and superior lumbar vertebrae. The mechanism by which the vertebrae were injured is not discussed.

Carty [3] notes that flexion and extension injuries may result from direct trauma or from impaction injuries as the child is forcibly thumped down on the buttocks. Galloway [17] adds that vertebral wedge fractures in the lower thoracic and upper lumbar region may also be found in cases where the child was shaken.

6.4.4 Sternum

Fractures of the sternum in children are uncommon. Along with ribs, they are very rarely fractured even during resuscitative maneuvers. When present, an abusive origin should be considered [27]. Hechter et al. [28], however, found that sternal fractures are not specific for child abuse. In 12 children who presented with such fractures, the mechanism of injury was suspicious for child abuse in only two. Both victims were 2 years old and younger. Other reported mechanisms for injury included forced accidental episodes such as falling from swings/monkey bars and jumping on the bed.

6.4.5 Ribs

The thoracic cage of infants and toddlers is very pliable and is therefore less prone to fracture than the more stable adult thorax. Normal daily interaction and child care such as bathing/dressing/picking up a baby or changing diapers will not produce rib fractures unless there is an underlying health condition that results in decreased bone mineral density [15]. Rib fractures are unlikely to occur during birth, even in traumatic vaginal deliveries. It is very rare for the ribs of young children to fracture in cardiopulmonary resuscitation efforts [29].

Rib fractures are, however, the most common fracture resulting from physical violence and are considered to be the most diagnostic of all abuse-related fractures [6, 8, 30]. Fracture frequencies per child will range depending on age category. Kogutt et al. [27] found that 15% of 52 abused children between 6 weeks and 2 years old displayed rib fractures. Kleinman et al. [12] found a fracture frequency of 35% of all infants in their study. Merten et al. [13] observed that 21% of all infants with skeletal surveys had rib fractures and that 61% of all rib fractures occurred in abused children less than 1 year old. Of all rib fractures sustained in child abuse, 90% were found in children less 2 years of age.

Rib fractures from abuse may occur anywhere on the rib, but they tend to be found more often at the anatomical head, neck, and costotransverse process [30]. Fractures are also found in the posterior, lateral, and anterior arcs [3, 12]. Anterior costochondral separations can also occur in abuse, where the end of the rib appears widened and clubbed [27]. Fractures resulting from abuse are frequently multiple, involving several contiguous ribs.

The most common action in which ribs are fractured is by shaking an infant held by the chest. Such excessive anteroposterior compression levers the rib head and rib neck against the transverse process of the vertebra, leading to fracture [3] (Fig. 6.2). This anterior–posterior compression also stresses the lateral aspects of the ribs, which can result in lateral rib fractures. Strouse and Owings [31] report on possible mechanisms for fractures found in the first ribs of abuse victims. Axial loads are produced when the child is shaken or slammed down. Additional forces result when the relatively heavy head moves violently forward and backward when the child is shaken. All these forces travel indirectly to first ribs via the muscles of the neck and may result in fracture. Direct trauma of sufficient force will also lead to rib fracture.

Trauma to the thorax may be just one component of a suite of injuries that make up the "shaken baby syndrome." As the infant is held and squeezed by the thorax, it is violently shaken. The head is thrown back and forth in a whiplash movement and the limbs swing without restraint. These actions result in often lethal brain injury as well as skeletal trauma that can be observed in the chest and limbs.

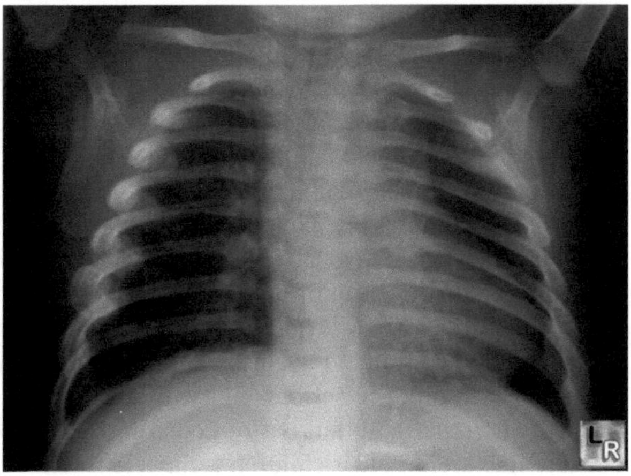

Fig. 6.2 Frontal radiograph illustrating multiple posterior rib fractures from excessive squeezing forces. Reprinted with permission from LearningRadiology.com

Rib fractures are often asymptomatic; it is estimated that approximately 80% of fractures do not lead to complaint [13]. They are rarely accompanied by external evidence of trauma [29] and are also difficult to visualize on radiographs. Fractures of the rib head and the costochondral junction are particularly difficult to observe, even with callus formation [12]. Therefore, rib fractures are in all likelihood underdiagnosed in the clinical setting. Anthropologists are in a much better environment to macroscopically visualize rib fractures (or any other skeletal trauma) as the elements can be manually freed from obscuring soft tissue.

Rib fractures may be the only skeletal evidence of child abuse. Barsness et al. [30] found that rib fractures were the only skeletal trauma as a result of child abuse in 29% of their study population. When such fractures are found, it may be in an accidental finding in a child that is examined for other reasons, or a finding within the scope of a full radiological examination upon suspicion of abuse.

As rib fractures carry such diagnostic weight in child abuse investigations, it is important to consider differential diagnoses. Rib fractures have been associated with violent coughing [32], chest physiotherapy [33–35], and prematurity [36].

6.5 Shoulder and Pelvic Girdles

6.5.1 Clavicle

The clavicle is the most commonly fractured bone in children, due mainly to its superficial location and its function as part of the supportive girdle for the upper limb in an active child. However, only 2–7% of all fractures due to child abuse are found in the clavicle [13, 27]. Midshaft fractures are not specific and should be considered significant only when associated with other injuries that may suggest child abuse. Fractures of the lateral end of the clavicle, however, are much less common and not usually encountered except as part of birth trauma or in child abuse, where they result from violent shaking or twisting [27].

It is nearly impossible to differentiate between clavicular fractures caused by birth trauma, by accident, or by abuse. Dating the fracture may help determine whether a fracture was caused by birth trauma. Generally, any fracture found 10 days to 2 weeks postdelivery that does not show radiographic evidence of soft callus formation was not the result of delivery.

Once birth injuries are excluded, clavicular fractures are rare as a result of accidents under the age of 2 years [3]. Fractures to the clavicle found in children this age and younger are the result of sudden traction to the arms by violent shaking. In children of preschool age, clavicle fractures become more common. They are caused by falls with the arm held against the side of the body. Falls from a short distance are unlikely to produce serious injury. In a study of 207 children under the age of 6 years who reportedly fell out of bed/crib, Lyons and Oates [37] found only one clavicle fracture. In older children a clavicle fracture tends to be more the result of an accident. Generally, it will be midshaft and mostly due to a fall on the shoulder.

6.5.2 Scapula

Fractures of the scapula are generally associated with high-energy impacts such as motor vehicle accidents and direct, sports-related blows [15]. Such accidental fractures are extremely rare, especially in children under 2 years of age. Fracture of the acromial process may occur, however, from severe twisting or shaking [27]. Fractures in the glenoid fossa are usually the result of a fall on the upper arm. Concomitant trauma/dislocation/avulsion of the acromio-clavicular joint may also be seen.

6.5.3 Innominates

Fractures to the innominates are rare; most are due to significant impact injury such as motor vehicle accidents [15], and trauma to this region is not usually included among those considered specific for child abuse. Johnson et al. [38], however, report on the occurrence of disruption or fracture to the pubic rami and sacroiliac joint that were associated with sexual assault.

Starling et al. [39] note that pelvic fractures are unlikely to occur in isolation, and patients who present with fractures to any part of the pelvic ring may also have concomitant trauma to other bony elements.

Any fracture to the innominates that occurs outside of a documented high-energy scenario, such as a motor vehicle accident, is suspicious for child abuse.

6.6 Extremities

6.6.1 Diaphyseal Trauma

Diaphyseal fractures in abused children are relatively more common than fractures found in other regions, such as the metaphyses. Various studies report a wide range in relative frequencies of the shaft fractures to the long bones, spanning from 33% to almost 100% [40–42].

When fractures to the long bones are observed, the investigator must consider the context of the clinical history and make a judgment whether the history, the clinical presentation, and the fracture type are all compatible. Transverse diaphyseal fractures of child abuse may be the result of direct trauma such as a blow. Spiral diaphyseal fractures may occur when an infant is grabbed by a limb; the weight of the suspended child, who may struggle against the fixed adult hand, applies twisting forces to the shaft of the bone.

Accidental transverse, oblique, greenstick, and spiral fractures in children under 2 years of age certainly do occur, but they are relatively rare in comparison with older children [3]. The 2-year mark is an important age at which trauma is critically judged regarding abuse, as children this age and younger are smaller and less able to protect themselves against attack.

6.6.2 Growth Plate Injuries

True Salter-Harris injuries to the growth plates are more often the result of accidental trauma. Indeed, they account for up to 30% of all accidental trauma-related fractures in mobile children and are therefore not primarily suspicious for abuse [43]. They may occur from non-accidental episodes, but they are relatively rare sequelae from child abuse [2].

Physeal fractures with separation of the epiphysis result from traction or rotation forces and shaking. Such fractures are uncommon in abused children [4]. A buckle fracture at the juncture of the femoral diaphysis and metaphysis, however, may result from forcibly thumping a young child on his leg on a hard surface [2].

6.6.3 Metaphyseal Lesions

Metaphyseal fractures are much less common than diaphyseal or epiphyseal fractures [8], but are much more specific for child abuse [6, 44]. Percentages of all long bone fractures that involve the metaphysis have been reported at 1–44% [40–42, 45] and even reached 50% in one study [8].

These lesions occur very close to the growth plate, unlike accidental metaphyseal fractures (usually of the torus variety), which occur at the junction of the diaphysis and metaphysis. Metaphyseal injuries are also called "bucket-handle" or corner fractures due to slight angulations in radiographic projection (Fig. 6.3).

Fractures to the metaphysis are most often caused by a shaking injury which can also inflict life threatening brain damage [2]. Hymel and Spivak [46] maintain that violent shaking of a child may lead to simultaneous avulsion fractures of the distal femur and the proximal and distal tibia accompanied by fractures of the posterior ribs and inflicted skull/brain injuries. This is the 'whiplash shaken infant syndrome', or 'shaken baby syndrome', originally described by Caffey [9].

In addition to rib fractures, metaphyseal fractures are the most specific injury for child abuse, especially when no reasonable explanation is offered for how the injury occurred. However, metaphyseal injuries are rarely the reason that a child is brought in for medical attention. They are often very difficult to detect and will usually not be verified unless they are specifically sought in high-detail skeletal surveys [12].

Metaphyseal fractures are the result of horizontal movement through the metaphysis, which is not present in a fall or blunt trauma. Indeed, the biomechanical forces necessary to produce fractures in this area are unlikely to be generated from falls or other accidents [4]. However, such forces are produced when a child is shaken while holding on to the hands or feet, or when the child is held around the chest with the extremities swinging back and forth [47]. Metaphyseal fractures occur most often from these acceleration and deceleration forces indirectly applied during shaking, but they may also occur when either twisting or shearing forces are applied when a child is taken by the arm or leg [3]. Symmetrical fractures are usually caused by indirect, violent shaking whereas single lesions and are more likely to occur by direct force [2].

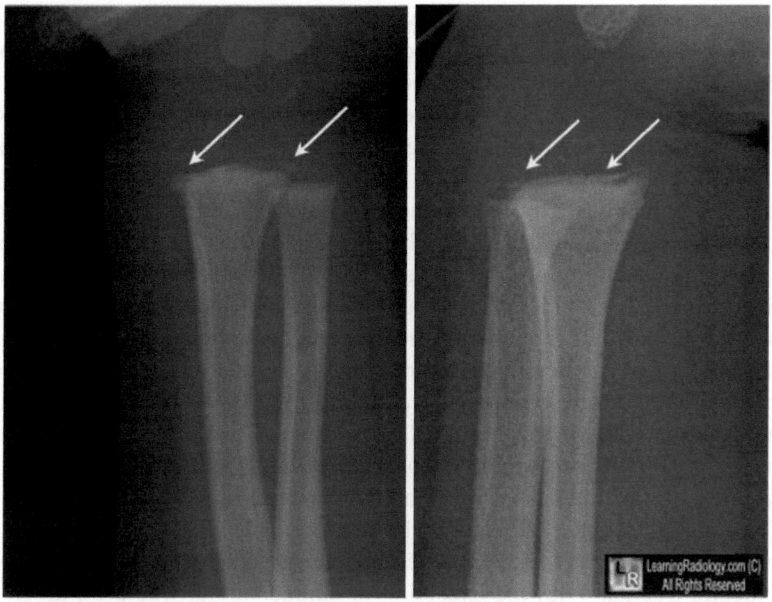

Fig. 6.3 Metaphyseal fractures of the distal radius. Both of these images are of the same element. The injuries appear as corner fractures in the frontal view (*left*) and bucket-handle fractures in the oblique view (*right*). Reprinted with permission from LearningRadiology.com

Metaphyseal fractures are most frequently found in the distal femur, the proximal and distal tibia, and the proximal humerus [15]. The tibial metaphysis is the most prevalent location for avulsion fractures [48]. Between 39 and 50% of children under the age of 18 months suspected of being physically abused will have one or more of these fractures. They are most often seen in children less than 2 years of age.

Since most cases of metaphyseal fractures do not cause severe pain, these lesions may not be obviously diagnosed in a clinical setting [2]. Often, the only evidence that may exist is radiological, and films must be of superior quality to observe these often very subtle lesions. This subtlety is because subperiosteal new bone formation does not occur because the periosteum in this area is tightly adherent and is not disrupted, therefore the usual marker of periosteal reaction for fracture will be either very subtle or not present at all [4].

6.6.4 Humerus

In determining the origin of humeral fractures, differential diagnoses are dependent upon general age groups. In neonates, humeral fractures result mostly from birth trauma, where delivery is difficult and/or the infant is macrosomal. In children less than 3 years of age, fractures to the humerus, especially spiral and oblique fractures, are going to result more often from abuse. Children in the toddler years are small and light enough to be handled in such a way that produces fracture, and they are unable to fight off an assault as an older child might do. The presence of any underlying medical condition that includes some degree of osteological involvement, and thus possible bone weakness, will naturally need to be considered as well.

Fractures to the midshaft of the humerus should be carefully assessed to exclude child abuse in children under 15 months [6]. While never an absolute indicator of child abuse, midshaft spiral fractures are caused by twisting forces, and unless a plausible scenario is provided, they should always raise suspicion for non-accidental trauma. Spiral midshaft fractures of the humerus may, however, result from accidental twisting that mimics fractures from abuse. Hymel and Jenny [49] report on documented cases where children were simply rolled over onto their backs from a prone position. The caregiver pulled them over by one arm, which allowed the opposite arm to be twisted behind the back, resulting in spiral fractures.

Fractures of the medial condyle of the humerus are another frequent fracture found in child abuse. These can be produced by violent torsion on the arm and involve both the trochlear groove and the growth plate [50]. They are rare in accidental trauma. With the exception of supracondylar fractures, all fractures of the humerus in children under the age of 3 years are generally suggestive of abuse [2].

In children 10 years of age and older, humeral fractures are more often the result of direct (impact against the shoulder or a fall on the posterolateral part of the shoulder) or indirect trauma (a fall backward on the extended arm) from contact sports, play, or motor vehicle accidents. Supracondylar fractures are nearly always the result of an accident and result when the child falls on the extended arm or elbow. Fractures to the lateral condyle are commonly seen after falls experienced during an active childhood.

6.6.5 Radius/Ulna

Of all bone trauma due to child abuse, 10–20% are fractures of the radius and ulna [51]. In general, fractures of the forearm in children less than 1 year old are highly suspect for abuse. Transverse fractures may occur when the older toddler holds up the arm to ward off a blow [3].

In the general population of mobile children, fractures of the forearm are usually the result of accidental trauma. These fractures tend to be sustained from falls, with indirect forces applied to the lower arm as the child tries to break the fall by outstretching the arm and hand. The majority of the force is transferred and applied to the radius. In younger children, this type of accident generally produces greenstick or torus fractures [15]. When an older child is held by the arms and swung, the triceps muscle is stronger than the cartilaginous insertion point on the olecranon process, and the centrifugal forces applied to this specific area can result in tearing off at the olecranon process [17].

6.6.6 Femur

Spiral fractures to the diaphysis are caused by torque (rotation along the longitudinal axis of the bone). Torque may occur in child abuse, such as when the leg is grabbed and twisted. In non-ambulatory children, child abuse should be considered when no plausible reason for the injury is given. Torque, however, can produce spiral fractures of a purely accidental nature, especially in mobile children, and can occur from actions as simple as slipping and falling while running [3].

Transverse and oblique fractures of the femoral diaphysis and are due to compression, tension, shearing, and bowing forces, and can result from accidental and non-accidental situations and from direct and indirect forces.

The age and associated level of motor development of the child who presents with a femoral fracture will provide clues regarding the true circumstances in which the injury incurred. Approximately 60% of diaphyseal fractures of the femur in children under 1 year of age are due to abuse [52, 53]. In children above 5 years, a shaft fracture is more likely due to high-energy impact, such as a motor vehicle accident. Johnson et al. [38] present a few rare cases of femoral fractures due to sexual abuse.

Kempe et al. [6] find the most common location of femoral fracture in both abused and nonabused children to be the midshaft of the diaphysis. Additionally, these authors found no significant difference in the frequency of transverse, spiral, or oblique fractures between abused and nonabused children.

6.6.7 Tibia/Fibula

In young, non-ambulatory children, fractures of the tibial shaft should be highly suspicious for child abuse. Spiral fractures can result from grabbing the lower leg and twisting but may also be the result of accidents [2], especially in mobile children 3–4+ years of age [54]. For example, "toddler's fractures" (non-displaced spiral tibial shaft fractures) are common and tend to be the result of accidental trauma [4]. These fractures can occur in youngsters who fall while running and should not be mistaken for abuse [3]. Similar to the femur, transverse and oblique fractures of the tibia may occur from direct force applied to the diaphysis.

Simultaneous fractures to the tibia and fibula are more often the result of accidents, such as spoke injuries. Such fractures can occur when a child is seated in a child's seat on the back of an adult's bicycle and their foot gets caught and becomes twisted between the frame and the spokes of the wheel [55, 56].

Isolated fibular fractures are rarely seen in child abuse. When they occur, they tend to be the result of direct-impact force to the shaft.

6.6.8 Hands/Feet

Fractures of the hands and feet are unusual, for any scenario. When present, they should be suspect for abuse in any age.

Trauma resulting from abuse tends to present as torus fractures to the metacarpals, metatarsals, and/or the proximal phalanges of the hands [15]. It often concerns multiple fingers and/or toes, perhaps in multiple stages of healing [57]. They result from direct impact, hyperflexion and hyperextension [15], or by squeezing the extremity or trampling on them [3]. In 11 abused infants with fractures of the feet, Nimkin et al. [58] found that 4 of 6 metatarsal fractures involved the first digit. In older children, fractures to the hands and feet are more often the result of accidents.

6.7 Subperiosteal Hemorrhage

Subperiosteal reaction resulting from trauma needs to be distinguished from normal physiological periosteal reaction. Physiological periostitis is commonly observed on the femoral, humeral, and tibial diaphyses of infants aged 6 weeks to 6 months. There is occasional extension to the metaphysis. It is idiopathic in nature and is usually symmetrically distributed [59]. Such physiological new bone is smooth and lamellar and observed mostly on the medial aspect of the diaphysis [3].

Traumatic periosteal reaction may also be bilateral, but there is usually other evidence of trauma, such as fracture or hematoma [59]. Caffey [60], however, previously suggested that periosteal reaction may also occur without a fracture, where rough gripping leads to periosteal damage and subsequent reaction. It has now been shown that the lesions can result from simply shaking, where the unsupported limbs are affected by acceleration and deceleration forces [1]. In child abuse, the periosteal reaction often extends to the metaphysis. Note that in periosteal reactions due to infection, new bone will not affect multiple bones symmetrically [59].

6.8 Harris Lines

Skeletal indicators such as Harris lines may be used as a proxy to determine generalities concerning overall physical health and environmental stress. Indeed, trauma resulting from child abuse is often accompanied by Harris lines. These lines (best observed radiographically) are formed in the metaphyses and are evidence of disturbances in longitudinal growth. They occur during the course of any illness involving metabolic stress (for example, malnutrition), but they are also encountered in cases involving failure to thrive and lack of bonding [15].

Harris lines are formed after an initial slowing or cessation of growth, followed by a period of resumed growth. Since the child must live through whatever nonspecific stress was encountered in order to form the Harris line, the lines represent periods of stress that have since passed. Harris lines may be multiple and represent more than one period of delayed growth followed by a period of resumed growth [61]. The lines will remain visible until puberty, at which point they will begin to shorten and eventually disappear.

References

1. Kleinman PK. "Multiple fractures in the long bones of infants suffering from chronic subdural hematoma"- a commentary. AJR 2006;187:1403–1404.
2. Carty HML. Fractures caused by child abuse. J Bone Joint Surg [Br] 1993;75-B:849–857.
3. Carty H. Non-accidental injury: a review of the radiology. Eur Radiol 1997;7:1365–1376.
4. Cramer KE, Green NE. Child abuse. In: Green NE, Swiontowski MF, editors. Skeletal trauma in children. Philadelphia, PA: Saunders, 2003;587–605.
5. Hymel KP, Makoroff KL, Laskey AL, Conaway MR, Blackman JA. Mechanism, clinical presentations, injuries, and outcomes from inflicted versus noninflicted head trauma during infancy: results of a prospective, multicentered, comparative study. Pediatrics 2007;119: 922–929.
6. Kemp AM, Dunstan F, Harrison S, Morris S, Mann M, Rolfe K, Datta S, Thomas DP, Sibert JR, Maguire S. Patterns of skeletal fractures in child abuse: systematic review. BMJ 2008;337:a1518.
7. Meservy CJ, Towbin R, McLaurin RL, Myers PA, Ball W. Radiographic characteristics of skull fractures resulting from child abuse. AJR 1987;149:173–175.
8. Worlock P, Stower M, Barbor P. Patterns of fractures in accidental and non-accidental injury in a comparative study. BMJ 1986;293:100–102.
9. Caffey J. The whiplash shaken infant syndrome: manual shaking by the extremities with whiplash-induced intracranial and intraocular bleedings, linked with residual permanent brain damage and mental retardation. Pediatrics 1974;54:396–403.
10. DiMaio DJ, DiMaio VJM. Forensic pathology. New York, NY: Elsevier, 1989.
11. Gerber P, Coffman K. Nonaccidental head trauma in infants. Childs Nerv Syst 2007;23: 499–507.
12. Kleinman PK, Marks SC, Richmond JM, Blackbourne BD. Inflicted skeletal injury: a postmortem radiologic-histopathologic study in 31 infants. AJR 1995;165:647–650.
13. Merten DF, Radkowski MA, Leonidas JC. The abused child: a radiological reappraisal. Radiology 1983;146:377–381.
14. Lancon JA, Haines DE, Parent AD. Anatomy of the shaken baby syndrome. Anat Rec 1998;253:13–18.
15. Bilo RAC, Robben SGF, van Rijn RR. Forensic aspects of pediatric fractures. Berlin Heidelberg: Springer, 2010.
16. Knight B. Forensic pathology. New York, NY: Oxford University Press, 1991.
17. Galloway A. Broken bones: anthropological analysis of blunt force trauma. Springfield, IL: Charles C Thomas, 1999.
18. Naidoo S. A profile of the oro-facial injuries in child physical abuse at a children's hospital. Child Abuse Negl 2000;24:521–534.
19. Hatton MP, Watkins LM, Rubin PA. Orbital fractures in children. Ophthal Plast Reconstr Surg 2001;17:174–179.
20. Lustmann J, Milhem I. Mandibular fractures in infants: review of the literature and report of seven cases. J Oral Maxillofac Surg 1994;52:240–245.
21. Kittle PE, Richardson DS, Parker JW. Two child abuse/child neglect examinations for the dentist. J Dent Child 1981;48:175–180.
22. Blain SM, Winegarden T, Barber TK, Sognnaes FR. Child abuse and neglect: II. Role of dentistry [abstract]. J Dent Res 1979;58:367.
23. Kellogg N. Oral and dental aspects of child abuse and neglect. Pediatrics 2005;116: 1565–1568.
24. Vialle R, Mary P, Schmider L, lePointe HD, Damsin JP, Filipe G. Spinal fracture through the neurocentral synchondrosis in battered children: a report of three cases. Spine 2006;31: 345–349.
25. Levin TL, Berdon WE, Cassell I, Blitman NM. Thoracolumbar fracture with listhesis – an uncommon manifestation of child abuse. Pediatr Radiol 2003;33:305–310.

26. Cullen JC. Spinal lesions in battered babies. J Bone Joint Surg 1975;57-B:364–366.
27. Kogutt MS, Swischuk LE, Fagan CJ. Patterns of injury and significance of uncommon fractures in the battered child syndrome. Am J Roentg 1974;121:143–149.
28. Hechter S, Huyer D, Manson D. Sternal fractures as a manifestation of abusive injury in children. Pediatr Radiol 2002;32:902–906.
29. Cadzow SP, Armstrong KL. Rib fractures in infants: red alert! The clinical features, investigations and child protection outcomes. J Paediatr Child Health 2000;36:322–326.
30. Barsness KA, Cha ES, Bensard DD, Calkins C, Patrick DA, Karrer FM, Strain JD. The positive predictive value of rib fractures as an indicator of nonaccidental trauma in children. J Trauma 2003;54:1107–1110.
31. Strouse PJ, Owings CL. Fractures of the first rib in child abuse. Pediatr Radiol 1995;197: 763–765.
32. Thomas PS. Rib fractures in infancy. Ann Radiol 1977;20:115–122.
33. Chalumeau M, Foix-L'Helias L, Scheinmann P, Zuani P, Gendrel D, Ducou-le-Pointe. Rib fractures after chest physiotherapy for bronchiolitis or pneumonia in infants. Pediatr Radiol 2002;32:644–647.
34. Gorincour G, Dubus JC, Petit P, Bourliere-Najean B, Devred P. Rib periosteal reaction: did you think about chest physical therapy? Arch Dis Child 2004;89:1078–1079.
35. Chaneliere C, Moreux N, Pracros JP, Bellon G, Reix P. Rib fractures after chest physiotherapy: a report of 2 cases. Arch Pediatr 2006;13:1410–1412.
36. Helfer RE, Scheurer SL, Alexander R, Reed J, Slovis TL. Trauma to the bones of small infants from passive exercise: a factor in the etiology of child abuse. J Pediatr 1984;104:47–50.
37. Lyons TJ, Oates RK. Falling out of bed: a relatively benign occurrence. Pediatrics 1993;92:125–127.
38. Johnson K, Chapman S, Hall CM. Skeletal injuries associated with sexual abuse. Pediatr Radiol 2004;34:620–623.
39. Starling SP, Heller RM, Jenny C. Pelvic fractures in infants as a sign of physical abuse. Child Abuse Negl 2002;26:475–480.
40. Akbarnia B, Torg JS, Kirkpatrick J, Sussman S. Manifestations of the battered-child syndrome. J Bone Joint Surg [Am]1974;56-A:1159–1166.
41. Barrett IR, Kozlowski K. The battered child syndrome. Aust Radiol 1979;23:72–82.
42. Galleno H, Oppenheim WL. The battered child syndrome revisited. Clin Orthop 1982;162: 11–19.
43. Mann DC, Rajmaira S. Distribution of physeal and nonphyseal fractures in 2,650 long bone fractures in children aged 0–16 years. J Pediatr Orthop 1990;10:713–716.
44. Taitz J, Moran K, O'Meara M. Long bone fractures in children under 3 years of age: is abuse being missed in Emergency Department presentations? J Paediatr Child Health 2004;40: 170–174.
45. King J, Diefendorf D, Apthorp J, Negrete VF, Carlson M. Analysis of 429 fractures in 189 battered children. J Pediatr Orthop 1988;8:585–589.
46. Hymel KP, Spivack BS. The biomechanics of physical injury. In: Reece RM, Ludwig S, editors. Child abuse – medical diagnosis and management. Baltimore, MD: Lippincott Williams, 2nd ed., 2001; 1–22.
47. Kleinman PK, Marks SC, Blackbourne B. The metaphyseal lesion in abused infants: a radiologic-histopathologic study. AJR 1986;146:895–905.
48. Kleinman PK. The lower extremity. In: Kleinman PK, editor. Diagnostic imaging of child abuse. St. Louis, MO: Mosby, 2nd ed., 1998; 26–71.
49. Hymel KP, Jenny C. Abusive spiral fractures of the humerus: a videotape exception. Arch Pediatr Adoloec Med 1996;150:226–228.
50. DeBoeck H, Castelyn PP, Opdecam P. Fracture of the medial humeral condyle: report of a case in an infant. J Bone Joint Surg [Am] 1986;69:1442–1444.
51. Brodeur AE, Monteleone JA. Child maltreatment: a clinical guide and reference. St. Louis, MO: GW Medical Publishing, 1994.

52. Thomas SA, Rosenfield NS, Leventhal JM, Markowitz RI. Long-bone fractures in young children: distinguishing accidental injuries from child abuse. Pediatrics 1991;88:471–476.
53. Beals RK, Tufts E. Fractured femur in infancy: the role of child abuse. J Pediatr Orthop 1983;3:583–586.
54. Kleinman PK. Diagnostic imaging of child abuse. Baltimore, MD: Williams and Wilkins, 1987.
55. Roffman M, Moshel M, Mendes DG. Bicycle spoke injuries. J Trauma 1980;20:325–326.
56. D'Souza LG, Hynes DE, McManus F, O'Brien TM, Stephens MM, Waide V. The bicycle spoke injury: an avoidable accident? Foot Ankle Int 1996;17:170–173.
57. Jaffe AC. Multiple metatarsal fractures in child abuse. Pediatrics 1977;60:642–643.
58. Nimkin K, Spevak MR, Kleinman PK. Fractures of the hands and feet in child abuse: imaging and pathologic features. Radiology 1997;203:233–236.
59. DeSilva P, Evans-Jones G, Wright A, Henderson R. Physiological periostitis; a potential pitfall. Arch Dis Child 2003;88:1124–1125.
60. Caffey J. Multiple fractures in the long bones of infants suffering from chronic subdural hematoma. AJR 1946;56:163.
61. Park EA. The imprinting of nutritional disturbances in growing bone. Pediatrics 1964;33: 815–862.

Chapter 7
Scene Investigation in Juvenile Death

Bobbi Jo O'Neal and Jennifer Schindell

Abstract The primary goal of a scene investigation is to identify, protect, document, and collect potential evidence that may provide information regarding the circumstances of the death. The scene investigation can provide valuable information regarding the identity of the deceased, postmortem interval, cause of death, manner of death, and may provide information about persons who may have contributed to the death. This chapter reviews basic scene investigation procedures as well as their application in child death investigations.

7.1 Introduction

While this chapter will focus on cases where abuse or neglect has led to death of a juvenile, the tenets set forth may be readily applied to scene investigations involving living children. Discovery of child abuse, neglect, or death often occurs some time after the original event(s) and in a location away from the original scene.

For a number of reasons, it is relatively uncommon that a deceased child is found and examined at the scene of the original event. Discovery of a critically ill or injured child will cause most people to seek immediate medical assistance, and as a result, child death investigations often begin in a medical facility. To further complicate matters, when a child dies as a result of abuse or neglect, the offender(s) may seek medical care yet provide a false or misleading history. The offender(s) may also wait until the child is "discovered" by someone else or hide/dispose of the body. Each of these situations presents unique scene investigation challenges that will be discussed in this chapter.

The scene investigation provides important information when attempting to determine, explain, and understand the circumstances of any death. The scene investigation helps answer the question "What happened?" and, just as importantly, "What didn't happen?" Other sources of information gathered during a child death investigation include terminal circumstances; medical history; social history; witness interviews and statements; initial external physical examination of the body;

B.J. O'Neal (✉)
Charleston County Coroner's Office, North Charleston, SC 29405, USA
e-mail: boneal@charlestoncounty.org

A.H. Ross, S.M. Abel (eds.), *The Juvenile Skeleton in Forensic Abuse Investigations*,
DOI 10.1007/978-1-61779-255-7_7,

autopsy findings to include radiology, toxicology, and other specialized laboratory testing; and doll reenactments as indicated. Many questions surrounding the circumstances of a death are answered by combining and comparing information from a number of these sources.

A prompt and thorough scene investigation is fundamental to an accurate cause and manner of death determination and increases the likelihood that the innocent may be exonerated and the guilty may be held accountable. In cases where the child is a victim of noncriminal, but preventable death, information gathered at the scene may impact statistics, which in turn will impact funding, education, and research directed toward the prevention of similar deaths [1].

7.2 Goals of the Scene Investigation

The primary goal of any death investigation is to determine "cause" and "manner" of death. Cause of death is the underlying disease or injury progression that results in death. Examples of cause of death determinations include "Gunshot Wound of Head," "Viral Myocarditis," "Asphyxia by Drowning," or "Subdural Hematoma (due to) Blunt Force Trauma (due to) Fall from Height." Manner of death will generally be classified in one of the following categories:

NATURAL: due exclusively to natural disease
ACCIDENT: the result of an outside action not intended to cause death
SUICIDE: caused by acts of the decedent with the intent to end life
HOMICIDE: death at the hand of another person [2]

If an investigation is lacking sufficient evidence or information, it may not be possible for the manner of death to be identified. In those circumstances the death may be classified as an "undetermined" manner until the time that evidence or information is obtained to accurately classify the death.

Contrary to popular belief, few cause and manner of death determinations can be made from autopsy findings alone [2]. Scene findings are essential to understanding how and why an individual died. Even when the cause of death is readily apparent, i.e., gunshot wound to the head, the scene findings may clarify whether the injury was a result of homicide, suicide, or accident. Accurate manner of death determination requires understanding of circumstances surrounding the event. The scene investigation provides this critical contextual information.

The primary goal of a scene investigation is to identify, protect, document, and collect potential evidence that may provide information regarding the circumstances of the death. The scene investigation provides valuable information regarding the identity of the deceased, the postmortem interval, the cause of death, and the manner of death, and may provide evidence and information about persons who may have contributed to the death. Information and evidence gathered at a scene of a death investigation may be further analyzed for identification, comparison, and individualization.

Child death investigation may involve many scenes such as the location where the decedent was initially injured, the location where they later died, and/or any place where the body may have been placed or kept after death. The primary residence should be examined, regardless of where the body is eventually found. The child's primary residence may provide much information regarding the child's normal activities of daily living, which in turn will provide valuable information about the child's normal and abnormal routines. These findings may be important for the cause and/or manner of death determination.

7.3 Impact of Growth and Development

Growth and development is an important consideration in any child death investigation. The investigator must correlate a child's actual abilities with events reported by caregivers and must maintain awareness of possible risk factors during different stages of development.

"Neonates" are infants between the ages of 1 day and 1 month. These children are at the greatest risk of accidental suffocation while bed-sharing with adults because they lack the ability to move out of a position that compromises their breathing. Two-year-olds may be more prone to an accidental drowning than a younger child as they are able to transport themselves to hazardous locations when not monitored. An 8-year-old child may be more prone to a bicycle or ATV accident, while a pre-teen or teen may be more prone to a drug overdose or motor vehicle collision based on their individual risk-taking behavior. Each stage of development has unique characteristics that may place those children at risk for certain types of injury/death. The scene investigation is an important tool to help determine the child's stage of development and/or determine circumstances that may have contributed to the death.

7.4 SUID/SIDS: What's the Difference?

In 1992, the US Senate and House of Representatives made a recommendation that a standard death scene protocol be developed for Sudden Unexplained Infant Deaths (SUIDs). Research suggested that data collected during infant death investigations were inconsistent across the county and that the manner in which these deaths were being classified on death certificates was also inconsistent [3, 4]. The classification of infant deaths is an important aspect to child death investigations and to the prevention of infant deaths. Lack of uniformity makes it difficult to monitor and identify infant death trends, which then alter statistics that ultimately impact research and prevention programs. It is important that professionals who classify or certify the cause of infant death use standardized criteria.

Often the terms Sudden Unexpected Infant Death (SUID) and Sudden Infant Death Syndrome (SIDS) are used interchangeably; however, they are two distinct terms that should be used with care. The SUID classification is a larger umbrella classification that includes all infant deaths with no obvious cause at the time of the infant's death [5]. The SUID category may include such causes of death as suffocation, neglect, choking, and SIDS, to name a few.

SIDS has been defined as the "death of an infant under 1 year of age that remains unexplained after a thorough case investigation, including performance of a complete autopsy, examination of the death scene, and a review of the clinical history." [6, 7]. In order for an infant death to be properly classified as SIDS, all of the above criteria must be met. If the autopsy, death scene investigation, or review of clinical history reveals any information that may offer a potential cause of death, then the term SIDS should not be used. In those cases the death should remain classified as a SUID with conditions that may have contributed to the death listed as a possible contributing factor to that death. Conditions that may contribute to a death with no obvious physical findings often include unsafe bed-sharing practices and inappropriate bedding. Placing infants to sleep in a prone position on unsafe bedding, can result in accidental asphyxia [8] (Fig. 7.1).

Fig. 7.1 Dangerous bedding conditions that contributed to the accidental asphyxial death of an infant

7.5 Doll Reenactments

Doll reenactments are an important scene investigation tool first mentioned in the 1996 Guidelines for the Death Scene Investigation of Sudden, Unexplained Infant Deaths and Investigative Report Form (SUIDIRF) developed by the Centers for Disease Control and Prevention (CDC). In 2006, the CDC released the Sudden, Unexplained Infant Death Investigation (SUIDI) Reporting Form [5] and associated training material that placed more emphasis on doll reenactments. The use of reenactment during the investigation of the death of a juvenile provides investigators with significant information that they may not be able to be obtained by other methods. Although it is beyond the scope of this text to provide detailed information regarding the use of doll reenactments, this very valuable technique should not go without mentioning.

Doll reenactments are a remarkably effective way for caregivers and witnesses to provide additional information regarding the circumstances of the event. The reenactment also provides investigators an opportunity to elicit information about how the infant was handled prior to and after the death (i.e., shaking, CPR demonstration, position placed in a crib, etc). This demonstration method should be used as a supplement to information described verbally or in a written statement [1].

7.6 Evidence Basics

The investigation of any death scene is driven by an attempt to identify and locate potential evidence. Specific types of evidence vary greatly between child death types and locations, but general concepts and procedures can be applied to all death scenes.

7.6.1 What Is Evidence?

> Evidence is "... anything that tends to logically prove or disprove a fact at issue in a judicial case or controversy" [9].
> Evidence is "... information ... that is given in a legal investigation, to make a fact or proposition more or less likely" [10].

There are many types of evidence and infinite methods for categorizing it. Regardless of how the evidence is categorized, the role of the scene investigator is to identify potential evidence; protect the integrity of that evidence from being altered or destroyed; document its existence, location, and context; and finally to collect the evidence in such a manner that the integrity and chain of custody are maintained.

7.6.1.1 Physical/Real Evidence

Physical or real evidence are tangible, material objects or items. Examples are weapons, soiled linens, sleeping surfaces, clothing, etc. Physical evidence has the potential to provide valuable information regarding abuse or neglect of a child, to include the following:

1. Information on corpus delicti (objective proof that a crime occurred)
2. Linkage of individuals to objects and scenes
3. Identification of suspects, witnesses, substances, and items involved
4. Proving or disproving witness statements
5. Possibility for reconstruction of events [11, 12]

7.6.1.2 Demonstrative/Illustrative Evidence

Demonstrative or illustrative evidence are representations of an item or location used when the original item/location cannot be collected, maintained, and secured for the remainder of an investigation. This type of evidence must fairly and accurately represent the real object at the time in question. Examples include photographs, x-rays, animation, maps, doll reenactments, etc.

7.6.1.3 Transient/Conditional Evidence

Transient or conditional evidence are temporary, easily altered, or expected to degrade or disappear with time. Examples of such evidence at a scene are ambient temperature, odors, heat from an engine, standing water in a bathtub, etc. Examples on a body are rigor mortis (stiffening of the muscles), livor mortis patterns (blood settling in dependent areas of the body), and algor mortis (body temperature).

7.6.1.4 Trace Evidence

Trace evidence are smaller pieces or quantities of evidence that may be overlooked or misplaced without deliberate attempts to locate and protect them. Examples are hair, fibers, dried saliva, etc.

7.6.2 Locard's Exchange Principle

Locard's Exchange Principle (also known as Locard's Theory of Exchange) refers to the concept that information is exchanged every time two things come into contact. Although some transfers may be undetected, the idea that every contact leaves a trace should direct decisions and actions during scene investigation. Not only does this theory apply to the recognition and identification of potential evidence, but it also logically extends to concerns regarding possible scene contamination.

Scene investigators must try to minimize their impact on a scene by avoiding unwanted or unnecessary transfer into the scene. Investigators, first responders, and bystanders may inadvertently alter and contaminate that scene as every individual who enters a scene risks leaving footprints, fingerprints, DNA, or other unintended transfer. The greater the number of people who have access to a scene, the greater the risk that the scene will be contaminated. Additionally, as more people move within a scene, there is greater risk that evidence of minute transfers may be obscured or lost.

> Wherever he steps, whatever he touches, whatever he leaves, even unconsciously, will serve as a silent witness against him. Not only his fingerprints or his footprints, but his hair, the fibers from his clothes, the glass he breaks, the tool mark he leaves, the paint he scratches, the blood or semen he deposits or collects. All of these and more, bear mute witness against him. This is evidence that does not forget. It is not confused by the excitement of the moment. It is not absent because human witnesses are. It is factual evidence. Physical evidence cannot be wrong, it cannot perjure itself, it cannot be wholly absent. Only human failure to find it, study and understand it, can diminish its value. Paul Kirk, 1953 [12]

7.6.3 Chain of Custody

For physical evidence to retain value from the scene to the courtroom, a "chain of custody" must be initiated and maintained. The chain of custody is a chronological record of individuals who have had physical possession of each item of evidence. A proper chain of custody offers documented proof that the evidence presented in court is the same as that collected at the crime scene. It maintains integrity of the evidence by recording who had contact with the evidence, when the contact was made, and what changes may have been made to the evidence. It is best if "links" on a chain of custody are kept to a minimum. The fewer the number of people who handle a piece of evidence, the fewer the questions that may arise about its integrity.

Chain of custody begins once evidence is recognized and collected. If a child is transported to a hospital, there may be a delay in recognizing and collecting evidence present on the body. Clothing, diapers, and other items may be removed by medical providers and unwittingly discarded without documentation. Medical staff may inadvertently return personal effects and/or other items over to family not recognizing their evidentiary value. It is critical to identify individuals who may have removed, altered, or discarded items brought in with the child. Those items must then be identified and, whenever possible, retrieved.

7.6.4 Specimen Collection and Storage

In order for evidence to retain its integrity, scene investigators must use appropriate techniques and equipment for collection, transport, and storage. Proper handling will increase the likelihood that useful information is obtained and ensure that the information will be admissible in a court of law.

Evidence packaging methods vary greatly between types of evidence, the condition of the evidence, and the type of analysis that may be requested on that evidence. Therefore, it is recommended that local crime scene procedure manuals be consulted for the techniques most likely to protect the integrity of a specific type of evidence. As a general rule:

- Paper bags should be used for biological evidence such as blood-soaked clothing or skeletal remains. Whenever possible, items should be dried thoroughly, using proper procedures, before packaging for storage or transport.
- Paper envelopes or druggist folds/bindles may be used to hold trace samples such as hairs, fibers, and paint chips.
- Cardboard boxes may be used for larger items or items with sharp edges such as guns, knives, and sections of glass.

7.6.5 Personal Protective Equipment (PPE)

Because every contact at a scene may leave trace evidence, appropriate protective gear must be worn to protect against contamination. The scene needs protection from contamination by the investigator, and the investigator needs protection from potential biohazards at the scene. Gloves must be worn at all scenes, and booties and masks may be appropriate in certain circumstances. Protective equipment must be changed often, particularly when it has become pierced or soiled, or when handling new items of evidence. As discussed above, Locard's Theory applies to everyone and everything. Professional responders must be aware of the impact their mere presence in a scene may have on the potential evidence.

7.7 Roles and Legal Authority of Professionals Responding to Scene(s)

Prior to conducting an investigation of any potential scene, it is critical that those at a scene clearly understand their roles and legal authority. Investigation into the death of a child may result in a large interdisciplinary or even multi-agency response. An understanding of each other's roles will improve efficiency and efficacy, while an understanding of legal authority will protect the integrity of any information obtained during the investigation.

In order for evidence to be admissible in court, it must be legally obtained. Protection against unlawful search and seizure is granted by the Fourth Amendment to the US Constitution in the Bill of Rights. As a result, there are numerous situations in which a search warrant must be granted prior to initiating a search. In addition to the US Constitution, requirements for a warrant may be dependent on Supreme Court decisions, state law, and case law [13]. Local laws may also differentiate between the rights and responsibilities of law enforcement and coroners/medical examiners. There are situations in which a search warrant may not be necessary, but if there is any chance that authority to search may be challenged, a search warrant should be obtained prior to entry.

Questions to answer prior to beginning any scene investigation:

- Who owns the property? Is the location private, public, or owned by the government? Do the investigating agencies have authority/permission to be present? Has consent been granted, or has a search warrant been executed?
- Is the scene safe to enter?
- Has the medical examiner/coroner been notified?
- Are other available resources being used appropriately?

7.8 Jurisdiction over Body and Scene(s)

Once the legal authority to be at the location has been established, jurisdiction over specific portions of the investigation must be determined. Each state/jurisdiction has its own laws, interpretations, duties, and relationships between law enforcement, medicolegal death investigators, and other agencies that may respond to a scene. In most cases, the body and/or human remains will fall under the jurisdiction of the coroner or medical examiner. Laws granting the coroner or medical examiner authority over the body may include items on the body, personal effects of the deceased, or implements that were involved in the act. Investigators are encouraged to review their individual state statutes. A team approach between law enforcement investigators and investigators representing the coroner or medical examiner's office is essential. A well-planned, collaborative approach will benefit all involved. The body and scene are inextricably linked, and a team approach provides for greater efficiency, more detailed investigation, and greater exchange of information.

7.8.1 First Responder Duties: Sequence of Events

The actions taken by the first individuals at a scene have the potential to dramatically alter the course of an investigation, for better or worse.

First responders have numerous responsibilities and their actions may be pivotal in any scene investigation. Most importantly, they must protect themselves and any other professional responders by determining whether the scene is safe to enter. No one should enter any scene until safety concerns have been addressed. Potential hazards are numerous and may include structural, electrical, chemical, animal, and environmental.

First protect people and then protect evidence.

Ensuring safety of those responding to a scene must remain the highest priority. The next priority is to render aid to those in need and provide life-saving care. Ultimately, people are more important than evidence, and patient care must never be compromised in an effort to protect evidence. However, first responders must maintain "forensic awareness" while providing life-saving care. In situations involving violent crime, accidental injury, environmental injury, or public health threats, the patient, family, and community are better served when this forensic awareness is maintained. Professional first responders must receive regular training related to this topic so that they fully appreciate the rationale for minimizing their impact on the scene. First responders should also be encouraged to report any actions that may have altered the scene, regardless of how inconsequential those actions may seem. If investigators are made aware of these alterations, they will not use limited resources and time attempting to understand or explain these findings.

If professional responders arrive on scene to find a child clearly deceased, their focus must change from "life-saving" to "information-saving." This may be an extremely difficult transition for professional first responders to make, as they are being asked to switch into a role that is often unfamiliar and extremely uncomfortable. Whenever possible, the deceased child should be left at the scene, in the location and position found. Transfer of a clearly deceased child to a hospital can have devastating effects on the investigation and may ultimately impact the ability to provide accurate cause and manner of death determination. Once an EMS provider enters a scene and verifies the death, additional emergency medical personnel should not enter the scene unless there are other persons in need of medical assistance. Allowing unnecessary responders or bystanders to enter the scene greatly increases the risk of scene contamination and evidence destruction.

7.8.2 Scene Investigators

Once investigators arrive, they must remain aware of scene safety while developing a plan of action for processing the scene. This plan must take into consideration location of the scene(s), size and scope of the scene(s), condition of the human remains, weather, daylight, types of potential evidence available, and resource availability. Investigators must implement a methodical approach to the scene to ensure that the greatest percentage of potential evidence is recognized, documented, and collected. This plan must be well thought out, but must frequently be reevaluated as new information becomes available. During the early stages of a child death investigation, investigators must proceed with caution and awareness that foul play may be a factor. Failing to consider this as an option increases the risk that critical evidence will be overlooked. Concerns regarding suspicious activity or will either be corroborated or eliminated as information comes to light in the investigation.

At the earliest opportunity, scene boundaries should be established. An outermost perimeter can be set out far beyond the bounds of the anticipated area of evidence collection in order to keep onlookers and media at a safe distance. These boundaries can always be made smaller, but they cannot be expanded without significant risk of losing evidence. These barriers should be set to include potential routes of access and egress from the scene. These borders may be determined using natural boundaries, existing structures, crime scene tape, well-positioned vehicles, or any other resources at the investigator's disposal. Within the outermost barrier, at least two additional boundaries may be set up: one to indicate the broad search area and another to protect the core location within the scene. For example, police vehicles may be used to block a road providing access to a property. Yellow crime scene tape may be set up to include an entire residence, including the driveway and surrounding yard. An inner perimeter of red tape may then be set to include only the particular area where the child's body was found or where an event occurred. Using a different color of tape on the innermost perimeter will draw attention to the fact that even nonessential law enforcement should not enter.

Once boundaries of the scene have been secured, a crime scene log should be established to document anyone who enters the scene. This document, like a Chain of Custody form, provides formal record of all persons who have come in contact with the scene and potential evidence from that scene.

7.9 Double-Team Approach to Child Death Investigations

A double-team approach is a useful process for investigating the death of any child that has been transported from the location of the original event. Children are frequently transported from the scene by caregivers or EMS and, as a result, are often pronounced deceased in a medical facility rather than at the incident location. In a double-team approach to a child death investigation, two investigators simultaneously conduct investigations at two separate locations. One investigator will respond to the location where the child was pronounced deceased, while the other investigator will responded to the incident location where events that led to death occurred. This approach provides investigators an opportunity to gather more information and to compare scene findings and witness statements immediately.

The investigator responding to the medical facility will first conduct an initial physical assessment of the child and will then interview medical providers and professional first responders who may still be present at the medical facility. This investigator will also be able to conduct initial interviews with caregivers who are present at the medical facility as well as begin the process of collecting copies of medical records, antemortem x-rays, laboratory samples, etc. Simultaneously, the investigator responding to the incident location will document the scene and begin to interview caregivers/witnesses who did not respond to the medical facility. The two investigators will frequently communicate their findings to determine if the physical assessment of the child, the scene investigation, and the initial interviews with caregivers and witnesses are consistent. The investigators will then develop a plan to further investigate the areas of concern [1].

7.10 Communication

Information sharing is essential during the acute phase of a child death investigation. Law enforcement, medicolegal death investigators, professional first responders, forensic pathologists, and hospital staff are among a few of the individuals who hold information that may impact the direction of any investigation. As the investigation unfolds, other individuals/agencies may be identified as possessing information germane to the investigation including family members, caregivers, primary care physicians, social service representatives, home health providers, and employers to name a few. Thoughtful communication with the family is also of paramount importance throughout the entire investigation process.

7.10.1 Caregivers/Family Members

It is imperative that caregivers and family members are treated with great consideration. The cause and manner of infant death are not often obvious from the outset, and the role of caregivers and family members will only emerge with time. An investigator's choice of words and actions can have a profound impact on grieving victims who are suffering the tragic loss of a child. In those cases where the caregivers or family members are guilty of harming the child, the investigation stands to benefit from suspects who continue to freely talk with investigators. Individuals treated with compassion may be more likely to share information than those that are treated with overt suspicion.

7.10.2 Hospital Staff

Communication with hospital personnel is essential when a child is transported to a medical facility. Hospital staff may hold vital information regarding the condition of the body when it arrived at the medical facility, may have interacted with caregivers, and may have overheard communications between witnesses who responded to the hospital. Investigators should also clearly communicate their needs to these medical providers. Historically, medical professionals receive little, if any, training in evidence protection and documentation. Investigators should specifically inquire about items that have been thrown away, destroyed, or returned to family members (memory boxes, dirty diapers in garbage, etc.). Hospital staff most likely to have information relevant to the case include emergency room physicians, nurses, technicians, front-desk staff, radiologists, social workers, and hospital chaplains. If the child is taken to surgery, transported to another hospital, or admitted as an inpatient, the list will grow exponentially.

7.10.3 Forensic Pathologist/Autopsy Facility

Communication between scene investigators and the forensic pathologist who will be conducting the autopsy is crucial. The pathologist will require specific information prior to the autopsy and will then provide law enforcement investigators with autopsy information that may direct further investigation. The pathologist will require specific information prior to the autopsy and will then provide law enforcement investigators with autopsy information that may direct further investigation. In 2005, the National Association of Medical Examiners (NAME) proposed recommendations for the minimum information required during an infant death investigation. A complete list of their recommendations may be found on NAME's website at http://thename.org [14].

7.11 Scene Considerations

A variety of locations may become the focus of a child death investigation, but a few bear specific mention. Unique considerations at any private residence and daycare/child care facilities will be discussed along with those in which skeletal remains are located. As mentioned earlier, each scene must be examined for the unique and valuable information it may hold. Regardless of the number of scenes, the goal at each is to identify, protect, document, and collect potential evidence. All scenes are susceptible to alteration, contamination, and destruction, so a prompt response is critical if scenes are to be examined in their most pristine state. Although indoor scenes may be better protected from exposure to weather and insect/animal activity, they may be more susceptible to alteration from humans. Well-meaning family/friends may inadvertently alter a scene as they attempt to assist the family by taking out the trash or by washing dishes for example. Subjects may attempt to hide evidence of abuse or neglect against the child, and other individuals may attempt to conceal evidence of illegal activity unrelated to the child's death. Investigators should pay close attention to the presence of small amounts of body fluids such as frank blood or purge on clothing worn by caregivers, which may still be worn by the individual, in the laundry, or in the garbage (Fig. 7.2).

Regardless of the location, the goal is to ensure that all potential evidence is recognized, documented, and collected. It is highly recommended that each area be

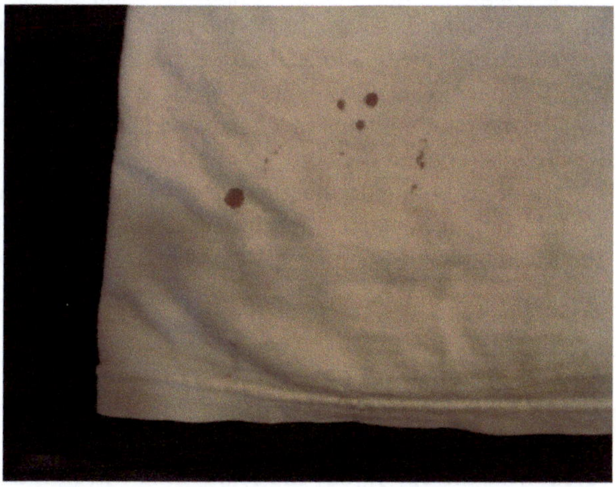

Fig. 7.2 Bloody purge found on discarded clothing associated with a crime scene

examined by more than one investigator. Having multiple sets of eyes on each area decreases the likelihood that potential evidence/information will be missed.

7.11.1 General Indoor Scene Considerations

Indoor scenes may be searched using a room-by-room or logical association method. The entire structure should be examined to include all potential entrances and exits to and from the building. The entire area within the structure should be photographed even if the death/injury event appears to have been confined to only one room. Findings that may seem unrelated at the outset may become key pieces of evidence once more details are revealed. Therefore, a methodical approach to the scene is recommended to ensure that all areas are thoroughly assessed.

Following are specific items to assess in a child death investigation with an indoor scene:

1. Type and condition of structure: singe home, apartment, etc.
2. Number of and location of doors: locked or unlocked
2. Windows: open or closed, locked or unlocked; blinds/shutters
3. Thermostat setting (in varying locations throughout residence)
4. Ambient temperature (in varying locations)
5. Heating/cooling source(s): gas, electric, and wood stove, AC, fans, other
6. Water source: city water, private well, public well, bottled water, other
7. Presence and number of stairs/stairways
8. Presence of animals (domestic and otherwise)
9. Presence of insect activity and infestation
10. Potential carbon monoxide sources
11. Strangulation hazards (blinds, swings, etc.)
12. Standing bodies of water (pool, buckets, bathtub)
13. Damage to walls and doors (patterned impressions, punch marks, etc.)
14. Safety hazards accessible to the child (unlocked or open safety gates, cleaning chemicals, medications, drugs, exposed wires, lead paint)
15. Garbage/trashcan contents
16. Refrigerator contents (adequate and appropriate food)
17. Toilets (contents)
18. Contents of laundry hampers and washing machines
19. Sleeping areas (sleeping surfaces, crib safety, etc.)
20. Mold, asbestos, or other potential household toxins

7.11.2 Special Scene Considerations for the Child's Residence

Regardless of where a child dies, an investigation of their primary residence may reveal what the day-to-day life of the child was like, as well as what their final hours may have entailed. Investigators should thoroughly document the child's sleeping area(s), play area(s), and clothing and hygiene items or the lack of those items. Additionally, the refrigerator should be checked for the presence and quality of food (Fig. 7.3).

7.11.3 Special Scene Considerations for Daycare/Child Care Facility

If an investigation involves a daycare or childcare facility, investigators should familiarize themselves with the specific licensing and operational requirements applicable in that scenario.

7.11.4 Scene–Body Interaction

During a death investigation, the scene and body are inextricably intertwined. Information found on the body must be considered within the context of scene findings and vice versa. If the child's body is at the scene of the original event, the investigator should work with the medical examiner/coroner to document the condition of the body including location found, exact positioning, type and condition of clothing/diaper, signs of external injury, and time of death indicators (postmortem changes). Preliminary documentation of these findings should be completed prior to moving the body whenever possible. Any evidence of traumatic injury should be noted at this time and those findings relayed immediately, but the investigators must bear in mind that a lack of obvious external injury does not preclude the presence of fatal internal injury. Transient or fragile evidence such as fibers, hairs, blood stains, saliva around bite marks, and patterned impressions may be readily lost during the process of moving and storing the body and should therefore be documented and potentially collected from the body before transport from the scene.

Regardless of where a body is examined, investigators must pay particular attention to patterns within livor mortis distribution. Because livor will not form in areas under pressure or tension and will become "fixed" after approximately 8-12 hours, it can provide clues about both time of death and positioning. If the lividity is not fixed, it will blanch to fingertip pressure (Fig. 7.4) and patterns that have formed may disappear when the body is moved (Fig. 7.5).

Investigators must clarify every location the body was placed after the time of discovery. As an example, family may have moved the child from an adult bed to the living room couch, and professional first responders may have moved the child from the couch to the floor. Each of these locations should be thoroughly assessed and documented for pertinent information.

Once the body has received a thorough external exam, the coroner or medical examiner representative may "release" it from the scene or hospital. This release is conditional and only allows for the transportation of the body to a secure facility

Fig. 7.3 Refrigerator contents may provide information on the day-to-day life of the child. The refrigerator contents in photo (b) are more consistent with providing adequate and age-appropriate nutrition for a child than the contents revealed in photo (a)

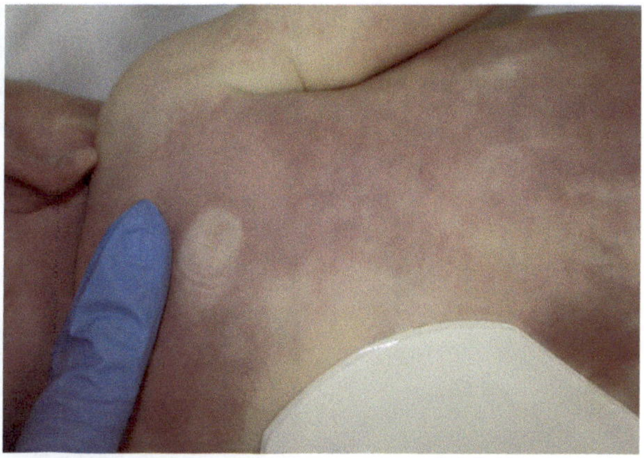

Fig. 7.4 Lividity less than 8–12 h old will generally blanch to fingertip pressure

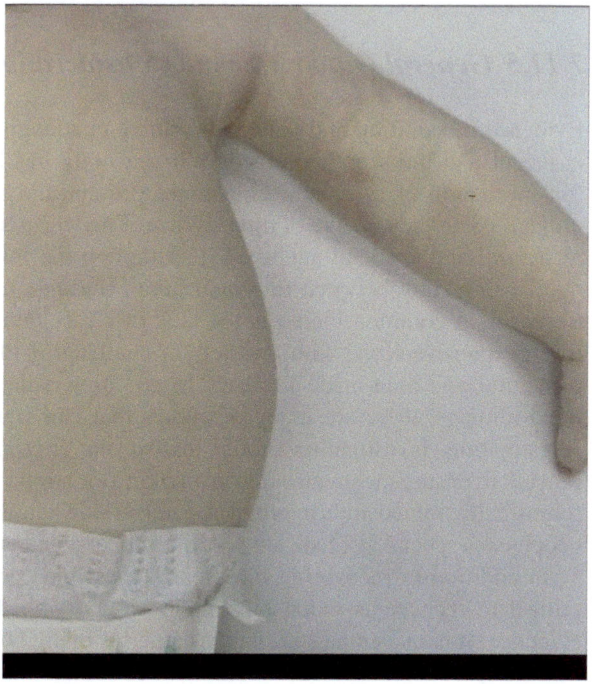

Fig. 7.5 The left arm of this infant was likely bent while lividity was forming

where it will await autopsy. The body must not be altered, cleansed, or dressed by the funeral home or medical staff. The body itself is evidence, and therefore chain of custody must be maintained until the time of autopsy. This may be accomplished in a variety of ways including by placing a numbered plastic lock on the body bag, container, or cooler (Fig. 7.6). In some cases, diagnostic imaging may be completed in a hospital setting prior to transport for an autopsy. In these cases, chain of custody is maintained by the investigators who accompany the body.

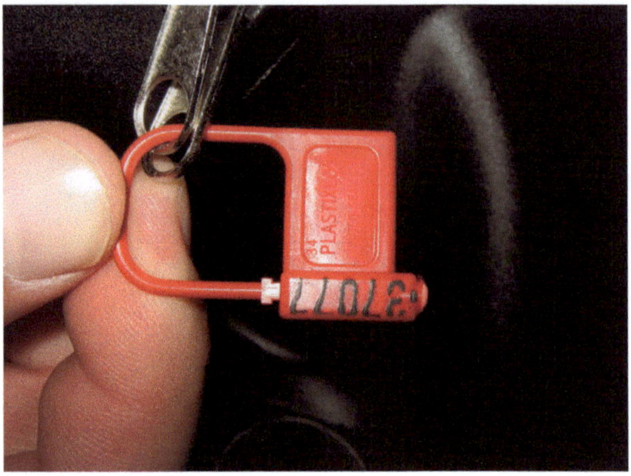

Fig. 7.6 Numbered plastic locks may be used to supplement chain-of-custody documentation

7.11.5 General Outdoor Scene Considerations

Evidence recognition and collection can be challenging even in cases where death is recent and the scene confined. When a body has been placed or left outdoors for any length of time, new challenges present and additional resources must be utilized. With the passage of time, evidence may be dispersed or altered by a variety of natural and artificial agents [15]. Although the influence of an outdoor setting may vary greatly between rural and urban settings, from state to state and season to season, a common theme is the lack of easily defined borders. The result may be an expansive scene with a variety of challenging elements including all manner of natural and man-made features. In all cases, whether involving burial or scattered remains, there are many resources that can significantly improve the scene investigation. Investigators should involve the appropriate specialists early in the process to ensure the greatest retrieval of information. These specialists may include forensically trained anthropologists, cadaver dog handlers, botanists, archaeologists, geophysics specialists, fish and wildlife officers, and entomologists, among others.

In addition to recovering the greatest possible percentage of the remains, it is critical to recover as much information as possible from the site and associated evidence. It is inadequate to simply gather as many bones or body parts as possible and transport to an expert for evaluation. There are many steps that must be taken, in sequence, in order for the maximum amount of detail to be salvaged from the scene. The value of including a forensic anthropologist in the early stages of recovery of skeletal remains cannot be overstated (Figs. 7.7 and 7.8).

Even if the identity of the victim is known, inclusion of the forensic anthropologist in the scene recovery will increase the amount of information that they may be able to provide during the subsequent evaluation of the remains. In cases where unidentified remains are located, the forensic anthropologist will be of even greater value as they create a biological profile of the individual. Armed with information about age, race, sex, stature, and unique physical characteristics, the investigator is able to begin the process of elimination and identification in the field. Obtaining

Fig. 7.7 One of the many benefits of including forensic anthropologists in the recovery of remains is the immediate identification and inventory of remains

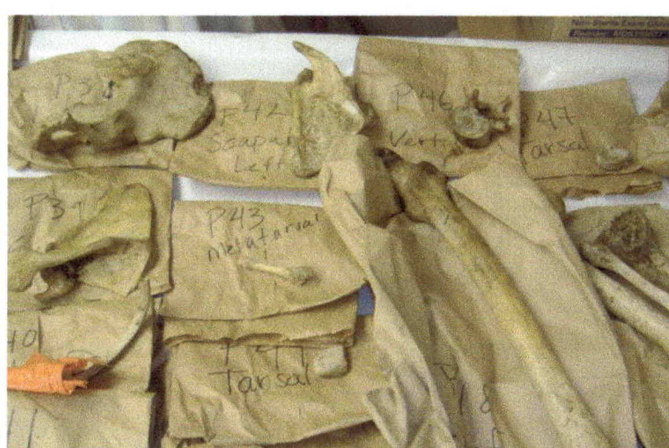

Fig. 7.8 In order to preserve details regarding relative location of remains, elements should be individually photographed, labeled, and mapped prior to removal from the scene

this information early in an investigation is of great benefit for the allocation of additional resources.

Questions a forensic anthropologist may be able to address in the field include the following:

- Is this item a bone?
- Is it a human bone?
- Are the remains contemporary or archaeological?

- Is there a single individual or multiple individuals?
- Which bones have been recovered? Which bones are missing?
- What are the subject's age range, race/ancestry, sex, and stature? Are the remains potentially Native American/historical and thereby protected by specific regulations/guidelines?
- What identifiable characteristics can be used to identify the subject?
- Are there any obvious injuries?
- Is damage to a bone the result of perimortem trauma, postmortem activities, or postmortem animal scavenging?

Use of archaeological methods may optimize evidence recovery and documentation in a burial or surface scatter scenario and these techniques may be second nature to many forensic anthropologists. For the same reason, archaeologists can be invaluable assets in efforts to excavate, document, map, and interpret the stratigraphic features or spatial context of buried items.

When properly processed, a burial or scattered remains scene can reveal great detail about what happened as well as what did not happen. The original position of the remains and associated evidence hold great value, so all findings must be documented horizontally and vertically. As with any scene investigation, the individuals processing the scene have only one opportunity to recognize, document, and recover relevant information. Processing can be equated to a "careful destruction" of evidence. While attempting to uncover information, other information is inevitably destroyed. Therefore, great care must be taken in the planning phase. Weather, daylight, and resource availability are just a few of the factors that must be taken into consideration in order to provide the most optimal environment for data recovery.

If remains are left outdoors for any length of time, they will likely be influenced by environmental factors such as weather, erosion, topography, and scavengers. As a result, with time, they may become scattered over a relatively large area and take on the color of the surrounding matrix (Fig. 7.9).

Basic procedures for recovery of these remains are similar to any other evidence search. The extent and breadth of the search should be dictated by resource availability, topography, and common sense. The search should continue well beyond the location where the most peripheral remains have been located, particularly when traveling in a downhill direction. Scavengers may take remains along their usual path of travel or to any other location where they feel more protected or elevated above possible threats. Items may be transported into trees, nests, and burrows. Search teams should be directed to flag any item that did not naturally occur in that location, regardless of whether they think it relates to the particular event being investigated. Items can always be disposed of at a later time if they are determined not to be related to the case at hand.

Methods used to search large outdoor areas include line, grid, strip, wheel, and spiral searches [13]. Each of these names indicates the shape of the search pattern, but more important than the shape of the search pattern is the fact that no ground is missed. Initial searches for a scene location may involve searching from a standing position at some distance apart. Once a scene is located and the detailed physical

Fig. 7.9 Skeletal remains will eventually take on the same color as the surrounding soil

evidence search begins, the searching should be performed on hands and knees with very little space between searchers. Specially trained search and rescue personnel can be an invaluable asset when conducting evidence searches in an outdoor setting (Fig. 7.10).

Fig. 7.10 Search and rescue workers at an outdoor scene. Searchers are close to the ground and in close proximity to each other to reduce the chance of overlooking evidence

Regardless of the search method employed, it is critical that high-probability locations are identified and searched exhaustively with significant overlap of the areas covered by adjacent searchers.

In situations where search dogs may be used, it is imperative that handlers are consulted early in the process. Decreasing the amount of distraction at scenes may increase the odds that dogs will be of assistance. Smoking, eating, and using perfume should be discouraged when dogs are working. Individual handlers are the best source for particular requirements/requests as they know the capabilities and needs of their animals.

Search and rescue teams a resource whose value cannot be overstated. The searchers will have the greatest chance of success when investigators educate them about what to expect based on terrain, method of disposal, and passage of time. Investigators should provide searchers with as much detail about the case as possible without compromising the investigation or eventual prosecution. In addition to details regarding specific items to watch for (such as clothing last seen on the individual), they must be reminded that bones take on the color of their environment and may be very difficult to recognize. They should also be given an introduction to the soil alterations and changes in vegetation that may be expected around a clandestine burial. Searchers must be instructed to flag all potential remains or associated evidence and to leave those items in the place without picking them up. Once all items have been flagged, they should be sketched, mapped, photographed, and finally retrieved.

The method of mapping best suited for a case will vary with the terrain. In urban or heavily wooded locations that do not permit the line-of-sight required for Total Data Station operation, a baseline method is an acceptable alternative. In either case, a datum (fixed point) must be selected. This datum may consist of a natural feature or may be created by driving a section of rebar into the ground. The benefit of using rebar is that it will not be lost if the natural feature is removed and it may be located with the assistance of a metal detector in the future. The site location should be documented by GPS coordinates as well as in relationship to local permanent features such as roadways or water bodies.

Detailed instruction for excavation of buried remains is outside the scope of this chapter, and the manner in which to best proceed will vary greatly on a case-by-case basis. Numerous factors influence the preferred methods of recovery, but in all cases the chosen method must result in a systematic and meticulously documented process. Burial scenes are generally more compact than their scattered counterparts, but they are complicated by a multitude of other factors.

Proper excavation of buried remains is a specialty that requires significant training and experience. Participation in a hands-on skeletal recovery class will greatly improve chances of success in an actual case (Fig. 7.11).

The following key points should be kept in mind during the processing of outdoor scenes:

- Include appropriate expert assistance early in the process.
- Assign photography, mapping, sketching, screening, and excavating duties to appropriately trained individuals.

Fig. 7.11 Hands-on skeletal remains recovery classes are offered across the country and offer valuable information to the investigator

- Photograph every body part, item, or bone.
- Closely inspect surface items such as leaf litter, loose soil, and vegetation for associated items of evidentiary value.
- Stake a grid around the burial (or concentration of surface remains) to aid in measurement and diagramming.
- Use plastic, blunt tools to reduce likelihood of inadvertent destruction/damage to the bones and associated evidence.
- Remove soil in a systematic, layer-by-layer approach.
- Meticulously document each finding in a three-dimensional context.
- Attempt to "pedestal" the findings (i.e., remove surrounding soil without disturbing the position).
- Screen soil as it is excavated.
- Photograph, sketch, and map items in relation to the fixed datum point before they are retrieved.
- Examine the surface under the remains for shoe prints, tool marks, cigarette butts, etc.
- Continue to dig a reasonable depth below the lowest recovered remains as small items can filter down through the soil.

7.12 Scene Documentation

Meticulous documentation of scene findings is essential in any death investigation. This documentation is a record of the evidentiary findings and aids the overall accuracy of data collection, analysis, and potential interpretation. Forms of documentation that will be discussed here include photo documentation, video photography, note-taking, diagrams, sketches, and maps.

7.12.1 Photo Documentation

Photo documentation is one of the most widely used, accurate, and objective forms of scene documentation. Photographs capture scene findings that may have otherwise been overlooked and record details as they were at that moment in time. Photographs also serve to aid in the description of findings and details that may otherwise be difficult to articulate.

The scene should be photographed as soon as possible in an effort to capture findings in an undisturbed state. The entire scene should be photographed prior to evidence collection except in rare cases where fragile/transient evidence may be lost during the time it takes to acquire photographs.

Photographic documentation should include a combination of long-range, medium-range, and close-up photographs to allow investigators to set the scene, reveal relationships between items, and present specific details.

Long-range (overall) photographs are used to provide context, reveal the surrounding environment, and show where individual items of interest are located within the greater scene. It is good practice to begin photo documentation of any scene with overlapping 360° photographs taken from a vantage point at the entrance to, and/or near the middle of, the scene. If the scene is located indoors, this same procedure should be used to document the surrounding outdoor setting. Additional long-range photographs may include all entrances and exits to a structure as well as routes of access/egress. Once inside a structure, the same technique of overlapping 360° photographs can be used within each room. Smaller rooms may require use of a wide-angle lens or an increase in the number of photographs to adequately capture the entire room.

Medium-range photographs reveal less of the scene but show where particular items are in relationship to their immediate surroundings. Any item of interest should be photographed from at least two sides to reveal spatial relationship and allow for depth perception.

Close-up photographs are intended to reveal the greatest detail about a particular item and can later be used for comparison and/or identification purposes. To obtain a quality close-up photograph, it may be necessary to diffuse the lighting and utilize the macro-photography feature present on most digital cameras. Items of evidence that may later be compared for size or shape (patterned injuries, bite marks, tool marks, etc.) must be photographed from a precise 90° perspective to prevent distortion with the camera aligned such that the back of the camera is parallel to the surface being photographed. If a scale is used to record the size of the item, the scale must be in the same plane as the item of interest. Evidentiary quality photographs should be composed such that the item of interest fills the frame and unrelated items are excluded. Whenever possible, an item must first be photographed as found before being photographed with evidence markers or scales.

The use of a photo log may be beneficial whenever multiple photographers document a scene or when there is a high likelihood that the photographs will be presented in a courtroom setting. This log provides a way to easily present the photographs to peers, experts, or jurors. It will also aid in identifying items of interest years after the event when the investigator has long forgotten the significance of the photographs or if the photographer is no longer a member of the investigating team. The simplest photo log may include only the name of the photographer, date, case number, photograph number, and brief description of the photograph. The photo log is used only to identify the items in the photograph and not to interpret them.

Following are the key points for scene photography:

- Take photographs as soon as possible. The more time that passes, the greater the likelihood that items will be moved or conditions will change.
- Never delete digital photographs. Even the blurry, seemingly useless, and poor-quality photographs must be maintained. Not only are they a form of evidence that must be accounted for, but they may also hold some important piece of information that is not yet recognized.
- When photographing close-up items, use a macro-lens or the macro-setting on your digital camera. This setting is routinely indicated by a small flower icon and allows your camera to focus on items much closer to the lens. When using the macro-setting, the flash will often need to be manually turned off or diffused in some manner (Fig. 7.12).
- Impressions and imprints often benefit from the use of oblique lighting. Light coming from the side will create shadows and may reveal the contrast, depth, and texture.
- Use photography to document a sequence of events or removal of layers. Take photographs before and after the scene is altered in any way.
- Use photographs to record what is present as well as what is not.
- A poor-quality photograph is usually better than no photograph at all.
- During child death investigations in which doll reenactments are being utilized, still photographs should be taken of doll placement in the position in which the child was last known to be alive as well as the location and position where the child was found deceased.
- Photographs should include overall as well as close-up views of areas of interest. The mouth and nose are of particular concern in cases where suffocation/asphyxiation is a possibility.

7.12.2 Video Photography/Recording

Video photography is an excellent supplement to still photography. It is good practice to videotape the entire scene prior to the scene being processed. It may be helpful to assign an individual to help guide the videographer through the scence and to prevent unintentional disturbance of evidence. Audio recording capabilities should be turned off during video recording, or all persons in the vicinity should be informed that their comments are being recorded.

During child death investigations, video recording the doll reenactment has shown to be a powerful tool for documenting the witness's description and placement of the doll. The video recording captures their choice of words and provides a

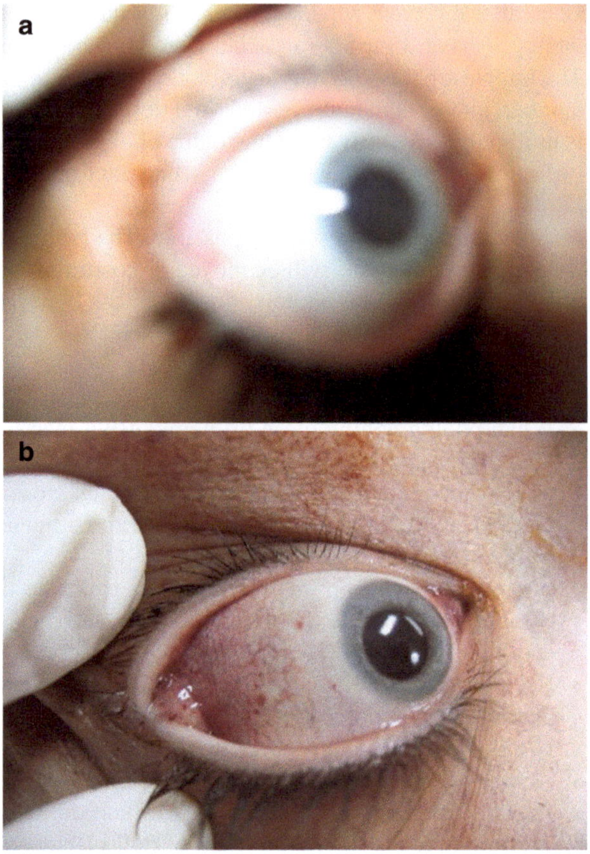

Fig. 7.12 Macro-settings are useful for close-up photography. (**a**) This photograph was taken without engaging the macro-setting and with the flash on. Notice that not only is the photograph blurry, but the details are also obscured by the "hot spot" created by the flash. (**b**) This photograph was taken with the flash turned off and the macro-setting engaged

visual permanent record of their description of the incident, which may prove to be useful later in the investigation [16].

7.12.3 Note-Taking

The importance of meticulous note-taking cannot be overstated. Many investigations begin with copious notes and end with scant illegible scribbles that are later unable to be deciphered and are therefore useless. Whether notes are placed on a standardized form or are free flowing, it is critical to take the time to record findings and actions. The most astute observations will be useless if the investigator cannot remember them at the time of writing a report or testifying in court.

Scene notes should include, at a minimum, the following:

- Time of arrival and departure
- Initial observations of conditional evidence (lights, doors, temperature, smells)

- Verbatim statements
- Conditions or items that cause you to form an opinion about what happened
- Findings that make other scenarios unlikely or impossible

7.12.4 Sketches/Diagrams/Maps

Scene sketches, diagrams, and maps are useful in providing context, orientation, and spatial relationships. They may serve as an investigative aid during interviews and may serve as demonstrative aids in court. Key features of any diagram include compass orientation, permanent reference points, measurements from reference points to items of interest, and associated objects that aid in establishing location (roads, walls, water bodies, light poles, fire hydrants, etc.). Most diagrams are not drawn to scale, and this should be clear on the legend. Scene investigators should indicate whether metric or English measurements were utilized.

7.13 Conclusion

Scene investigation is a critical component of any death investigation and a child death investigation may involve more than one scene. A prompt, thoughtful evaluation of each scene will increase the likelihood that key evidence is recovered and that an accurate cause and manner of death determination can be made.

Suggested Reading

American Board of Medicolegal Death Investigators, Inc. (ABMDI), http://www.slu.edu/organizations/abmdi/.

Byers S. Introduction to Forensic Anthropology, 3rd rev. ed. Boston, MA: Allyn and Bacon Press, 2007.

Center for Disease Control and Prevention, Sudden Unexplained Infant Death Investigation Initiate (SUIDI): Overview, available at http://www.cdc.gov/SIDS/SUID/htm.

Center for Disease Control and Prevention, Sudden Unexplained Infant Death Investigation Reporting Form. Additional Investigative Scene Forms: Body Diagram forms, available at http://www.cdc.gov/SIDS/PDF/SUIDIforms.pdf.

Haskell NH, Williams RE, editors. Entomology & Death: A Procedural Guide. Clemson: East Park Printing, 2008.

Melbye J, Jimenez SB. Chain of Custody from the Field to the Courtroom. In: Haglund WD, Sorg MH, editors. Forensic Taphonomy: The Postmortem Fate of Human Remains. Boca Raton, FL: CRC Press, 1997:65–75.

Miller MT. Crime Scene Investigation. In: James SH, Nordby JJ, editors. Forensic Science: An Introduction to Scientific and Investigative Techniques. Boca Raton, FL: CRC Press, 2009:167–192.

National Association of Medical Examiners (NAME). http://www.thename.org.

Pasquale-Styles MA, Tackitt PL, Schmidt CJ. Infant Death Scene Investigation and the Assessment of Potential Risk Factors for Asphyxia: A Review of 209 Sudden Unexpected Infant Deaths. J Forensic Sci 2007 July;52(4):924–929.

Scott DD, Connor M. Context Delicti: Archaeological Context in Forensic Work. In: Haglund WD, Sorg MH, editors. Forensic Taphonomy: The Postmortem Fate of Human Remains. Boca Raton, FL: CRC Press, 1997:27–38.

Spitz WU, Spitz DJ, editors. Medicolegal Investigation of Death: Guidelines for the Application of Pathology to Crime Investigation. Springfield: Charles T. Thomas, 2006.

Ubelaker D. Taphonomic Applications in Forensic Anthropology. In: Haglund WD, Sorg MH, editors. Forensic Taphonomy: The Postmortem Fate of Human Remains. Boca Raton, FL: CRC Press, 1997:77–90.

U.S. Department of Justice, Office of Justice Programs, National Institute of Justice. Crime Scene Investigation: A Guide for Law Enforcement. Washington, DC: U.S. Department of Justice, 2000. www.ncjrs.gov/pdffiles1/nij/ 178280.pdf.

U.S. Department of Justice, Office of Justice Programs, National Institute of Justice. Death Investigation: A Guide for the Scene Investigator. Washington, DC: U.S. Department of Justice, 1999. www.ncjrs.gov/pdffiles/167568.pdf

American Academy of Pediatrics, Hymel KP, Committee on Child Abuse and Neglect, National Association of Medical Examiners. Distinguishing sudden infant death syndrome from child abuse fatalities. Pediatrics 2006 Jul;118(1):421–427.

References

1. O'Neal BJ. Investigating Infant Deaths. Boca Raton, FL: CRC Press, 2007.
2. Adams VI, Flomenbaum MA, Hirsch CS. Trauma and Disease. In: Spitz WU, editor. Spitz and Fisher's: Medicolegal Investigation of Death, 4th ed. Springfield: Charles C Thomas, 2006:436–459.
3. Shapiro-Mendoza CK, Tomashek KM, Anderson, RN, Wingo J. Recent national trends in sudden, unexpected infant death: More evidence supporting a change in classification or reporting. Am J Epidemiol 2006;163(8):762–792.
4. Malloy MH, MacDorman M. Changes in the classification of sudden unexpected infant deaths: United States, 1992–2001. Pediatrics 2005;115(5):1247–1253.
5. Center of disease, control and prevention. Guidelines for death scene investigators of sudden, unexplained infant deaths: Recommendations of the interagency panel on sudden infant death syndrome. Morbid Mortal Wkly Rep 1996;45:RR–10.
6. Willinger M, James LS, Catz C. Defining the sudden infant death syndrome (SIDS): Deliberations of an expert panel convened by the National Institute of Child Health and Human Development. Pediatr Pathol 1991;11(5):677–684.
7. American Academy of Pediatrics, Committee on Child Abuse and Neglect and National Association of Medical Examiners. Pediatrics 2006;118:421–427. Retrieved February 1, 2010, from http://aapolicy.aappublications.or/cgi/content/reprint/pediatrics;118/1/421.pdf
8. http://thename.org – Writing Cause of Death Statements in SIDS 2002 A Guide for Manner of Death Classification, 1st ed. pp 15–18 Sudden Infant Death Syndrome and Related Infant Deaths
9. Swanson CR, Chamelin NC, Territo L, Taylor RW. Criminal Investigation, 9th ed. Boston, MA: McGraw-Hill, 2006.
10. Houck M, Siegel, J. Fundamentals of Forensic Science. Oxford: Elsevier, 2006.
11. James S, Nordby J, editors. Forensic Science: An Introduction to Scientific and Investigative Techniques, 3rd rev. ed. Boca Raton, FL: CRC Press, 2005.

12. Kirk PL. Crime Investigation: Physical Evidence and the Police Laboratory. New York, NY: Interscience, 1953.
13. Geberth, VG. Practical Homicide Investigation: Tactics, Procedures, and Forensic Techniques, 4th ed. Boca Raton, FL: CRC Press, 2006.
14. Corey TS, Hanzlick J, Nelson C, Krous H. A Functional Approach to Sudden Unexpected Infant Death. Prepared by the NAME Ad Hoc Committee on Sudden Unexplained Infant Death. Approved by the NAME Board of Directors on October 14, 2005. http://www.thename.org
15. Dirkmatt D, Adovasio JM. The Role of Archeology in the Recovery and Interpretation of Human Remains from an Outdoor Forensic Setting. In: Haglund WD, Sorg MH, editors. Forensic Taphonomy: The Postmortem Fate of Human Remains. Boca Raton, FL: CRC Press, 1997:39–64.
16. O'Neal BJ, Wooten RH. Child Death Investigation from Beginning to End. Presented at the International Association of Forensic Nurses Scientific Assembly. Pittsburg, PA, October 2010.

Chapter 8
Medicolegal Issues of Battered Baby Syndrome

Erin H. Kimmerle and Leszek Chrostowski

Abstract Battered baby (child) syndrome has been recognized for nearly half a century and is defined as repeated non-accidental trauma of various ages. In medicolegal death investigations, it is often avoided, due to its alleged controversy, or more accurately, due to the challenges it presents in court. In this chapter, we discuss some of the medicolegal issues of a battered baby syndrome diagnosis for the cause of death and the legal issues surrounding the prosecution and defense in these types of cases. A case example involving a 5-month-old infant is presented. Additionally, the importance and challenges in timing fractures and using skeletal trauma as evidence of abuse are discussed. Finally, this case is contextualized among infant and child homicides and recommendations for best practices are outlined.

Children begin by loving their parents. After a time they judge them. Rarely, if ever, do they forgive them.
Oscar Wilde

8.1 The Speaker for the Dead

Pediatric forensic pathology is one of the most challenging fields within the specialty; it can charge the investigators, pathologists, and anthropologists to their limits. The issues we face in these cases are not confined to "just" determination of the cause and manner of death and scientific evidence shedding light on the circumstances of death, but also include ethical and emotional aspects. We do not want to over-call or under-call the diagnosis, since the consequences of each may be quite severe. One can also easily find himself/herself framed as a "speaker for the defense" or a "speaker for the prosecution." This must be avoided with great care: we have to bear in mind that we are neither. If we do speak for somebody, we can be considered *The Speakers for the Dead.* At times it is difficult to avoid being emotional in these cases; after all, we are human, and often parents ourselves. However, despite the subtle (or not so subtle) push from the attorneys to elicit emotional responses from jurors, we should stay within the limits of science and clearly indicate the gray areas of scientific uncertainty.

E.H. Kimmerle (✉)
Department of Anthropology, University of South Florida, Tampa, FL 33620-8100, USA
e-mail: Kimmerle@usf.edu

A.H. Ross, S.M. Abel (eds.), *The Juvenile Skeleton in Forensic Abuse Investigations*,
DOI 10.1007/978-1-61779-255-7_8,

The first challenge of death investigation of a child is to gather the background information. To begin with, the available information usually originates from the caretakers. Even in a benign controversy of natural vs. accidental manners of death, difficulties may arise, since the source of information are emotionally challenged people who just suffered a loss and often fear the investigation. This may result in the omission or commission of information that eventually may affect the cause and manner of death opinion, for example, a "probable SIDS" case in a child that was reportedly found supine in his crib, but has fixed anterior lividity. A prone position would not exclude SIDS. On the other hand, one starts to wonder *what else was I not told*, and that may result in an opinion of "undetermined" due to inconsistency in the investigation.

In cases of child abuse, it is typical for the responsible parent or caregiver to tell authorities that the child fell or had an accident, even while seeking medical treatment for inflicted trauma. Therefore, it is incumbent upon detectives, medical examiners, and forensic anthropologists working in cases of child deaths to present clear evidence that will either support or refute such claims. In some cases, distinction between accidental versus non-accidental injuries may be difficult or outright impossible [1]. In such cases, clues may be buried in the investigation data, provided by autopsy findings or anthropological analysis, or found in the ancillary studies. Another issue may be dating of the injuries, e.g., various ages of fractures to bone or bruises; at times such determinations are pertinent to the diagnosis, and in other cases, they may be of paramount importance for the prosecution or defense, even when they bear no significant influence on the cause and manner of death opinion. Establishing a timeline for injuries may provide the attorneys with physical evidence that is necessary for demonstrating custody and control in cases of child abuse.

The correct interpretation of the findings may allow for reconstruction based on the injuries of the events surrounding the death and determination of whether or not a crime was committed. When accidental versus inflicted trauma can be clearly differentiated, and patterns of repeated abuse or neglect established, issuing an opinion seems to be a straightforward task. Having said that, even in some cases where significant amounts of inflicted trauma are present, the actual mechanism of death may not be clear, thereby challenging death investigators and courts.

In this chapter, we present a case of a 5-month-old infant, whose death was opined as resulting from battered baby syndrome with a laceration of the small bowel and rib fractures, and the manner of death as homicide. The case details, including ante- and perimortem trauma, are discussed, with attention to radiography for fracture diagnosis and histological timing. Further, key issues arising at the trial in the attempted prosecution of this case are discussed, including the prosecution and defense tactics, and the debate over the specific mechanism of death, diagnosis, and the dating of the rib fractures. Finally, we present some of the general trends among cases involving battered baby syndrome and child homicides to illustrate the difficulty in employing this syndrome as the diagnosis; we hope to dispel common misperceptions, offer some recommendations for best practice, and highlight the areas where further research may be beneficial.

8.1.1 Case in Point

The decedent was a 5-month-old infant boy, who was visiting family with his father, from another state. They were staying in their family's apartment for 3 weeks, occupying one bedroom. Reportedly, the vacation from their home state and from the child's mother was not quite voluntary, due to financial problems associated with job loss back home. There was neither history of domestic violence in this family, nor history of any medical problems. During the stay, the child was healthy. Their hosts described the father as a person loving and caring for the child; they never noticed any evidence of him abusing the boy. In the bedroom, the boy was co-sleeping with his father in a queen-size bed. One night the father emerged from the bedroom, extremely upset, screaming and kicking furniture; he stated that he found the child unresponsive.

The father claimed that the baby rolled off the bed and was found "wedged" face down in between the bed and the dresser, with his feet on the bed. When he picked the baby up from the floor, the infant gasped and then became unresponsive. Reportedly, the decedent's father attempted resuscitation; he said that he was compressing the boy's abdomen while the child was on the bed. Then, the aunt (who is a nurse) started resuscitation, and the paramedics were summoned. The initial recorded heart rhythm was asystole, and the Glasgow coma scale score was 3. The child was transported to a hospital. The baby did not regain consciousness or heartbeat, and since the therapeutic efforts were ineffective, he was pronounced dead in the emergency room. The elapsed time of resuscitation, including by-stander efforts, was nearly 2 h. The death was reported to medical examiner's office as suspicious, due to external evidence of blunt impact trauma, i.e., multiple bruises.

The scene was in a ground-floor apartment, neat and clean, in a new, gated apartment complex. The bedroom that was occupied by the decedent and his father was equipped with a queen-size bed. There was a dresser against the wall parallel to the side of the bed, with an 18-inch-wide gap between the dresser and the bed. In that space, there was a carpeted floor (about an inch thick carpet with sponge padding) with a large pillow filling the space between the bed and the dresser. The pillow had dried clear stains of mucus, on the entire surface, i.e., close to the bed and close to the dresser.

The autopsy revealed multiple contusions in the skin, subcutaneous tissue, and muscles on the abdomen in the inguinal and umbilical regions and at the rib arches. Small contusions were in the back muscles, in the thoracolumbar region, and in the scalp on each side. There were also contusions on the buttocks. The distribution of the inguinal and buttocks contusions had pattern consistent with fingers of adult hands; the grip that could have caused such a pattern would be with a child's body flexed forward, with thumbs of the holding hands on the buttocks, and fingers in the inguinal regions of abdomen; such hold would account for some, but not all, bruises on the abdomen and thighs. The perianal skin had two shallow lacerations oriented radially from the anus, but not extending to the anus, each less than 1 cm long.

Internally, the child had almost completely lacerated small bowel within the ileal portion, which was associated with 75 mL hemoperitoneum, but with no peritonitis.

There were hemorrhages in the Treitz ligament and in the periadrenal adipose tissue. Skeletal trauma included several healing posterior rib fractures on the right and left sides; at least one of the calluses had a recent re-fracture. The radiological imaging of the entire skeleton was completed prior to the internal examination; however, due to the child's age-related weak mineralization of the bones, the rib plates were dissected and examined with a mammography machine (Figs. 8.1 and 8.2). This allowed for better visualization of the calluses. All areas with fractures or potential fractures were identified and sampled for histological assessment.

The histological examination revealed healing fractures, with periosteal fibrosis, residual thrombus, and no bony union. There was young scarring with neovascularization and beginning of cartilage formation. All the fractures had similar appearance, indicative of approximately the same age, which was estimated at 5–10 days antemortem. Histology also confirmed the recent re-fracture with fresh hemorrhage (Figs. 8.3, 8.4, and 8.5). The toxicological tests and other additional studies, i.e., bacterial and viral cultures, and genetic metabolic studies were negative.

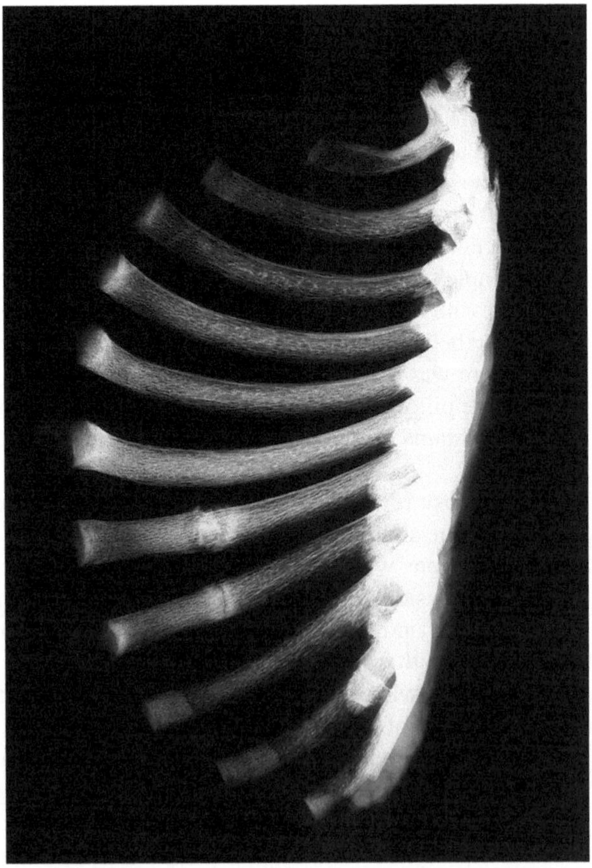

Fig. 8.1 Radiographic images from mammography machine of right rib fractures

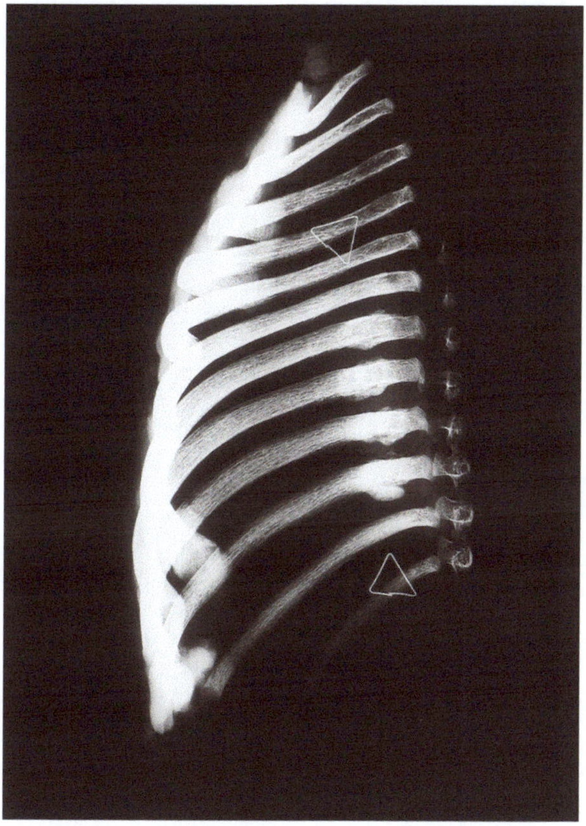

Fig. 8.2 Radiographic images from mammography machine of left rib fractures

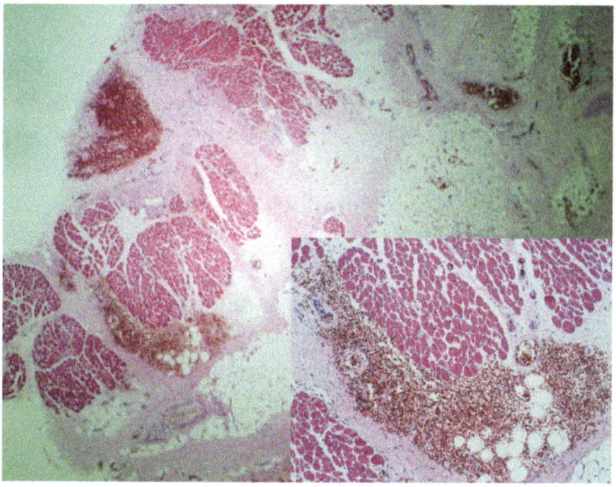

Fig. 8.3 Recent hemorrhage in muscle adjacent to callus

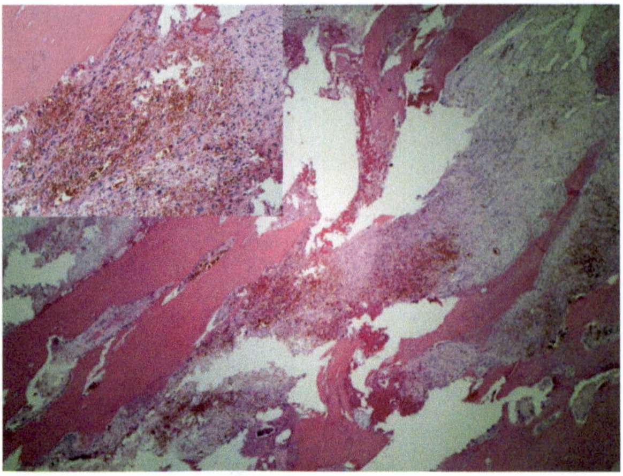

Fig. 8.4 Recent hemorrhage in a callus (re-fracture)

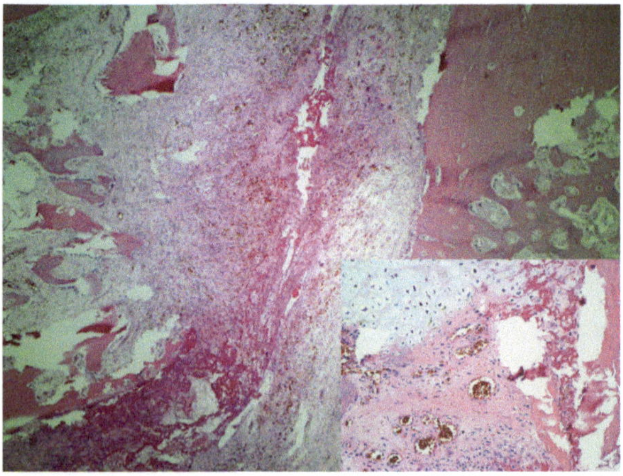

Fig. 8.5 Callus without bony union

After thorough review of the gathered data, the following opinion was rendered: Cause of death *Battered Baby Syndrome with Rib Fractures and Laceration of the Small Bowel* and the manner of death a *homicide*. The reasoning behind this opinion is as follows: there was no clearly identifiable mechanism of death in this case, with several reasonable possibilities.

- The child could have been smothered with a pillow.
- The child could have had positional asphyxia.
- The child could have had hemorrhagic shock. The volume of hemoperitoneum plus hemorrhages in the contusions could have resulted in hypovolemia.
- The child could have had neurogenic shock associated with ruptured bowel and peritoneal irritation.

Given his stage of development, the infant could roll over in bed, but would not crawl. If the boy fell from the bed, why would he stay in the face-down position without movement, while suffocating? There was enough space to not restrict his movement. Also, according to witnesses in the house and the father, the baby did not cry. Why did the child have so many bruises on his body? What explains the prior skeletal rib fractures?

Cardiopulmonary resuscitation that is correctly administered results in approximately 50 mmHg blood pressure, which is barely enough to perfuse the brain, and certainly too little to perfuse the skin or muscles of the torso and extremities. Bruising, i.e., hemorrhage into the tissue, needs blood pressure to occur. Almost all the children seen at the medical examiner's office have undergone resuscitation attempts before death, some for prolonged periods of time. However, they do not have bruises. If the child was dead when found on the floor, the subsequent manipulation would not result in bruising. In the literature, there have been reports of ruptured bowel and retroperitoneal hemorrhages resulting from resuscitation attempts [2–4]. However, in this case the only time when the alleged resuscitation was incorrect enough to cause any injuries was reportedly performed by the boy's father, on a soft bed. In addition, the child had healing rib fractures, in portions pathognomonic for inflicted trauma, just distally to the costo-transverse joints.

The cause of death is an injury or disease that initiates the chain of events ending in a person's death. Its definition does not include the mechanism of death. The battered child syndrome is a diagnosis defined by multiple inflicted injuries of various ages. In our opinion, the presented case meets the criteria for a battered child syndrome diagnosis, regardless of the actual mechanism of death. As such, it was also opined as homicide.

8.2 Battered Baby (Child) Syndrome

"Battered Baby Syndrome" was first diagnosed and described in 1962 by Dr. C. Henry Kempe and is described as follows [5; p. 28]:

> . . . the extreme form of a whole spectrum of non-accidental injury and deprivation of children. At one end of the spectrum is the child who is frankly battered and may have repeated serious injuries. These injuries often occur in a crescendo of increasing severity from mild bruising to subperiosteal bleeding seen on x-ray, to fractures of the long bones and ribs, to subdural hematoma with or without skull fracture.

The majority of children who are abused and neglected survive, and so it is typically incumbent on pediatricians and emergency room doctors to recognize abuse or the failure to thrive as non-accidental or nonpathological. Repeatedly among cases of inflicted trauma, caregivers or parents tell authorities that the injuries result from an accident. This trend is observed in families regardless of the socioeconomic or demographic patterns of those involved. The literature on battered baby (child) syndrome reports similar findings in that child abuse and neglect occur across all social and economic boundaries [6–8]. Therefore, debate surrounding the frequency and diagnosis of this syndrome has not been without controversy. Similar questions arise for forensic pathologists and anthropologists, who are presented with the challenge of differentiating between accidental and inflicted trauma and the timing of those injuries.

The evaluation of battered baby (child) syndrome as a cause of death includes evidence of repeated abuse. However, the presence of prior injuries does not necessarily prove prior abuse, as those injuries may have been caused by accidental trauma. Likewise, the presence of skeletal or dental anomalies associated with starvation or malnutrition may be present in the form of delayed growth, insufficient bone density, or skeletal lesions, such as *Harris Lines*, *dental hypoplasias*, *vitamin deficiencies*, or *skeletal osteopenia*. Adelson [9] presents five cases of homicide by starvation among infants. Skeletal evidence of starvation or neglect may also be detected in bone tissue, without the presence of soft tissue. For example, *vitamin D deficiency* may result in *rickets, osteomalacia*, or marked bowing of the tibia, whereas *vitamin C deficiency* may be evident in the form of scurvy, including skeletal lesions, cribra orbitalia, ectocranial porosis, and lytic lesions of the sphenoid, zygomatic, maxillary, and temporal bones.

8.3 Methods of Analysis, Radiography, and Histology

It is well accepted that fractures in various stages of healing at the time of death are an important tool for demonstrating a history of abuse in cases of child deaths. A similar approach has been taken to document patterns of torture in human rights cases and among elder abuse. The protocol used for osteological analysis of trauma (Table 8.1) should be based on standard practices for forensic medicine and anthropology, including gross observation of bony tissues, examination of the clothing, and the radiological analysis of skeletal remains (i.e., Buikstra and Ubelaker [10] and Kimmerle and Baraybar [11]). There are several radiographic references that provide specific and useful guidelines for radiographic use and methodology for the

Table 8.1 Protocol for the documentation, analysis, and timing of skeletal trauma

Inventory of all affected bones.
Description, measurement, and documentation of each location of the specific affected areas on bone, including the side/region/aspect of each fracture or defect.
Description of the number, type(s), and size of fractures or defects.
The presence of any abnormal bone shape, growth, or loss.
The severity, state, and distribution of abnormal bone changes.
Histological sectioning or decalcification of bone tissue for internal and/or microscopic analysis.
Documentation of any radiographic evidence (fractures, bone healing, callus formation, or weaponry). Depending on the availability, multiple radiographic methods may be of use for differentiating mechanisms of trauma and neglect.
Analysis of affected clothing (defects, tears, burning, or weaponry).
Estimation of the mechanism of injury, class of weapon, and victim's position relevant to the direction of the force.

interpretation of postmortem examinations [12–16]. The identification of fractures or skeletal defects at autopsy through direct observation or radiography can depend on what tools are available. It has been demonstrated how the elucidation of fractures through CT scanning or 3D modeling can detect fractures missed in traditional radiographs. In large part, modern radiographic tools such as CT scanning, mammography, and virtual autopsies have demonstrated the detection of minute fractures not visible in standard radiographs. Employment of these sophisticated techniques highlights the importance of using multiple tools when possible. Still, the need for direct observation of skeletal tissue remains, e.g., through maceration of soft tissues, in addition to the use of any radiographic tool to confirm or refute patterns of injury.

The detection of antemortem injuries is evident from signs of healing such as new bone growth, callus formation, abnormal bone shape or displacement, necrotic tissue, periostitis, osteomyelitis, or myostitis ossificans. The timing of bone remodeling can be assessed macroscopically and histologically, with varied rates depending on age. Among adults, the edges of a fracture begin to become rounded after about 1 week following the injury [17] and eventually form into a "V" shape as the two elements reunite. Within approximately 4–6 weeks, a bony callus begins to form [17]. New bone growth is structurally different in form and may be best summarized as *disorganized*. New bone growth is evident both visually and radiographically, though this process may be altered or significantly delayed or disrupted due to a lack of blood supply to the region from surrounding soft tissue damage or necrotic bone tissue.

Several methods specific to the timing of antemortem injuries based on direct and radiographic observation include O'Conner and Cohen [18] and Islam et al. [19]. Additionally, histological analysis of bone remodeling may produce a narrow and reliable timeframe for injuries. Very limited experimental data is available regarding the sequence of changes in a healing fractured bone. Most of the current knowledge we have on rates of healing and bone remodeling is based on accumulated observations, which is severely limited. The cumulative body of knowledge on this topic was summarized in an article "Dating of Healing Rib Fractures in Fatal Child Abuse" [20], published in *Advances in Pathology and Laboratory Medicine* in 1990, which still remains the standard text for forensic evaluation of the time for fracture healing.

Rates of bone remodeling and healing among children is expected to be faster than it is in adults, assuming growth, development, and healing occur at normal rates. A lack of medical treatment or continued stress or injury to the area may also impede or delay the healing process. According to O'Conner and Cohen [18], soft tissue restoration typically begins 2–10 days following injury in children. Periosteal thickening occurs within 2–3 days, and the earliest reported was within 24 h. Early periosteal bone growth such as rounding along fractured edges typically occurs 4–21 days and soft callus formation on bone typically occurs 7–21 days following injury. Soft tissue restoration in this case was present, with periosteal and callus formation. Islam et al. [19] observed that sclerosis along the fractured margins is evident in radiographs by 5 weeks following injury among children in 85% of cases. No sclerotic changes were observed on the radiographs. No bony union was observed microscopically in any of the fractures. Such union should be present within 3–6 weeks, with the earliest observed reportedly after 18 days [20]. The scarring within the fractures had the appearance typical for about a week, with extensive neo-vascularization and fibroblastic activity. Given these findings, the antemortem rib fractures in this case most likely occurred 1–2 weeks prior to death.

8.4 The Legal Issues: What Happened at Trial?

After the pre-trial hearings, the Grand Jury decided to prosecute the father of the decedent in our case example. Initially, the prosecution offered him a plea agreement, in which case he would plead guilty of manslaughter and serve 8 years of imprisonment. The public defender presented the offer to the accused, informing him that the charge in court could result either in him walking free or alternatively in a possible life sentence. The defendant decided to accept the trial.

The prosecution charged the father with *First Degree Murder with Aggravated Child Abuse*, following their algorithm for this type of cases, and subsequently the case went to trial.

The jurors decided that the defendant was not guilty of these charges, and the defendant was acquitted.

It is always difficult for the prosecutors to file charges or win convictions in cases of battered baby syndrome or homicidal violence without a specific mechanism of death. The task of the defense is a bit less demanding, due to the presumption of innocence.

In this particular case, the defense initiated the proceedings by filling a *Motion in Limine* (at threshold), requesting that the judge forbids the pathologist to use the diagnosis of "Battered Baby Syndrome" and orders exclusion of the rib fractures from the trial. Their argument was that since the fractures were old, they were irrelevant to the child's death. The defense argued that "Battered Baby Syndrome" was not an established diagnosis because it was not present in the International Classification of Diseases (ICD) or in the library of the National Institute of Health. However, their claims were disproved during the hearing, based in part on the overwhelming amount of literature and research establishing "Battered Baby Syndrome," as well as the fact the rib fractures were in fact part of the diagnosis. Indeed, the term "Battered Baby Syndrome" is nearly half a century old, yet today's forensic pathologists rarely use it. The diagnosis is listed in the ICD code 995.5, but more often, other wording is favored, e.g., "Homicidal Violence," which interestingly does not have an ICD code. Consequently, the motion was denied and a full discussion of the rib fractures was allowed.

Overall, the defense team was very well prepared, and after calling into question the very diagnosis for the cause of death, they also questioned the timing of fractures, the investigation procedures, and the credibility of the medical examiner. The forensic expert hired by the defense (who, parenthetically, was recommended to the defense attorney by the pathologist that performed the autopsy) was a retired, very accomplished forensic pathologist. During his deposition he signaled his disbelief in some microscopic findings, specifically hemorrhages, and disagreed with the histological dating of the rib fractures. Anticipating his denial of the findings, the prosecution introduced microphotographs of the fractured ribs and bruises at trial. As a result, the presence of recent hemorrhages, e.g., in the re-fractured rib, was not in question, and his assessment of timing of rib fractures shrank from "over 4–5 weeks" during the deposition to "3–4 weeks" during the trial.

Second, the defense team questioned the investigation procedures. They were concerned with handling of the pillow from the floor, specifically, why it had not been tested for the presence of transfer DNA? The answer was that such a test would have no evidentiary value, since the child lived in the room for 3 weeks prior to his death and his DNA would be expected on any of the objects found there. The defense then asked whether the police investigators followed up with the defendant so as to explain how the child could have been held to leave a specific pattern of bruises in the inguinal regions. However, this was a moot point since police investigators do not release information about the inconsistencies between the findings and their interviews to suspects.

Third, the autopsy report came under scrutiny and this lead to questioning about the medical examiner's credibility. One mistake was found in the autopsy report. In the report it was erroneously noted that the infant was "slightly underdeveloped" although not out of range for his age (5 months, 26 days). The weight (6,760 g) and height (67 cm), given his age, placed him "below the 5th percentile for weight and the weight to height ratio." The error was due to a slightly misplaced line marking the age of the child on a CDC Growth Chart, which resulted in a false reading. The child was in fact in 50th percentile for age. However, since there was no documented history of prior medical problems, abuse, or illness, and it was a single reading of these numbers, it was dismissed as diagnostic tool and not considered in the final determination for the cause of death. During the cross-examination of the pathologist, the defense attorney questioned the meaning of the child being below the 5th percentile; he suggested that it may mean "failure to thrive," a child abuse feature. The medical examiner pointed out that since such a conclusion would be based on a single reading, with no additional clinical information, it was of no value and could not influence the process of arriving at the diagnosis. Regardless, during the examination of the defense expert on the next day, the attorney reintroduced the issue, revealing the mistake on large posters and spending about 15 min discussing it.

At the end of any direct or cross-examination of the pathologist, the defense attorney would ask a litany of questions following list of injuries from the autopsy report:

Defense attorney: Was the contusion in muscle at the right rib arch the injury that killed the child?

Pathologist: No, sir, it was not.

Defense attorney: Was the healing fracture of the right eight rib the injury that killed the child?

Pathologist: No, sir, it was not.

And so forth. The defense expert, when asked what in his opinion actually killed the child, stated that he did not know, “maybe SIDS, maybe suffocation,” but argued that prolonged resuscitation could have introduced artifacts to the body, which in the end were misinterpreted as injuries.

The defense tactics proved effective, since it introduced a reasonable doubt to the jurors.

8.5 Discussion

In Hillsborough County, Florida, where this case study originated, there have been just over 580 criminal homicides from 1997 to 2010 among local law enforcement agencies in the county solved by the following police agencies and included in our database: the Hillsborough County Sheriff's Office, the Tampa Police Department, and the Temple Terrace Police Department. Among this sample, approximately 45 involved juveniles under the age of 7 years. In addition to the solved juvenile cases, there are five homicide investigations involving infants and children that remain open since 2007. The open cases are unsolved for a variety of reasons, but several key issues challenge investigators and prosecutors as discussed in this chapter, such as the difficulty of timing injuries, particularly when they occur over a several-day period and the fact that multiple people may have had access to the child during the time frame prior to the death. In some cases, the manner of death is opined as homicide, but the specific mechanism of death may be more elusive or attributed to homicidal violence or battered baby (child) syndrome.

Given the high number of variables that contribute to understanding the epidemiology of battered baby (child) syndrome, these findings are presented only as general trends, without specific incidence reporting. The primary goal is to share our findings in an effort to help dispel some common misperceptions about diagnosing battered baby (child) syndrome, such as the relationship between soft and skeletal tissue injuries. These findings further highlight areas where future research could benefit this discussion for investigators.

In the majority of solved juvenile cases from this sample, parents reported that the infant “fell” accidentally upon seeking medical treatment, though inflicted trauma was determined as present at autopsy. Overall, victims tended to have multiple blunt impact injuries throughout the body. The most common areas affected included the head, followed by the extremities and then thorax. Through comparison of injury patterns among known cases of accidents and inflicted trauma, common threads emerge. For example, in addition to specific patterns, i.e., affecting the specific body parts, accidents tend to create far fewer injuries than cases of abuse, accidental trauma tends to be more focused, and rarely are there multiple incidents of repeated accidental trauma.

- Overall, more than half of the victims under the age of 10 years are male, yet there is a higher ratio of female victims involving infants and children under the age of 3 years.

- In approximately half of the cases, the body was moved following the death. In four cases, the scene was actually altered, and in one case, the scene was staged to look like something other than a murder.
- In the majority of cases, the offenders are a parent (17/32), the boyfriend or girlfriend of the parent (2/32), or another family member (1/32). In six cases, children were killed by a nonrelated babysitter. The majority of offenders who inflicted trauma and committed murder were male.
- In just over 56% (18/32) of cases, the primary mechanism of injury was blunt impact trauma followed by gunfire, strangulation, smothering, drowning, and nonspecific violence including beating, stomping, and the throwing of infants against walls, across the room, or from moving vehicles.
- It is rare to find no evidence of injury upon external examination of the body. However, typically when soft tissue injuries to the face or head are evident, only a fraction have cranial fractures (typically around 20%). More commonly, fractures to the ribs or extremities are present.
- Only about half of cases reveal physical evidence of prior neglect or abuse at autopsy.

In only a very small number of fatal cases are kidnapping or child rape a factor. A higher frequency is classified as *victim precipitated. Victim-precipitated* homicide refers to instances in which the victims' actions contribute to their own demise; i.e., the deceased may have made a menacing gesture or was first to pull a weapon. In cases of child abuse, these typically reflect events where the offender is responding to the child who is crying or *acting up* when administering physical punishment. It is precisely these types of cases that can be challenging to prosecute as jurors tend to view the parent as having lost control but not intending to fatally harm the child. The key legal issue for investigators in those types of situations is to show a pattern of repeated abuse, rather than the intent to kill for that single incident.

8.6 Recommendations for Best Practice and Future Research

Mapping out the case factors that take into account intrinsic, extrinsic, and circumstantial variables helps clarify the events surrounding the death and ultimately speaks to whether a crime was committed. The general patterns of injury and presence of repeated trauma illustrate trends consistent with inflicted injuries that vary from accidental trauma. The ability for forensic pathologists and anthropologists to create a differential diagnosis of trauma patterns at autopsy increases when these practitioners work together and apply a range of radiographic technologies. Likewise, soft tissue injuries do not always occur in the same pattern or distribution as skeletal fractures. Direct observation of skeletal tissue by forensic anthropologists provides medical examiners and prosecutors a second opinion on the type of injuries, mechanisms of trauma, and timing of fractures. As documented in this example, the ability to accurately time antemortem or healed injuries (physical evidence of past abuse) is fundamental to investigators. Therefore, increased research into the histological changes of bone remodeling for different age groups, particularly among populations under stress or enduring repeated abuse, would be highly beneficial.

Acknowledgments We would like to thank our colleagues at the Hillsborough County Sheriff's Office, the Tampa Police Department, and the Temple Terrace Police Department who have been working with us on researching homicide patterns for the Tampa Bay area. In particular we thank Major Harold Winsett, Captain Alan Hill, Sgt. Frank Losat, Det. Herb Saumell, Det. Chuck Massucci, and Det. Eric Houston for their assistance in collecting data and preparing this manuscript. We also thank Chris Moody and Gregory Hill, the prosecution and defense attorneys, respectively.

References

1. Plunkett J. Fatal pediatric head injuries caused by short-distance falls. Am J Forensic Med Pathol 2001;22:1–12.
2. Feldman KW, Brewer DK. Child abuse, cardio-pulmonary resuscitation, and rib fractures. Pediatrics 1984;73:339–342.
3. Bush CM, Jones JS, Cohle SD, Johnson H. Pediatric injuries from cardiopulmonary resuscitation. Ann Emerg Med 1996;28:40–44.
4. Dolinak D. Rib fractures in infants due to cardiopulmonary resuscitation efforts. Am J Forensic Med Pathol 2007;28:107–110.
5. Helfer RE, Kempe CH, editors. The Battered Child. Chicago, IL: University of Chicago Press, 1968.
6. Curphey TJ, Kade H, Noguchi TT, Moore SM. The battered child syndrome: responsibilities of the pathologist. Calif Med 1965;102(2):102–104.
7. Kempe HC. Paediatric implications of the battered baby syndrome. Arch Dis Child 1971;46:28–37.
8. Smithey M. Infant homicide: victim/offender relationship and causes of death. J Fam Violence 1998;13:285–297
9. Adelson L. The nutritional variant of the "Battered Child." J Am Med Assoc 1963;186: 458–460.
10. Buikstra JE, Ubelaker DH, editors. Standards for data collection from human skeletal remains. Proceedings of a seminar at the Field Museum of Natural History. Arkansas Archaeological Survey Research Series No. 44, 1994.
11. Kimmerle EH, Baraybar JP. Skeletal Trauma: Identification of Injuries Resulting from Human Rights Abuse and Armed Conflict. Boca Raton, FL: CRC Press, 2008.
12. Ortner DJ, Putschar WGJ. Identification of Pathological Conditions in Human Skeletal Remains. Smithsonian Contributions to Anthropology. Washington, DC: Smithsonian Institution Press, 1981;28.
13. Brogdon BG. Forensic Radiology. Boca Raton, FL: CRC Press, 1998.
14. Meyers J, Okoye M, Kipple D, Kimmerle EH, Reinhard K. Three dimensional (3-D) imaging in post-mortem examinations: elucidation and identification of cranial and facial fractures in victims of homicide utilizing 3-D computerized imaging reconstruction techniques. Int J Legal Med 1999;113:33–37.
15. Brogdon BG, Vogel H, McDowell JD. A Radiological Atlas of Abuse, Torture, Terrorism, and Inflicted Trauma. Boca Raton, FL: CRC Press, 2003;328.
16. Thali MJ, Kneubuehl BP, Vock P, Allmen G, Dirnhofer R. Highspeed documented experimental gunshot to a skull-brain model and radiologic virtual autopsy. Am J Forensic Med Path 2002;23:223–228.

17. Sauer NJ. The timing of injuries and manner of death: distinguishing among antemortem, perimortem and postmortem trauma. In: Reichs KJ, editor. Forensic Osteology, 2nd ed. Springfield, IL: Charles C. Thomas Publisher, 1998;321–332.
18. O'Conner JF, Cohen J. Dating Fractures. In: Kleinman PK, editor. Diagnostic Imaging of Child Abuse. Baltimore, MD: Williams and Wilkins, 1987;103–113.
19. Islam O, Soboleski D, Symons S, Davidson LK, Ashworth MA, Babyn P. Development and duration of radiographic signs of bone healing in children. Am J Roentgenol 2000;175:75–78.
20. Zumwalt RE, Fanizza-Orphanos AM. 1990. Dating of Healing Rib Fractures in Fatal Child Abuse. In: Fenoglio-Preiser CM, editor. Advances in Pathology. St. Louis, MO: Mosby, 1990;193–205.

Chapter 9
Evidence of Neglect from Immature Human Skeletal Remains: An Auxological Approach from Bones and Teeth

Hugo F.V. Cardoso and Teresa Magalhães

Abstract Child neglect is the most common form of child maltreatment and failure to thrive is one of its most common manifestations. Although growth failure has many etiologies, recognizing it is very important in aiding the identification of neglect in living children and in fatality cases, particularly in the detection of severe malnutrition. Although the forensic anthropologist may deal with a fatal case of child neglect, the assessment of growth failure from osteological observations is considerably limited. The expert relies on the assessment of dental and skeletal growth and development for the estimation of age and the assessment of growth failure. Although dental development is susceptible to environmental insults, such as malnutrition, it is more stable than skeletal growth and maturation, which is more susceptible. This chapter cautions the use of dental development for age estimation in suspected cases of child neglect and offers two general approaches for the detection of growth failure from observations in bone and teeth. One approach relies on comparing height estimates and long bone lengths to sex and age-specific references of height and long bone length, while the other relies on assessing the discrepancy between dental and skeletal age. A sample of identified Portuguese human immature skeletons is used to illustrate the consistency of results between the two approaches. Although an auxological approach to the study of bones and teeth can provide important insights into the growth status of individuals represented by their hard tissues, it cannot be definite about the diagnosis of malnutrition and, particularly, neglect as the cause of the child's death.

9.1 Introduction

Immature human skeletal remains can be found in a variety of forensic contexts, although actual forensic anthropology cases involving children are rare. In non-conflict areas, perhaps the most common circumstances are those of homicide and maltreatment. Several studies are devoted to the development and testing of

H.F.V. Cardoso (✉)
Museu Nacional de Historia Natural & Centro de Biologia Ambiental, Universidade de Lisboa, Lisbon, Portugal; Faculdade de Medicina, Universidade do Porto, Porto, Portugal
e-mail: hfcardoso@fc.ul.pt; hcardoso@med.up.pt

A.H. Ross, S.M. Abel (eds.), *The Juvenile Skeleton in Forensic Abuse Investigations*,
DOI 10.1007/978-1-61779-255-7_9, © Springer Science+Business Media, LLC 2011

techniques employed in the identification of child remains by the forensic anthropologist, and the literature provides numerous examples of methods for determining age, sex, height, and ancestry from immature skeletal remains [1, 2]. However, few advances have been published in recognizing the circumstances surrounding the child's death. Children are by definition immature and, as such, are particularly susceptible to various forms of maltreatment, and physical and nonphysical violence. Neglect is the most common form of child maltreatment, but has received much less attention than child physical or sexual abuse [3]. Up until recently, forensic anthropologists rarely have had the opportunity to examine cases of child abuse [4], and in various circumstances, they are now frequently called upon for an assessment of bone trauma in suspected cases of abuse. This is in contrast with child abuse identified in an archeological context [5, 6], where most cases go unidentified for a variety of reasons [2], including the fact that few child skeletons may survive in the burial record. This is also true for cases of neglect, with the possible exception of abandonment and infanticide in an archeological context [7, 8], but the reasons why these cases remain unidentified are different.

In general terms, child neglect results from acts of omission from the caretaker who fails to provide basic necessities to the child [3]. In cases of neglect the child is exposed to a variety of invisible insults, such as malnutrition, recurrent infection, and injury, which may not be detected from human skeletal remains. The most common problem resulting from physical and emotional neglect during infancy is growth failure [9, 10], but since growth disruption has many etiologies, neglect may remain "hidden" and be difficult to distinguish from other causes. In a forensic context, an auxological approach to the study of immature skeletal remains may provide important clues in the detection of growth deficit from bones and teeth. Subsequently, this can aid the expert in the identification of physical and/or emotional abuse. This chapter deals with forms of neglect that will lead to growth failure. It will provide a brief overview of the clinical literature on child neglect and on failure to thrive as a common manifestation of neglect and abuse. This is followed by a brief review of fatal cases of neglect, as well as by a discussion of the diagnostic criteria for growth failure when a fatality is involved. The conditions under which growth failure can be detected from immature skeletal remains and the implications of nutritional neglect on age estimation are mentioned. Specifically, two general approaches for the detection of growth failure from immature human skeletal remains are proposed and a discussion of their limitations is presented.

9.2 Child Neglect and Failure to Thrive in a Clinical Setting

Neglect is the most common form of child maltreatment. For example, using 2008 data on cases of child maltreatment known to Child Protection Services agencies in the United States, of the approximately 760,000 children found to be victims of child maltreatment, more than half (71%) suffered from neglect [11]. In cases of neglect, boys and girls are equally likely to be physically neglected, and the incidence is higher among children between 0 and 11 years old [12]. There are marked differences in the rates of physical neglect for family income, with the highest rates in low-income families [12].

Legal definitions of child neglect vary [3], but most agree on nine components of neglect: inadequate food, inadequate clothing, inadequate shelter, inadequate supervision, inadequate medical care, inadequate emotional care, inadequate education, exploitation, and exposure to unwholesome circumstances. The basic principle underlying each component is that neglect occurs when a child's basic needs are not met by the caregiver, regardless of the circumstances leading to the inadequacy of care [3, 13, 14]. Therefore, neglect refers to regular acts of omission, and it is not included in physical abuse classifications. Situations of neglect require a detailed analysis of the context in which they occur, since not all negligence is intentional and criminally prosecuted, but instead may represent simpler cases of social and health risk.

Since child neglect usually results from a heterogeneous collection of situations, some professionals have categorized it into several types, on the basis of its different components, frequently as medical, physical, safety, educational, and emotional neglect [3, 13, 15]. In educational neglect, the caregiver fails to fulfill the child's educational needs and include endorsed or tolerated school absenteeism, families never enroll their child in school despite the child reaching the mandatory age, and families fail to take the necessary steps to assess and meet the needs of children with disabilities. Inattention to child's needs of attention, affection, and emotional support, as well as exposure to domestic violence, is among the most common type of emotional neglect. Medical neglect is usually distinct from physical neglect because it involves the expertise of the healthcare providers in detecting this type of neglect. It is usually manifested in disregard for routine health care, delay in seeking healthcare assistance, and refusal of appropriate medical care for treatable diseases. Physical neglect results from inacceptable parenting, usually a lack of reasonable supervision or little attention to creating and maintaining a safe environment. It can be identified as single or multiple circumstances where there is an obvious disregard toward the child's hygiene, health, or nutritional status. Abandonment of a child is generally considered safety neglect, as well as leaving the child in places where they are put at a significant risk. Since individual cases usually involve more than one type of neglect, it is, perhaps, more useful in the assessment to conceptualize it in terms of the basic needs that are not met when neglect exists, rather than in terms of the type of neglect.

Screening for neglect by the healthcare professional involves the assessment of the child and adult caregiver to identify signs and symptoms related to neglect [16]. Failure to thrive is a common manifestation of various types of neglect and of physical abuse. For example, according to a 2004 report by the Massachusetts Department of Public Health covering 6 years of statewide experience, 1700 children were referred to for failure to thrive, and most of these children would fulfill at least one of the criteria for neglect [17]. Failure to thrive has been defined as a significantly prolonged cessation or deccelaration of growth compared to age-

and sex-specific references for normal children [10, 14, 17] and is often considered another separate type of neglect or is included in physical neglect as a nutrition-related form of neglect [14, 15]. However, failure to thrive or the inadequate growth of infants and children is more of a sign or consequence, rather than a diagnosis, and is also not synonymous to neglect. In addition, child neglect represent a wide range of care-giving deficits, and not all will manifest in growth failure. Some of the most common signs include poor hygiene and grooming, irregular feeding habits, recurrent infections, and injuries; some of the most common symptoms include delay in social skill acquisition and learning, appetite and sleeping disturbances, antisocial behavior, and reduced peer interaction [18].

In nutritional neglect cases, failure to thrive usually occurs when the child's basic nutritional needs are not met, namely when the child is not offered sufficient nutrients. The main factor behind abusive malnutrition is then protein-energy deprivation. However, most cases of failure to thrive actually result from emotional abuse and psychosocial stress, usually concomitant with nutritional deprivation [9, 14]. For example, the care givers may be uninformed about proper nutritional requirements, they may be psychologically or mentally impaired, or there is a history of domestic violence and physical abuse in the family. In these circumstances, the child will develop psychosomatic pathologies and digestive dysfunctions, which will lead to digestion of inadequate amounts of offered nutrients, low retention of ingested nutrients, or increased metabolic demands that exceed ingested nutrients. Endocrine factors are thought to be at play when retarded growth results from emotional abuse or stress rather than from nutritional deprivation. Emotionally abused or neglected children usually show depressed growth hormone levels, whose production by the pituitary may be affected by the amygdala and limbic cortex when subjected to emotional stress [19]. Consequently, one of the clinical manifestations of the "battered child syndrome" is also malnutrition [20] and, consequently, growth failure. The nutritional and psychosocial causes of failure to thrive are also demonstrable by growth recovery by long-term physically neglected and emotionally abused children when placed in foster care [21]. The pervasiveness of growth failure in cases of child neglect and abuse may likely result from the fact that infants and toddlers are more exposed to basic needs such as nutrition and preventable diseases, as acts of omission from the caretaker. They have great nutritional demands due to growth, have immature immune systems and are totally dependent on adults for feeding, care and attention.

The differential diagnosis of failure to thrive is vast, but the primary etiology of many cases of growth failure is malnutrition and infection, with insufficient nutrients to meet metabolic requirements [10, 22]. Growth reflects the balance between caloric intake and metabolic expenditure, and in physical neglect, malnutrition determines a low protein-energy intake sufficient for maintenance, fighting disease, activity, and growth. Thus, the economy of nutrients (protein and energy), which are being allocated to maintenance and fighting disease, is being diverted from physical activity (which decreases) and growth (which is delayed or retarded). In addition, malnutrition, by virtue of diminishing the available energy allocated to fight disease, exposes the child to more disease. In turn, in a diseased environment, nutrition intake is lowered, thus contributing to the escalade of this infection-nutrition synergistic cycle, which affects growth [22, 23]. Eventually, the nutrition-infection synergy will further contribute to growth retardation. Although almost every serious illness of childhood and infancy are included in the differential diagnosis of failure to thrive, major medical diagnoses such as cystic fibrosis, cerebral palsy, congenital heart disease, HIV infection or AIDS, cancer, as well as metabolic and several other chronic conditions are among the most important etiologies of growth failure [10, 17, 24]. In addition, more subtle causes of growth failure must be considered as well. These include oral motor deficiencies, breast-feeding difficulties, errors in baby formula preparation, poor diet selection, or improper feeding technique [10, 17, 24]. One important aspect in the differential diagnosis of failure to thrive is the prenatal history to distinguish in utero exposures to neglect from congenital infections and malformations. Alcohol and drug abuse during pregnancy are important causes of growth failure and must be considered [14]. Women who were physically abused during pregnancy also show a greater risk of preterm delivery [25], which may concur with postnatal neglect situations.

Since malnutrition is the main factor behind growth failure, depending on the duration and quality of the protein and energy deficiency, two main types of malnutrition can be recognized from growth: stunting and wasting. The first clinical sign of malnutrition is acute and refers to weigh loss or wasting. In the face of malnutrition, after weight gain has ceased, linear growth continues for a while. If conditions of malnutrition persist and become chronic, a reduction in height occurs and the child is said to be stunted. Clinicians usually diagnose failure to thrive in children whose physical development falls persistently below the third or fifth percentile in weight and/or height for no known medical reason [10]. Velocity of growth is frequently a better measure of growth deficiency than height or weight at a specific point in time, because it is obtained from a long-term follow-up history of the child [17, 26]. A fall downward over 2 or more percentile lines is sufficient for a diagnosis. However, a clinical evaluation for failure to thrive involves a comprehensive family history, physical examination, feeding observation, and a home visit by an appropriate healthcare professional.

There are three groups of risk factors associated with failure to thrive as a form of neglect: social, family, and individual factors [10, 13–15, 17]. Social factors include the wider social, cultural, and economic context of the family and neglected child. Poverty is the greatest single risk factor for failure to thrive worldwide and in the United States. Other social risk factors include lack of available extended family to help with child rearing, social isolation of the family, employment instability, and housing conditions. The family comprises the immediate environment of the child and their family characteristics, at the level of both parent and parent-child interaction. Risk factors at this level include parent attributes such as single parenthood, adolescent parents, and family violence. Infant-caregiver attachment issues are an example of parent-child interaction risk factor. The last group of risk factors includes individual factors at the level of the caregiver, such as substance abuse by the caregiver or a history of abuse of the parent as a child. At the level of the victim or child, individual risk factors include age and whether the infant was born preterm or with low birth weight.

9.3 Fatal Child Neglect and the Forensic Anthropologist

The death of a child is the most extreme outcome of child neglect or abuse. Omissions in child care can be so severely dangerous that death can occur. Over half of the child fatalities attributed to child maltreatment results from neglect [27]. Of the approximately 1600 deaths in 2008 known to have occurred from child maltreatment, 32% where associated with neglect alone and 40% resulted from a combination of physical abuse and neglect [11]. The majority of victims of fatal neglect are under 3 years [28, 29], and about one-third are younger than 1 year and two-thirds are males [28]. Although less severe forms of neglect can be generally handled by child protection services agencies, without police or prosecutor involvement, more serious cases of neglect, and particularly fatal cases, involve the criminal justice system.

Early reports on fatal child neglect examined cases where children died from "passive" neglect because they were abandoned, or when children died as an extreme consequence of deprivation, such as malnutrition, or when parents failed to provide adequate health care [28]. In its extreme form, failure to thrive secondary to neglect may be fatal [17]. The definition of fatal neglect has now broadened to include common injury deaths, and the role of parental supervision in these preventable injury deaths is now amply recognized [30]. In fact, most fatal cases of neglect appear not to involve chronic or severe malnutrition, but instead are associated with a single life-threatening incident [28, 30]. Although growth failure cannot be the cause of death (usually is starvation), diagnosing or detecting failure to thrive is, nonetheless, a strong indication of continuous child neglect in life [31].

The literature on fatal child neglect is relatively scarce, compared with that of fatal physical abuse. There are several cases of child neglect fatalities described in the literature [28, 29, 31–37], and most report circumstances of severe malnutrition or starvation, with documented growth failure. Although most reports also describe physical safety or medical neglect involving a fatal injury, none of these report on the growth status of the children involved. In these cases of fatal nutritional neglect, the most affected children are those under 1 year of age, and rarely are there children over 3 years involved. The exception is usually older children with special needs [31].

Failure to thrive is a clinical diagnosis made in a living child who is not growing or gaining weight as expected, but if a child dies as a result of nutritional neglect, the pathologic findings relate to the presence of severe malnutrition [29, 31]. In addition, even if the child dies as a result of a fatal injury, pathological changes associated with malnutrition may be present as well, as a consequence of concurring neglect. In fatal cases of malnutrition, weight loss and height retardation are so extreme that they are usually below weight and height percentiles. Consequently, other anthropometric criteria are needed to measure the amount of growth failure. Several classification systems have been developed to estimate protein-energy malnutrition in developing countries and these have proved useful in a forensic setting, because they allow an estimate of the degree of malnutrition [38]. The more simple classifications like the Gomez classification of protein-energy malnutrition [39] use the expected weight for the respective age group as standard, but these cannot distinguish acute malnutrition from chronic one. Taking into account not only weight but also height and the expected weight for the actual height is what the Waterlow classification of protein-energy proposes [40]. In addition, the Waterlow classification provides a grading to classify acute and chronic protein-energy malnutrition, according to the actual weight in percentage of normal weight of respective age group and the actual height in percentage of normal height of respective age group, respectively. In the most severe grade of malnutrition, actual height is below 80% of normal height for age [40]. Combining height and weight data can provide an indication of the persistence in neglect [38]. In acute malnutrition there may be a severe loss of body weight, while the reduction in body height may be only very slight. Conversely, impaired growth in height is a sequel of a chronic condition.

In fatal cases, the autopsy also provides additional diagnostic criteria for severe malnutrition. The most common autopsy findings are extreme emaciation, sunken eyes, and low body weight and organ weight, with the frequent exception of the brain, loss of subcutaneous and mesenteric fat, and atrophy of muscles of organs, in particular endocrine and reproductive glands [29, 34, 36, 37]. In addition to starvation as the cause of death and growth failure, in cases of lethal child abuse where a single or multiple injury incidents are the cause of death, emotional and psychosocial stress can also lead to growth failure in these children [9]. In these circumstances of fatal abuse, detecting growth failure can be important as a sign of abuse, in the final diagnosis.

In a forensic context, the anthropologist will deal with fatal cases of child neglect. In particular, the forensic anthropologist may be called upon when the child's body is decomposed and reduced to hard tissue to assess whether the child may have been neglected or abused. There are several cases in which forensic anthropologists have examined the skeletons of children, who were physically abused in life [4, 41]. In the archaeological record there are few reports, namely that by Blondiaux and co-workers [5], who describe a 2-year-old child skeleton, from fourth-century Normandy, suspected of having suffered child abuse, and that by Wheeler and co-workers [6], who examined another potential case of abuse in a 2–3-year-old child from fourth-century Egypt. Comparatively, the detection of neglect, namely severe malnutrition, has not been so successful in the forensic and archaeological context. Although growth failure is a common manifestation of neglect and abuse, its etiology may not result from intentional acts of neglect, and, consequently, it becomes "invisible" to the eyes of the expert. This is particularly true in the archaeological record, where the anthropologist has little contextual information and stunting was pervasive in past. Nonetheless, Walker and co-workers [4] describe a forensic case that revealed many Harris lines in the long bones suggesting episodes of malnutrition and infection. In the archaeological study by Blondiaux and co-workers [5], the child's skeleton also showed evidence of rickets, which is suggestive of nutritional deficiencies and of neglect as well. None of the forensic or archaeological reports explored further the growth status of the skeletons under analysis, namely the possible divergence between dental and skeletal age estimates.

In much the same way as diagnosing growth failure can provide useful insights into the detection of a child neglect case, the identification of skeletal growth failure is one of the most powerful tools to detect neglect from immature skeletal remains. Wasting cannot be detected from osteological findings because weight cannot be accurately estimated from the skeleton. Autopsy findings associated with cases of lethal starvation are also useless in the identification of growth failure and severe malnutrition from skeletal remains, because they rely on soft tissue changes. Consequently, only reduced bone size and delayed skeletal maturation as a result of chronic malnourishment can be identified. This means that, in practice, if height, linear growth, or maturation is unaffected, malnourishment cannot be recognized in children's skeletons.

Studies of human skeletal growth in the past have become increasingly popular, and there is a wealth of literature dealing with this topic [42–47]. The term "paleoaxology" has been proposed to group together growth and development studies of past populations from bone and teeth [48]. The study of growth patterns reconstructed from skeletal remains in bioarchaeological studies usually involve the construction of a skeletal growth profile to examine the cross-sectional age-progressive trend in growth in sex-pooled samples [49]. In skeletal growth profiles, a proxy for statural growth such as a long bone measurement, usually femur length, is plotted against a measure of chronological age, such as dental age. Under stressed environmental conditions, such as malnutrition or infection, a large number of individuals will show a bone growth deficit relative to dental age, and this relative difference indicates a delay in skeletal growth as a consequence of stress. Therefore, determining whether a child is stunted from skeletal remains involves the comparison of a measure of skeletal growth with a measure of dental age, which may not necessarily involve the construction of a growth profile. For instance, the use of skeletal maturation indicators, such as changes in size and shape of ossification centers, can be used as an alternative to long bone diaphyseal length. This alternative is particularly useful in cases where the skeleton is incomplete or badly preserved, lacking the long bones, and provides the opportunity to simply compare skeletal and dental age.

Although skeletal growth profiles from sex-pooled samples are commonly used in assessments of growth in archaeological populations, their use in a forensic context will allow the detection of differences in growth or maturation attained between the child case and the reference sample. The use of linear skeletal growth and skeletal maturation as measures of growth delay or deficit relies on the assumption that growth and maturation of the skeleton are more affected by external factors such as malnutrition and infection, whereas dental development is more buffered. For this reason, skeletal growth measures are normally employed to identify physiological stress in an individual, whereas dental development is used to estimate his/her chronological age.

9.4 An Auxological Framework for Aiding the Identification of Neglect from Immature Human Skeletal Remains

From an auxological perspective, the detection of neglect from immature skeletal remains is, ultimately, about identifying the effects of malnutrition and infection on growth and development of the skeleton and dentition. Since the cause of malnutrition and infection can be other than neglect, a human growth perspective can only aid the expert, while pursuing other lines of evidence that support a diagnosis of neglect. A diagnosis of growth failure or of severe malnutrition from osteological findings will not be able to establish the cause of death. Instead, the diagnosis of growth failure may contribute to the identification of a case of neglect, since failure to thrive is a common manifestation of neglect and abuse, and as such the cause of death may not be nutritional.

The greater sensitivity of skeletal growth and development to external factors, such as malnutrition and infection, compared to the more buffered dental system, is at the core of growth assessments from the skeleton. Although different studies use different approaches to measure skeletal and dental development, the literature largely supports this assertion. The lower sensitivity of dental development is suggested by relative greater delays in skeletal maturation than in tooth formation in children with major abnormalities affecting growth, diseases and malnutrition. For example, Vallejo-Bolaños and España-López [50] examined the developmental delay in dental and skeletal maturation of Spanish children with a growth disorder (short familial stature) and found that skeletal maturation was more retarded with respect to chronological age than permanent tooth formation. Ozerovic [51] examined the relationship between chronological age, dental formation, and skeletal maturation in Yugoslavian children with cerebral palsy and reported that chronological and dental age differed on average by 1–7 months, while skeletal age differed from chronological age by an average of 4–11 months. In several cases of ß-thalassemia major, the mean delay in skeletal maturation was 28% compared to a mean delay of 17% in dental formation [52]. Similarly, Garn and co-workers [53] reviewed a series of North American children with growth disorders of varying etiologies, including hypothyroidism, celiac disease, and anemia, and found that, in general, the degree of retardation in dental formation of this mixed group was approximately one-third the magnitude of the skeletal delay. Edler [54] arrived at very similar results in a sample of British patients with hypopituitarism, where average percentage delay in skeletal maturation was 27.9% in age groups between 7 and 12 years, while for tooth formation, the average delay was only 9.3%. Keller and co-workers [55] also found that, compared to skeletal development, the dental system is not noticeably affected by endocrine and metabolic diseases, except in pituitary insufficiency, hyperthyroidism, and delayed puberty. In a sample of children with sickle-cell anemia studied by Sears and co-workers

[56], skeletal age was also found to be significantly behind chronological age by approximately 17 months, whereas dental age was not found to be significantly different from chronological age. Finally, Holderbaum and co-workers [57] found that HIV-positive children showed delayed dental age, but the delay in skeletal age was much greater (approximately half as much), particularly before the administration of antiretroviral drugs.

Not many studies have directly examined the effects of malnutrition on dental and skeletal development, but the greater impact of nutrition on skeletal development is suggested by greater advancement of skeletal maturation relative to tooth formation in obese children [58]. Another example of the impact of nutrition and of general improvement in living conditions is the study by Melsen and co-workers [59]. These authors examined a group of Asian children, with inexact chronological age adopted by Danish families within 1 month after their arrival in Denmark and re-examined them 1 year subsequent to the first examination. At the time of the second examination the children showed an increment in dental age in accordance with the time interval between the two examinations but an increase in skeletal age that exceeded the corresponding time span. The authors suggest that the greater recovery of skeletal development reflected its greater environmental sensitivity.

More recently Cardoso [60] and Conceição and Cardoso [61] were able to further document that skeletal growth and skeletal maturation are more affected by environmental circumstances than dental formation. In these studies, dental and skeletal ages were contrasted against chronological age in a sample of fully identified known sex and age Portuguese child skeletons, which were divided into two subsamples of differing socioeconomic status. The father's occupation and the place of residence provided information about socioeconomic categorization of the sample that was meant to stratify the sample in two groups: one of individuals exposed to more negative environments (low socioeconomic status) and the other of individuals exposed to more positive environments (high socioeconomic status). This stratification assumes that children in a higher socioeconomic group have preferential access to fundamental resources, such as better nutrition, sanitary living conditions, and health care than do children in the lower socioeconomic group. Cardoso [60] found that, in addition to skeletal age showing a greater delay relative to chronological age when compared to dental age, the socioeconomic difference in skeletal age, obtained from diaphyseal femur length, was about 1 year, whereas the socioeconomic difference in dental age was only about 0.5 years. Conceição and Cardoso [61] found a similar socioeconomic difference in dental age, while the socioeconomic difference in skeletal age, obtained from skeletal maturation indicators at the knee, was about 1.2 years.

9.4.1 Age Estimation

As part of the identification process of the child, age estimation is crucial and is commonly obtained from dental and skeletal growth and development. Since growth failure is a common consequence of neglect, in a forensic anthropology situation, dental and skeletal growth have the dual purpose of providing age estimates and of aiding in the detection of neglect. Dental development is less affected by environmental influences than skeletal growth and maturation, and is the preferred method for estimating age in immature skeletal remains. However, neglect can influence the rate of tooth formation through the effects of malnutrition. As a consequence, although age can be usually estimated with confidence by forensic anthropologists, in suspected cases of neglect this technique can be seriously hampered.

Once considered very stable and free from environmental influences, dental development is now thought to be less buffered. Dental development comprises the processes of tooth emergence and tooth formation, and the latter is traditionally considered the most accurate age-at-death estimator [62, 63]. The influence of nutrition on the emergence of the deciduous and permanent dentition has been suggested and demonstrated for some time [64–70], but nutritional effects on tooth formation have been more contentious. However, some studies have been able to show an indirect effect of nutrition on tooth formation. This includes most of the studies cited above that support the assertion of lower sensitivity of dental development, relative to skeletal development, to major abnormalities and diseases affecting growth. For example, indirect impacts of nutrition on dental formation include the report by Garn and co-workers [53], who have found a dental delay in patients with celiac disease (0.67 years). In patients with ß-thalassemia studied by Laor and co-workers [52], dental age was also found to be significantly delayed by 12–24% of chronological age. The studies by Cardoso [60] and by Conceição and Cardoso [61] are other examples of the indirect influence of nutrition on tooth formation, where dental age was consistently behind chronological in low socioeconomic status children. More recently, Cardoso and co-workers [71], using samples of Portuguese children in the early and late twentieth century, were able to document the first consistent secular acceleration in dental formation, in response to improvements in social and economic conditions, which influenced the nutritional status of children over time.

Studies that have demonstrated a more direct effect of malnutrition on dental development are rare and include that by Murchison and co-workers [72], who carried out an experimental study with protein-deprived infant rhesus monkeys. In these monkeys, crown-root deciduous length in protein restricted monkeys was found to be significantly less than those of controls, although only for deciduous second molars. Hilgers and co-workers [73] also found a significant direct effect of nutrition on dental development, but in conditions of overnutrition. BMI status was determined in a sample of children between the ages of 8 and 15, where a mean dental age acceleration of 1.53 years was found for obese individuals, compared to 0.68 years for normal children. Finally, with respect to the third molar, Rai [74] using a sample of North Indian patients between the ages of 17 and 21 found that dental and chronological age did not differ in the group of well-nourished individuals, but dental age underestimated chronological age in the group of malnourished subjects. In this study, the patients were categorized according to the nutritional risk index, which incorporates information about the subject's weight and plasma albumin level [74].

Evidence also suggests that the deciduous dentition is less affected by malnutrition than by permanent dentition [75–80] by contrasting the delay in deciduous and permanent eruption in different studies. Although a delay in both dentitions have been associated with childhood malnutrition, no comparative studies have been carried out. In addition, this nutritional effect seems to be documented for tooth emergence but not for tooth formation. Given that older children have a greater chance of accumulating environmental insults, it is perhaps reasonable to assume that the formation of the permanent teeth will also likely show a greater possibility of delay in maturation, when compared to that of the deciduous teeth.

A clearer picture has been emerging with respect to the consequences of malnutrition, and other external factors, in dental formation. Malnourished children may show delayed dental development compared to what is expected for their age. Consequently, age estimation from tooth formation should be performed critically. In a forensic context, this is particularly noteworthy in cases of suspected abuse or neglect.

9.4.2 Assessing Growth Failure from the Skeleton

Two general approaches are proposed here for the assessment of growth status from immature human skeletal remains. The two approaches differ in that one requires age to be known and the other is better used when true age cannot be ascertained with accuracy. Once the child is identified, his/her true age is usually known from comparison with the date of birth. However, in some situations, age or date of birth may not be determined, such as in cases of an unreported non-hospitalized delivery or cases of immigrant families. Due to the rapid body changes associated with growth, accurate age determination is essential for an accurate assessment of growth status. Both approaches also require sex to be known with certainty due to sex-specific differences in growth. In the first approach, growth failure is assessed by comparing an estimation of height or the length of the long bones with sex- and age-specific reference data for height and long bone length. Since height or length is being compared with a reference, age must not be estimated. The risk of delay in tooth formation in neglect cases may jeopardize the identification of growth failure, through underestimation of true age. In the second approach, growth failure is assessed by determining the discrepancy between two estimates of age: dental age, which is more stable, and skeletal, which is more susceptible to malnutrition and other nutrition-related factors. The larger the discrepancy between ages, the greater the growth deficit.

Since both approaches will only detect cumulative insult on skeletal growth and development, they will only be indicative of chronic and not acute malnutrition. For that reason, it is also less likely that a young infant will be identified as stunted or maturationally delayed, because not enough time may have elapsed for the insult to become chronic. This may be related to fact that skeletal growth faltering is usually only detectable at about 6 months of age in studies of living infants and children from developing countries [81].

9.4.2.1 Assessing Growth Failure from Height Estimates and Long Bone Length

One possibility of identifying failure to grow is to compare the height of the child, estimated from long bone lengths, with an age-specific reference of height. A pre-requisite of this approach is that age has to be known with accuracy, once the remains are identified. If age is estimated from dental development, the effects of malnutrition may be underestimated due to a delay in tooth formation, as the child will appear younger than he/she is. A few methods have been proposed for estimating the height of immature skeletal remains, but most have important limitations. Only methods that provide regression formulae based on actual bone lengths are referred to here, and these include the studies by Telkkä and co-workers [82], Feldesman [83], Smith [84], and Ruff [85]. In these studies, height is obtained from living subjects, and the lengths of all six long bones (humerus, radius, ulna, femur, tibia, fibula) are collected from radiographs.

This approach may be useful because it will allow the expert to assess whether the child's height is below the 3rd or 1st percentiles of height for the age of the child. However, the initial problem is the choice of method for height estimation. Since the purpose is to compare the height estimate with a reference, the sample utilized by the height estimation method should match or be similar to the sample of reference children, against which the height estimate will be compared. In addition, due to issues of population mimicry in regression, the height estimated from a certain method will be the expected height for that bone size in the sample of children from which the regression formulae derive. If the sample utilized by the height estimation method is composed of shorter children than that of the reference sample, the case child will appear shorter than he/she is. Consequently, the choice of height estimation method will be dependent on the sample from which it is derived and the reference against which the height estimate will be compared.

The studies of Feldesman [83], Smith [84], and Ruff [85] are all based on the Child Research Council (Denver) data, but they differ in age range. While Ruff [85] has developed regression formulae for all six limb bones to estimate height from 1 to 17 years of age, Smith [84] has provided formulae only from 3 to 10 years. Feldesman's [83] equations only apply to the femur of 8–18-year-old children. Differences between Smith's and Ruff's methods result from the fact that Smith utilized only standing height and eliminated the years where height is measured from recumbent length, as well as the post-pubertal individuals. Changes in growth from puberty alter the relationship between height and long bone length. It is important to note that Ruff has corrected recumbent length for standing height in infants, so that Ruff's estimates cannot be used for comparison with reference data, since in this age group it is based on recumbent length. Finally, the study by Telkkä and co-workers [82] is based on Finnish data, which is not described in detailed. In a study by Cardoso [86] it was shown that in a sample of child skeletons of known height, children are tallest when height is estimated from Telkkä and co-workers' [82] formulae. Although this is not a sufficient indication that this is the most suitable method, the fact that the Child Research Council children are significantly shorter than the Fels Longitudinal Growth Study children (see also below), suggest that Telkkä and co-workers' method may be the best choice for estimating height with the purpose of comparing it with a height reference. The reason for this is that the Fels data was utilized to construct the 1977 NCHS growth charts [87]. Although the Fels data includes long bone lengths from 1 month to 18 years, no regression formulae for height estimation were developed from these series.

One major problem with comparing a height estimate with a reference is that Cardoso [86] showed that the methods devised by Telkkä and co-workers [82], Feldesman [83], and Smith [84] tend to underestimate true height consistently in a sample of stunted children. This results from altered body proportions in the stunted child, who is not simply a smaller version of a taller child, but has instead proportionally shorter legs relative to trunk [88–92]. In fact, since a significant proportion of abused and neglected children are stunted, they also show disproportionally short legs [93].Consequently, if the Waterlow classification (see above) is applied to the height estimates, the child will appear more stunted, as the estimated height in percentage of normal height of respective age group is smaller than the actual height (which is unknown).

One alternative to estimating the height of the child, which also requires the age to be known, is to use the long bone length directly to measure the growth deficit. However, reference data for long bone lengths is relatively scarce and is available only from radiographic sources. Maresh [94] provides mean long bone length for age between 1 month and 18 years and is based on the Child Research Council children. The Harvard School of Public Health Growth Study also includes long bone length reference information, which was published by Anderson and co-workers [95], for the tibia and femur between 1 and 18 years of age. Similarly, Ghantus [96] published reference values for the length of the radius and ulna from 3 to 24 months, based on the Brush Inquiry/Foundation Growth Study carried out at Western Reserve University (Cleveland). Since the Fels longitudinal growth data was utilized to construct the 1977 NCHS growth charts [87], the long bone data from this study may represent the best approximation of a reference for long bone length. Unfortunately, long bone length data for the Fels study is available only for the tibia and radius and for children from 1 month to 18 years of age, at 6-month intervals [97].

The Fels or Harvard data will most closely resemble a reference sample, in particular, because long bone lengths in the Denver sample are significantly shorter than those in the Fels and Harvard data. Since there are no percentiles for long bone lengths, the only option is to calculate a z-score from reference data. Actually, Maresh's [94] long bone data tables include the 10th, 50th, and 90th percentiles, but they are of little use in the detection of severe malnutrition. z-scores are calculated by subtracting the median bone length for age from the actual bone length divided by the standard deviation [98]. The advantages of the z-score are that it allows more precision in describing growth status and distinguishes between a child at (whose z-score may be –2.5) or below the 1st percentile (whose z-score may be –3.5 or lower). Although there are no grading schemes for stunting based on z-scores of long bone length, according to Waterlow and co-workers [99], when the child's actual height is 85% of normal height for age – close to the most severe grade of malnutrition of 80% – this corresponds to a z-score between –3.6 and –4.2, depending on the age of the child (under 6 years). However, long bones of the lower limb, namely the femur but particularly the tibia [22, 94, 100, 101], being the fastest growing segments of the body will be more sensitive to nutritional insults and to the detection of severe stunting and severe malnutrition. In addition to the z-score, the calculation of tibia length in percentage of normal tibia length for age may provide an approximation to the Waterlow classification. However, relative tibia length (as percentage of height) increases throughout the growth period, and this complicates its interpretation. Another problem is that long bone length data published by Maresh [94] are not corrected for magnification, and its use can confound interpretations of growth patterns, whereas data provided by Gindhart [97] has been corrected.

9.4.2.2 Assessing Growth Failure from Discrepancies Between Skeletal and Dental Development

Considering that dental development is negatively affected by nutritional status (especially severe and chronic malnutrition), rather than attempting to predict chronological age from tooth formation and plotting dental age against long bone length or a stature estimate to detect growth failure, it may be more useful to compare the level of attainment in dental development to the level of attainment in skeletal growth and development. This can be accomplished by calculating the difference between the two ages in years. Discrepancies between dental and skeletal development are simple subtractions, where a positive score indicates that dental age is advanced relatively to skeletal age and the score increases as the skeletal age lags increasingly behind the dental age. The basic premise in using these discrepancies for detecting growth failure in immature skeletal remains is that dental development is more stable and skeletal development is more susceptible to environmental insults. Discrepancies between dental and skeletal age are indicative of cumulative insult, such that the greater/longer and the more severe the insult the greater the discrepancy and the lesser chance of catch up growth. One important aspect of these calculated skeletal and dental ages is that they are attained ages and not predicted ages. That is, they are informative of how far the child has gone in his/her development, but are not necessarily a good approximation of his/her chronological age.

Contrary to the previous approach, assessing growth from discrepancies between dental and skeletal development does not require knowing the age of the child with certainty. Since these discrepancies are relative measures of growth status, it is only necessary that the methods utilized to determine dental and skeletal age are based on the same sample or on similar samples of children with similar developmental statuses. Otherwise, differences between dental and skeletal ages may result from differences in the samples in which the methods were based, rather than from real differences. This similarity is not easy to accomplish given the diversity of methodologies available for estimating both dental and skeletal age. Several methods have been proposed for assessing dental age and the most common use stages of tooth calcification obtained from radiographic data. Skeletal age is commonly assessed by measuring skeletal maturation or, less frequently, by examining growth in height (skeletal growth). Skeletal maturation is usually derived from radiographic data on the appearance and fusion of centers of ossification, such as those of the hand and wrist. Since skeletal maturation comprises changes in bone size and ossification of the growth plates, it implies the completion of skeletal growth and height [102]. Therefore, because these two developmental processes are closely related, linear skeletal growth can be used as a proxy for growth in height.

To the best of the authors' knowledge, only the Fels Longitudinal Growth Study has been the source for both skeletal and dental development data, which can be used for physiological age assessments. The studies on the formation of the deciduous and permanent dentition, carried out by Moorrees, Fanning, and Hunt [103, 104], are largely based on the Fels data and are among the few that provide information across the entire age range of the developing dentition. The Fels material was the source of data for the deciduous dentition and for the permanent posterior teeth (C-M3). Data published by Gindhart [97] is also based on the Fels data and can be used for skeletal age estimation from skeletal linear growth using the sex- and age-specific long bone length data between 1 month and 18 years of age. Skeletal maturation can provide an alternative measure of skeletal age by using the score methods published by Roche and co-workers for the hand and wrist [105] or knee [106], which also derive from the Fels study. In these methods, specific indicators of growth are scored as noted on radiographs and are then used to compute a skeletal age.

Moorrees, Fanning, and Hunt [103, 104] also utilized dental data from the Harvard School of Public Health Growth Study in their studies, and, consequently, the long bone length data provided by Anderson and co-workers [95] can provide a possible alternative for the assessment of skeletal age, for comparison with dental age obtained from the Moorrees standards. One problem with the use of Gindhart [97], or other similar reference values for long bone length, is that their tables are divided up in very few age groups, particularly in younger children where age changes are more rapid. Consequently, the calculation of attainment age for infants, in the case of Gindhart's data, is made with reference to only four expected ages. This may result in a frequent underestimation of the true skeletal age attained by these children.

Since there is a greater magnitude of growth deficit in older children, due to accumulated nutritional insult over time, there may be a tendency to standardize the differences by dental age. The purpose of the approach is to detect chronic cases of malnutrition, which will be obscured by standardized discrepancies. This is particularly true for the infants, whose relative small dental/skeletal age discrepancies may be amplified by their very young dental age with which the discrepancies are standardized. The use of long bone may also affect the accuracy with which dental/skeletal age discrepancies can detect cases of growth failure. Because the growth of the tibia will be more sensitive to insult, discrepancies between skeletal growth and dental development calculated from tibia data will tend to classify/identify more stunted individuals than when the discrepancies are calculated from femur or other long bone. However, the use of tibia and femur data as increasingly reflecting the conditions of malnutrition is consistent with the findings of Wales, who demonstrated that a significant proportion of abused children are short and have shorter lower limb lengths.

Skeletal maturation can provide an important alternative to skeletal growth when estimating skeletal age, but its assessment is problematical from skeletal remains. Although hand-wrist bone maturation is routinely used to calculated skeletal age in the living, it is difficult, if not impossible, to apply in skeletal material due to problems of recovery, preservation, and identification of ossification centers. Therefore, developmental indicators of bone maturation in the knee have a great potential to be used with a skeletal sample because the epiphyses of the knee are significantly larger than those of the hand, they preserve well, are more easily recovered, can be easily identified, and are already present from birth [61]. This is where the Roche and co-workers' method for determining skeletal age from maturational indicators at the knee proves most useful, particularly since it is based on the Fels data.

9.4.2.3 Illustrating the Two Approaches

In order to illustrate the similarities and/or differences between the approaches described above, as well as their usefulness and value, a sample of Portuguese documented child skeletons was selected from the Lisbon Collection housed at the National Museum of Natural History [107]. Individuals in the collection do not represent the contemporary population of Portugal, as they were mostly born and died in the first half of the twentieth century. In addition, they represent the middle to low socioeconomic strata of the Lisbon at this time period, as inferred from occupations of the male segment (mostly menial occupations) and from the origin of the remains (temporary graves at the local Lisbon cemeteries) [108]. This collection include over 100 fully identified skeletons of individuals under the age of 20 years, but only children under the age of 3 were selected, as this is the age group where neglect is more prevalent. Individuals in the collection can be described as representing populations experiencing lower levels of social and economic development, where the children may parallel those living under conditions of mild to moderate malnutrition and moderate to high infection.

In this sample of child skeletons, skeletal age was obtained as the age at which a certain long bone length was attained relative to the average long bone length measurements for each sex provided by Gindhart [97]. Dental age was calculated as the sex-specific mean age of attainment for the deciduous and permanent tooth stage of Moorrees, Fanning and Hunt [103, 104]. These studies were chosen because they are both based on the Fels Longitudinal Growth Study sample, making dental and skeletal age directly contrasted. In order for the results to be comparable with that of height, height was estimated from tibia length using Telkkä and co-workers method [82] and z-scores were obtained from the same reference data on the tibia [97]. Actual tibia length as percentage of expected tibia length for age was also calculated to assess its value as an alternative to the Waterlow classification for height. The z-score and tibia length as percentage of normal length should provide similar results to that of plotting height estimates against the WHO reference, when height is estimated from tibia length. Due to differential preservation, a total of

25 skeletons could have their physiological ages and height calculated from these methods.

Data from previous studies have shown that most children in this collection are stunted [60, 61, 86], so it is no surprise that the approaches described here confirm these previous findings. Of the 25 children analyzed, 19 (76%) are below the 15th percentile for height, 11 (44%) below the 3rd percentile, and 4 (16%) under the 1st percentile, compared to the WHO growth reference. z-Scores under –3.6 are all included below the 1st percentile, as well as estimated height in percentage of normal height under 90% and most cases of actual tibia length in percentage of normal tibia length for age under 80%. These four children show the greatest growth delay and are the most likely candidates for a diagnosis of severe malnutrition. Absolute discrepancies between dental and skeletal age in these children are, with one expectation, greater than 1 year and greater than 50% when standardized for dental age. However, other three other children showed standardized discrepancies greater than 50%. These children are the youngest in the sample and their large standardized discrepancies result from a slight overestimation of dental age combined with a very young dental age with which to standardize the discrepancies between dental and skeletal age.

Table 9.1 provides a summary of the results when the two general approaches are applied to the group of four children below the 1st percentile for height. With the exception of child #1, all indicators seem to provide consistent results. Due to problems in height estimation (see above) the Waterlow classification for protein-energy malnutrition cannot be applied straightforwardly and it is impossible to assess reliably how good % tibia length is a substitute for % height. Standardized discrepancies between dental and skeletal age may tend to overestimate the amount of growth delay, particularly in younger children. Absolute discrepancies may be more reliable, regardless of the child's age.

Table 9.1 Contrasting results of the two approaches proposed for the detection of growth failure from the skeleton, when applied to the identified immature skeletons in the Lisbon collection (<3 years of age). Only the children under the 1st percentile (WHO growth reference) for estimated height are depicted ($n = 4$)

Child#	Age	DA	SA	DA-SA	(DA-SA)/DA	Tibia	% Tibia	z-score	Height	% Height
1	1.20	0.93	0.25	0.68	73	96	80.3	–4.1	72.4	93
2	2.60	2.25	1.00	1.25	56	129	79.3	–4.5	84.0	91
3	2.80	2.30	1.00	1.30	57	127	78.0	–4.7	83.3	88
4	3.50	1.95	0.75	1.20	62	110	59.8	–8.1	77.3	77

Ages are in years; DA, dental age; SA, skeletal age; DA-SA, discrepancy between DA and SA in years; (DA-SA)/DA, standardized discrepancy in percentage; Tibia, tibia diaphyseal length in mm; % Tibia, tibia length as percentage of expected tibia length for age [97]; z-Score, z-score for tibia length [97]; Height, estimated height in cm from tibia length using Telkkä and co-workers [82] method; % Height, estimated height as percentage of expected height (WHO) for age

Available information obtained from civil registration of death and autopsy records (child #1 and #2 were autopsied), provides the opportunity to know in greater detail some aspects of the lives (and deaths) of these children, which may help understand the observed pattern of growth delay. Child #1 is a 1-year-old boy who died of giant cell pneumonia. The diagnosis was made at autopsy, whose records also described the child as being poorly nourished. From available documentary evidence, child # 2 may have been a victim of medical neglect. This 2-year-old boy died of purulent otitis and was autopsied because death was presumed to have occurred from lack of medical assistance. The family address in the civil registration of death suggests that they lived in a poor suburban neighborhood in the Lisbon outskirts. Bilateral bronchopneumonia was the cause of death of child #3, a 2-year-old illegitimate son of a docker, according to the civil birth registration. The family address in the same record also suggests a poor neighborhood, but in this case in the old core of the city of Lisbon. Child #4 died of tuberculous meningitis in 1913. This 3-year-old boy was son of a navy sailor who lived in one of the old port areas of the city of Lisbon. From cross-referencing records, it was found that he had a 14-month-old sister who died 7 months after him. All of the children under analysis show a large growth deficit and seem to have suffered from mild to severe malnutrition. The context of their lives and deaths points to several risk factors of child neglect cases, particularly poverty. However, with the possible exception of child #2, all cases also suggest that growth failure may have had other etiologies, particularly infectious diseases. Although data in Table 9.1 is not meant to provide the means for the diagnosis of child neglect, it may provide some guidance in the assessment of malnutrition from measures of growth delay from the skeleton.

9.5 Discussion and Conclusions

Assessing growth status from immature skeletal remains requires accurate methods for dental and skeletal age estimation and up-to-date sex- and age-specific reference data for skeletal growth. Reference data for dental and skeletal development of modern populations is generally lacking, and this can potentially represent a major obstruction in forensic and criminal investigations by complicating the detection of growth failure and, consequently, the identification of a potential case of neglect or abuse. Due to well-documented secular changes toward increase in height and acceleration in maturation, earlier standards may not be appropriate to modern forensic cases. In particular, references used by skeletal biologists to assess skeletal development, such as long bone length data from the Child Research Council or the Fels Longitudinal Growth Study, are dated to 1960s and 1970s and earlier. Although there is up-to-date developmental data for the permanent dentition and skeletal maturation, long bone reference values are lacking and are unlikely to be updated due to wide concerns of excessive x-ray exposure for research purposes. Consequently, experts will have to be aware of the limitations of the available data and make informed choices and cautious decisions. In addition, some of the methods or reference data do not provide age information with sufficient detail, particularly in the younger age groups where growth is fastest. This complicates the detection of growth failure in these children, who are already at greater risk for neglect. In addition, utilizing long bone lengths to assess growth failure are probably better than using height estimates, due to uncertainty in the later. On the other hand, there are no guidelines for classifying malnutrition according to long bone length, such as the Waterlow scheme devised for height.

The limitations of the reference sources for dental and skeletal development are directly related with the diagnostic limits of child neglect from ostelogical observations. Although the forensic anthropologist may be able to assess whether the child shows growth failure of some magnitude from developmental observations of bone and teeth, this alone will not warrant a case of fatal child neglect and cannot provide confirmation of death by starvation or severe malnutrition. Criteria described here are meant to provide guidance in the detection of growth failure from immature skeletal remains and not a straightforward diagnosis of neglect. In fact, failure to thrive as a manifestation of child neglect represents only a minority of children with failure to thrive [109] and a diagnosis of neglect must consider a history of withholding of food from the child and/or disregard for nutritional needs that endanger the child. Although a clinical evaluation for failure to thrive involve a comprehensive family history, physical examination, feeding observation, and a home visit by an appropriate health professional, when dealing with a fatal case in a forensic anthropology context, diagnosis relies on the post-mortem examination of the remains, on a comprehensive family history and, eventually, on previous information collected during a home visit while the child was alive or collected during a doctor's appointment (subsequent to an episode of injury or not). If available, medical records are essential to determine evidence of malnutrition from growth deficits. Finally, assessing the circumstances surrounding the death and the findings at the scene, such as sanitary conditions of the child's home, provide vital clues for the detection of case of neglect.

Although neglect should not be a diagnosis by exclusion in a clinical setting [109], this is even more compelling in a forensic anthropology situation, which requires greater care and precaution in the interpretation of the growth data, in the context of other evidence obtained. The forensic anthropologist and other experts working in the case must collect as much evidence as possible because it is the underlying cause of the starvation (i.e., withholding of food or neglect), and not the diagnosis of starvation itself, that will be valued in criminal proceedings [29]. In this context, it is essential to establish differential diagnosis of growth failure with other cases of natural etiology.

Since growth failure is not an enough condition for the diagnosis of child neglect, other skeletal indicators of malnutrition should be used to support the identification of a potential case of neglect. These include lines of arrested growth identified in radiographs of long bones, known as Harris lines [110], and the histological analysis of pathological striae of Retzius in enamel microstructure, known as Wilson bands, indicative of growth disruption [111]. However, these osteological and dental changes require that the individual survive and recover from the episode of malnutrition or disease. Although there are problems with the etiology of Harris lines, Walker and co-workers [4] considered them suggestive of episodes of stress in abuse cases. Failure to thrive may also be accompanied with lesions indicative of metabolic deficiencies, namely iron deficiency anemia, and vitamin D and C deficiencies [2]. Iron deficiency anemia, in particular, is the most common known nutritional deficiency, especially among young children and women. For example, in the 2004 report by the Massachusetts Department of Public Health, where 1700 children were referred to as showing failure to thrive in the previous 6 years, nearly 30% were anemic [112]. Consequently, skeletal development delay can concur with lesions indicative of various nutritional deficiencies, of growth disruption in long bone and enamel, and even changes in appositional bone growth [44]. Other findings, consistent with child neglect, are general poor dental health and greater prevalence of dental disease [113–115].

In the most severe cases of neglect it may be useful to use other indicators of developmental status which seem to be affected last. One example of such an indicator is the measurement of head circumference, since the brain is usually spared from malnutrition. Only in cases of extreme malnutrition or starvation will head size suffer a delay in growth. For example, in five cases of severe malnutrition in infants, four showed normal head circumference and only one showed reduced circumference [116]. Consequently, due to head size stability, head circumference is probably a more accurate indicator of extreme growth failure. However, postmortem changes to the skeleton are unlikely to preserve an intact and pristine skull which can be accurately measured. This is particularly true for the immature and fragile cranium of children. Even if the skull is not intact and the different elements are preserved, an accurate reconstruction of the skull may be difficult to accomplish due to postmortem modifications that may cause deformation and warping of the skull bones. If measurement or reconstruction is possible, a correction may have to be introduced while converting skull circumference to head circumference [117].

Assessments of growth status in a forensic context from osteological findings need careful consideration of the limitations of the evidence and of the auxological methods employed. Data suggest that a diagnosis of growth failure alone will likely identify several cases of moderate to severe malnutrition unrelated to child neglect or abuse. Only a careful examination of the circumstances surrounding the death and the findings at the death scene, as well as a thorough family and medical history will be able to associate growth failure with child neglect or abuse. Ultimately, a diagnosis of neglect requires the assessment of multiple lines of evidence and the work of a multidisciplinary team of experts and professionals involved in any given case.

References

1. Lewis ME, Rutty G. The endangered child: the personal identification of children in forensic anthropology. Sci Justice 2003;43:201–20.
2. Lewis ME. The bioarchaeology of children. Current perspectives in biological and forensic anthropology. Cambridge: Cambridge University Press, 2007.

3. Joffe MD, Giardino AP, O'Sullivan AL. Neglect and abandonment. In: Giardino AP, Alexander R, editors. Child maltreatment: a clinical guide and reference. St Louis: GW Medical Publishing Inc., 2005;153–93.
4. Walker PL, Cook DC, Lambert PM. Skeletal evidence for child abuse: a physical anthropological perspective. J Forensic Sci 1997;42:196–207.
5. Blondiaux G, Blondiaux J, Secousse F, Cotton A, Danze P.-M, Flipo R-M. Rickets and child abuse. The case of a two year old girl from the 4th century in Lisieux. (Normandy). Int J Osteoarchaeol 2002;12:209–15.
6. Wheeler SM, Beauchesne P, Williams L, Molto JE. Fractured childhood: a probable case of child abuse from ancient Egypt. SAS Bull: Newsl Soc Archaeol Sci 2007;30:6–9.
7. Mays S. Infanticide in Roman Britain. Antiquity 1993;67:883–8.
8. Smith P, Kahila G. Identification of infanticide in archaeological sites: a case study from the late Roman-Early Byzantine periods at Ashkelon, Israel. J Archaeol Sci 1992;19: 667–75.
9. Iwaniec D. The emotionally abused and neglected child. New York, NY: Wiley, 2006.
10. Kolagotla L, Sandel M, Frank D. Failure to thrive: a reconceptualization. In: Giardino AP, Alexander R, editors. Child maltreatment: a clinical guide and reference. St. Louis: GW Medical Publishing Inc., 2005;195–207.
11. US Department of Health and Human Services, Administration on Children, Youth, and Families. Child maltreatment 2008. Washington DC: US Government Printing Office, 2010.
12. Sedlak AJ, Broadhurst DD. Third national incidence study of child abuse and neglect. Washington, DC: US Department of Health and Human Services, 1996.
13. Cowen PS. Child neglect: injuries of omission. Pediatr Nurs 1999;25:401–16.
14. Joffe MD. Child neglect and abandonment. In: Giardino AP, Giardino ER, editors. Recognition of child abuse for the mandated reporter. St Louis: GW Medical Publishing, 2002;39–61.
15. Gaudin Jr. JM. Child neglect: a guide for intervention. US Department of Health and Human Services, Administration for Children and Families. Washington, DC: Westover Consultants, 1993.
16. Lewin D, Herron H. Signs, symptoms and risk factors: health visitors' perspectives of child neglect. Child Abuse Rev 2007;16:93–107.
17. Block RW, Krebs NF, the Committee on Child Abuse and Neglect and the Committee on Nutrition. Failure to thrive as a manifestation of child neglect. Pediatrics 2005;116: 1234–7.
18. Dubowitz H, Black M. Medical neglect. In: Briere J, Berliner L, Bulkley JA, Jenny C, Reid T, editors. The APSAC handbook on child maltreatment. London: Sage, 1993;227–42.
19. Patton RG, Gardner LI. Growth failure in maternal deprivation. Springfield, IL: Charles C. Thomas, 1963.
20. Kempe CH, Silverman FN, Steele BF, Droegemueller W, Silver HK. The battered-child syndrome. JAMA 1962;181:17–24.
21. Oliván G. Catch-up growth assessment in long-term physically neglected and emotionally abused preschool age male children. Child Abuse Negl 2003;27:103–8.
22. Bogin B. Patterns of human growth. 2nd ed. Cambridge: Cambridge University Press, 1999.
23. King SE, Ulijaszek SJ. Invisible insults during growth and development: contemporary theories and past populations. In: Hoppa RD, Fitzgerald CM, editors. Human growth in the past: studies from bones and teeth. Cambridge: Cambridge University Press, 1999;161–82.
24. Markowitz R, Duggan C. Failure to thrive: malnutrition in the pediatric outpatient setting. In: Walker WA, Watkins JB, editors. Nutrition in pediatrics. London: BC Decker Inc, 2003; 897–909.
25. Rodrigues T, Rocha L, Barros H. Physical abuse during pregnancy and preterm delivery. Am J Obstet Gynecol. 2008;198:171–6.
26. Edwards AGK, Halse PC, Parkin JM, Waterston AJR. Recognising failure to thrive in early childhood. Arch Dis Child 1990;65:1263–5.

27. Brown J, Cohen P, Johnson JG, Salzinger S. A longitudinal analysis of risk factors of child maltreatment: findings of a 17-year prospective study of officially recorded and self-reported child abuse and neglect. Child Abuse Negl 1998;22:1065–78.
28. Margolin L. Fatal child neglect. Child Welfare 1990;69:309–19.
29. Madea B. Death as a result of starvation: diagnostic criteria. In: Tsokos M, editor. Forensic pathology reviews, Vol. 2. Totowa, NJ: Humana Press, 2005;3–23.
30. Lawrence R, Irvine P. Redefining fatal child neglect. Child Abuse Prev 2004;21:1–23.
31. Berkowitz CD. Fatal child neglect. Adv Pediatr 2001;48:331–61.
32. Adelson L. Homicide by starvation. The nutritional variant of the battered child. JAMA 1963;186:458–60.
33. Asser S, Swan R. Child fatalities from religion-motivated medical neglect. Pediatrics 1998;101:625–9.
34. Benecke M, Lessig R. Child neglect and forensic entomology. Forensic Sci Int 2001;120:155–9.
35. Knight LD, Collins KA. A 25- year retrospective review of deaths due to pediatric neglect. Am J Forensic Med Pathol 2005;26:221–8.
36. Fieguth A, Gunther D, Kleemann WJ, Troger HD. Lethal child neglect. Forensic Sci Int 2002;130:8–12.
37. Piercecchi-Marti MD, Louis-Borrione C, Bartoli C, Sanvoisin A, Panuel M, Pelissier-Alicot AL, Leonettiet G. Malnutrition, a rare form of child abuse: diagnostic criteria. J Forensic Sci 2006;51:670–3.
38. Wehner F, Schieffer MC, Wehner HD. Percentile charts to determine the duration of child abuse by chronic malnutrition. Forensic Sci Int 1999;102:173–80.
39. Gomez F, Galvan RR, Cravioto J, Frenk S. Malnutrition in infancy and childhood with special reference to Kwashiokor. Adv Pediatr 1955;7:131–69.
40. Waterlow JC. Classification and definition of protein-caloric malnutrition. Br Med J 1972;2:566–9.
41. Kerley ER. Forensic anthropology and crimes involving children. J Forensic Sci 1976;21:333–9.
42. Merchant V, Ubelaker D. Skeletal growth of the Protohistoric Arikara. Am J Phys Anthropol 1977;46:61–72.
43. Saunders SR, Hoppa R, Southern R. Diaphyseal growth in a nineteenth century skeletal sample of subadults from St Thomas' Church, Belleville, Ontario. Int J Osteoarchaeol 1993;3:265–81.
44. Mays S. Linear and appositional long bone growth in earlier human populations: a case study from Mediaeval England. In: Hoppa RD, Fitzgerald CM, editors. Human growth in the past: studies using bones and teeth. Cambridge: Cambridge University Press, 1999;290–312.
45. Humphrey LT. 2003. Linear growth variation in the archaeological record. In: Thompson JL, Krovitz GE, Nelson AJ, editors. Patterns of growth in the genus Homo. Cambridge: Cambridge University Press, 2003;144–69.
46. Saunders SR. Juvenile skeletons and growth-related studies. In: Katzenberg MA, Saunders SR, editors. Biological anthropology of the human skeleton. New York, NY: Wiley-Liss Inc., 2008;117–48.
47. Cardoso HFV, Garcia S. The not-so-dark ages: ecology for human growth in Medieval and early twentieth century Portugal as inferred from skeletal growth profiles. Am J Phys Anthropol 2009;138:136–47.
48. Hoppa RD, Fitzgeral CM. From head to toe: integrating studies from bones and teeth in biological anthropology. In: Hoppa RD, Fiztgerald CM, editors. Human growth in the past: studies from bones and teeth. Cambridge: Cambridge University Press, 1999;1–31.
49. Hoppa RD. What to do with long bones: toward a progressive palaeoauxology. Anthropologie 2000;38:23–32.
50. Vallejo-Bolaños E, España-López AJ. The relationship between dental age, bone age and chronological age in 54 children with short familial stature. Int J Paediatr Dent 1997;7:15–7.

51. Ozerovic B. Correlation of dental and skeletal age in children with cerebral palsy. Eur J Orthod 1980;2:193–5.
52. Laor E, Garfunkel A, Koyoumdijsky-Kaye E. Skeletal and dental retardation in ß-thalassemia major. Hum Biol 1982;54:85–92.
53. Garn SM, Lewis AB, Blizzard RM. Endocrine factors in dental development. J Dental Res 1965;44:243–58.
54. Edler RJ. Dental and skeletal ages in hypopituitary patients. J Dent Res 1977;56:1145–53.
55. Keller EE, Sather AH, Hayles AB. Dental and skeletal development in various endocrine and metabolic diseases. J Am Dent Assoc 1970;81:415–9.
56. Sears RS, Nazif MM, Zullo T. The effects of sickle-cell disease on dental and skeletal maturation. ASDC J Dent Child 1981;48:275–7.
57. Holderbaum RM, Veeck EB, Oliveira HW, Silva CL, Fernandes A. Comparison among dental, skeletal and chronological development in HIV-positive children: a radiographic study. Braz Oral Res 2005;19:209–15.
58. Garn SM, Lewis AB, Kerewsky RS. Genetic, nutritional and maturational correlates of dental development. J Dent Res 1965;44:228–42.
59. Melsen B, Wenzel A, Miletic T, Andreasen J, Vagn-Hansen PL, Terp S. Dental and skeletal maturity in adoptive children: assessments at arrival and after one year in the admitting country. Ann Hum Biol 1986;13:153–9.
60. Cardoso HFV. Environmental effects on skeletal versus dental development using a documented subadult skeletal sample to test a basic assumption in human osteological research. Am J Phys Anthropol 2007;132:223–33.
61. Conceição E, Cardoso, HFV. Environmental effects on skeletal versus dental development II: further testing of a basic assumption in human osteological research. Am J Phys Anthropol 2011;144:463–70.
62. Ubelaker DH. Estimating age at death from immature human skeletons: an overview. J Forensic Sci 1987;32:1254–63.
63. Ubelaker DH. The estimation of age at death from immature human bone. In: Iscan MY, editor. Age markers in the human skeleton. Springfield, IL: Charles C Thomas Publisher, 1989;55–70.
64. Fanning EA. Effect of extraction of deciduous molars on the formation and eruption of their successors. Angle Orthod 1962;32:44–53.
65. Adler P. Effect of some environmental factors on sequence of permanent tooth eruption. J Dental Res 1963;42:605–16.
66. Lee MMC, Low WD, Chang SF. Eruption of the permanent dentition of southern Chinese in Hong Kong. Arch Oral Biol 1965;10:849–61.
67. Enwonwu CO. Influence of socio-economic conditions on dental development in Nigerian children. Arch Oral Biol 1973;18:95–107.
68. Garn SM, Jerrold MN, Sandusky SM, Trowbridge F. Economic impact on tooth emergence. Am J Phys Anthropol 1973;39:233–38.
69. Kaul S, Sushma S, Saxena B. Emergence of permanent teeth in school-children in Chandigarh, India. Arch Oral Biol 1975;20:587–93.
70. Alvarez JO, Navia JM. Nutritional status, tooth eruption, and dental caries: a review. Am J Clin Nutr 1989;49:417–26.
71. Cardoso HF, Heuzé Y, Júlio P. Secular change in the timing of dental root maturation in Portuguese boys and girls. Am J Hum Biol. 2010;22:791–800.
72. Murchison MA, Riopelle AJ, Owsley DW. Dental development in protein-deprived infant rhesus monkeys. Hum Biol 1988;60:383–94.
73. Hilgers KK, Akridge M, Scheetz JP, Kinane DE. Childhood obesity and dental development. Pediatr Dent 2006;28:18–22.
74. Rai B. Effect of nutrition on coronal displacement of cementum in impacted teeth. Ann Hum Biol 2009;36:431–6.

75. Neill JJ, Gurney JM, Kuti, OR, Akinkugbe DD, Hanafy MM, Kassem SA et al. Deciduous dental eruption time and protein-calorie malnutrition from different parts of the world. J Trop Pediatr ;1973;19(Special issue 2A):217–22
76. Truswell AS, Hansen DL. Eruption of deciduous teeth in protein-calorie malnutrition. J Trop Pediatr 1973;19:214–6.
77. Jelliffe EFP, Jelliffe DB. Deciduous dental eruption, nutrition and age assessment. J Trop Pediatr 1973;19:71–4.
78. Delgado H, Habicht JP, Yarbrough C, Lechtig A, Martorell R, Malina RM et al. Nutritional status and the timing of deciduous tooth eruption. Am J Clin Nutr 1975;28: 216–24.
79. Konigsberg LW, Holman D. Estimation of age at death from dental emergence and implications for studies of prehistoric somatic growth. In: Hoppa RD, Fitzgerald CM, editors. Human growth in the past. Cambridge: Cambridge University Press, 1999;264–89.
80. Holman DJ, Yamaguchi K. Longitudinal analysis of deciduous tooth emergence: IV. Covariate effects in Japanese children. Am J Phys Anthropol 2005;126:352–8.
81. Martorell R, Khanl LK, Schroederet DG. Reversibility of stunting: epidemiological findings in children from developing countries. Eur J Clin Nutr 1994;48(Suppl 1):S45–57.
82. Telkkä A, Palkama A, Virtama P. Prediction of stature from radiographs of long bones in children. J Forensic Sci 1962;7:474–9.
83. Feldesman MR. Femur/stature ratio and estimates of stature in children. Am J Phys Anthropol 1992;87:447–59.
84. Smith SL. Stature estimation of 3-10-year-old children from long bone lengths. J Forensic Sci 2007;52:538–46.
85. Ruff C. Body size prediction from juvenile skeletal remains. Am J Phys Anthropol 2007;133:698–716.
86. Cardoso HFV. A test of three methods for estimating stature from immature skeletal remains using long bone lengths. J Forensic Sci 2009;54:13–9.
87. Hamill PV, Drizd TA, Johnson CL, Reed RB, Roche AF, Moore WM. Physical growth: National Center for Health Statistics Percentiles. Am J Clin Nutr 1979;32:607–29.
88. Tanner JM, Hayashi T, Preece MA, Cameron N. Increase in length of leg relative to trunk in Japanese children and adults from 1957 to 1977: comparison with British and with Japanese Americans. Ann Hum Biol 1982;9:411–23.
89. Buschang PH, Malina RM, Little BB. Linear growth of Zapotec schoolchildren: growth status and yearly velocity for leg length and sitting height. Ann Hum Biol 1986;13: 225–34.
90. Frisancho AR, Guilding N, Tanner S. Growth of leg length is reflected in socioeconomic differences. Acta Med Auxol 2001;33:47–50.
91. Bogin B, Smith P, Orden AB, Varela-Silva MI, Loucky J. Rapid change in height and body proportions of Maya American children. Am J Phys Anthropol 2002;14:753–61.
92. Smith PK, Bogin B, Varela-Silva MI, Loucky J. Economic and anthropological assessments of the health of children in Maya immigrant families in the US. Econ Hum Biol 2003;1: 145–60.
93. Wales JKH, Herber SM, Taitz LS. Height and body proportions in child abuse. Arch Dis Child 1992;67:632–5.
94. Maresh MM. Measurements from roentgenograms. In: McCannon RW, editor. Human growth and development. Springfield: Charles C Thomas Publisher, 1970;157–88.
95. Anderson M, Messner MB, Green WT. Distribution of lengths of the normal femur and tibia from one to eighteen years of age. J Bone Joint Surg Am 1964;46A:1197–202.
96. Ghantus MK. Growth of the shaft of the human radius and ulna during the first two years of life. Am J Roentgenol 1951;65:784–6.
97. Gindhart PS. Growth standards for the tibia and radius in children aged one through eighteen Years. Am J Physis Anthropol 1973;39:41–8.

98. Markowitz R, Watkins JB, Duggan, C. Failure to thrive: malnutrition in the pediatric outpatient setting. In: Duggan C, Watkins JB, Walker WA, editors. Nutrition in pediatrics: basic science and clinical applications. Hamilton, ON: BC Decker Inc., 2008;479–89.
99. Waterlow JC, Buzina R, Keller W, Lane M, Nichaman MZ, Tanner JM. The presentation and use of height and weight data for comparing the nutritional status of groups of children under the age of 10 years. Bull World Health Organ 1977;55:489–98.
100. Eveleth PB, Tanner JM. Worldwide variation in human growth. 2nd ed. Cambridge: Cambridge University Press, 1990.
101. Smith SL, Buschang PH. Variation in longitudinal diaphyseal long bone growth in children three to ten years of age. Am J Hum Biol 2004;16:648–57.
102. Liliequist B, Lundberg M. Skeletal and tooth development: a methodologic investigation. Acta Radiol 1971;11:97–112.
103. Moorrees CFA, Fanning EA, Hunt EE. Formation and resorption of three deciduous teeth in children. Am J Phys Anthropol 1963;21:205–13.
104. Moorrees CFA, Fanning EA, Hunt EE. Age variation of formation stages for ten permanent teeth. J Dent Res 1963;42:1490–502.
105. Roche AF, Chumlea WM, Thissen D. Assessing the skeletal maturity of the hand-wrist. Springfield, IL: Charles C Thomas, 1988.
106. Roche AF, Wainer H, Thissen D. Skeletal maturity: the knee joint as a biological indicator. New York, NY: Plenum, 1975.
107. Cardoso HFV. Brief communication: the collection of identified human skeletons housed at the Bocage Museum (National Museum of Natural History), Lisbon, Portugal. Am J Phys Anthropol 2006;129:173–6.
108. Cardoso HFV. Patterns of growth and development of the human skeleton and dentition in relation to environmental quality [PhD dissertation]. Hamilton, ON: McMaster University, 2005.
109. Black MM, Dubowitz H, Casey PH, Cutts D, Drewett RF, Drotar D et al. Failure to thrive as distinct from child neglect. Pediatrics 2006; 117:1456–8.
110. Blanco RA, Acheson RM, Canosa C, Salomon JB. Height, weight and lines of arrested growth in young Guatemalan children. Am J Phys Anthropol 1974;40:39–48.
111. Simpson S. Reconstructing patterns of growth disruption from enamel microstructure. In: Hoppa RD, Fitzgerald CM, editors. Human growth in the past. Cambridge: Cambridge University Press, 1999;241–63.
112. Nyambose J, Cunningham K. The Massachusetts growth and nutrition program summary report FY 2003. http://www.mass.gov/Eeohhs2/docs/dph/com_health/nutrition/report_2003.pdf.
113. Kellogg N, Kellogg ND. Oral and dental aspects of child abuse and neglect. Pediatrics 2005;116:1565–8.
114. Mezzich AC, Bretz WA, Day B-S, Corby PM, Kirisci L, Swaney M et al. Child neglect and oral health problems in offspring of substance-abusing fathers. Am J Addict 2007;16: 397–402.
115. Valencia-Rojas N, Lawrence HP, Goodman D. Prevalence of early childhood caries in a population of children with history of maltreatment. J Public Health Dent 2008;68:94–101.
116. Househam KC, de Villiers JF. Computed tomography in severe protein energy. Arch Dis Child 1987;62:589–92.
117. Dayall MR, De Conti F, Henneberg M, Steyn M, Veitch D. Reconstruction of stature from head circumference. Am J Phys Anthropol 2006;129:81.

Chapter 10
Fatal Starvation/Malnutrition: Medicolegal Investigation from the Juvenile Skeleton

Ann H. Ross

Abstract Child deaths due to starvation are exceedingly rare and difficult to investigate, and it is difficult to obtain justice for the decedent. These deaths are considered to be the most severe form of maltreatment due to a prolonged period of abuse by the caregiver. Methods used in developing countries to assess malnutrition, starvation, and stunting are presented as they can be useful in medicolegal cases. A case study illustrating the utility of several biological indicators including lines of arrested growth, excessive metaphyseal porosity, growth deficits in long bones, and bone mineral density in medicolegal investigations of fatal starvation is presented. The complexity of these cases calls for multiple lines of evidence such as complete social, medical, and investigative history and investigation in order to rule on a cause and manner of death.

The death investigation begins at the scene
Dolinak et al. [1]

10.1 Introduction

According to the US Department of Health and Human Services 2008 Child Maltreatment Report, 31.9% or 555 of child fatalities were due to neglect. Data reported by 48 states show that 1740 children died from abuse or neglect and approximately 60% of cases reported to child protective services are neglect allegations [2–4]. Pediatric neglect can be defined as inadequately meeting a child's needs in the form of safety and protection, food, shelter and clothing, education, supervision, and medical/dental care by their caregiver [5, 6]. Most neglected children do not show evidence of physical abuse externally, but *failure-to-thrive* is observed in all cases [2]. Failure-to-thrive, or inadequate nutrition to support growth and development, can be from different causative factors, which can be unintentional (e.g., improper breast-feeding, underfeeding, etc.), organic diseases (e.g., cystic fibrosis, celiac disease, HIV, etc.), and neglect [7]. Thus, in order to determine the correct

A.H. Ross (✉)
Department of Sociology and Anthropology, North Carolina State University, Raleigh, NC 27695, USA
e-mail: ann_ross@ncsu.edu

A.H. Ross, S.M. Abel (eds.), *The Juvenile Skeleton in Forensic Abuse Investigations*,
DOI 10.1007/978-1-61779-255-7_10,

etiology, it is imperative that each case be fully examined [2]. For a more in-depth discussion of failure-to-thrive, please see Chapter 9 by Cardoso and Magalhães in this volume.

However, deliberate starvation resulting in the death of an infant or a child is considered extremely rare and is regarded as the most severe form of maltreatment. Even after a complete autopsy, starvation may be difficult to prove [5, 8, 9]. In their 25-year retrospective study of pediatric neglect, Knight and Collins [5] found that the average age of infants in malnutrition/starvation and dehydration cases was 6 months with a range of 6–18 months and that the primary caregiver at the time of death was usually the mother. These observations agree with conclusions by Kellogg and Lukefahr [8], who found that the age of the infant/child was the only statistically significant risk factor for death due to starvation. Starvation is more commonly observed in younger infants and children as older children can generally feed themselves if there is not some underlying type of physical and/or mental disability.

10.2 Neglect and Homicide

Child neglect has a legal definition, which varies from state to state. In the state of North Carolina, the following definition applies [10]:

Citation: Gen. Stat. § 7B–101

Neglected juvenile means a child:

- who does not receive proper care, supervision, or discipline from his or her parent, guardian, custodian, or caregiver
- who is not provided necessary medical or remedial care
- who lives in an environment injurious to his or her welfare
- who has been placed for care or adoption in violation of law

"In determining whether a child is a neglected juvenile, it is relevant whether that child lives in a home where another child has been subjected to abuse or neglect by an adult who regularly lives in the home."

Any person found guilty will be subject to Class 1 misdemeanor and sentenced to 120 days. For specific summaries of state laws for the definition of child abuse and neglect, please see http://www.childwelfare.gov/systemwide/laws_policies/statutes/define.pdf.

Citation: Gen. Stat. § 14–17 Homicide

"In North Carolina, a juvenile homicide resulting from abuse will fall under a felony murder charge for NC General Statute for first-degree murder (showing premeditation, deliberation, and malice) that will carry a punishment of life in prison or death, or second-degree murder (without premeditation and deliberation) that will carry a punishment of 94–480 months" [11].

10.3 Fatal Starvation (Fatal Child Neglect)

In cases of fatal neglect including starvation, review of family conditions shows that the last born is commonly the child dying from neglect, and in most cases the child is under the age of 1 due to their inability to procure food and nourishment on their own [6, 9]. Other risk factors include, but are not limited to, low socioeconomic status and single parents. Investigations of these cases have shown the following commonalities in living conditions:

- Filthy homes, smelling of urine and feces (both from humans and animals)
- Insect infestation such as flies and roaches
- Minimal baby food supplies (Figs. 10.1 and 10.2)

Another indication of lack of concern for the child's welfare may be observed in failing to keep well-baby appointments and/or not seeking medical treatment when the baby or child is ill.

The information gathered at the scene and other investigative information are crucial in the final ruling of cause and manner of death by the medical examiner or coroner. Likewise, it is imperative that medical examiners not work in isolation, but examine all case information including law enforcement scene reports, case and medical histories, and social and family histories before determining the cause and manner of death. Cases of fatal starvation due to their rarity are difficult to rule on without a multidisciplinary investigation and could result in the death of an infant to go unchallenged or unprosecuted. With a thorough scene and social and medical history to rule out a possible underlying illness, a homicide charge can be sustained [12].

Table 10.1 presents the physical traits generally exhibited in cases of pediatric starvation.

Fig. 10.1 Filthy living conditions commonly observed in fatal neglect/starvation cases

Fig. 10.2 Minimal baby food supplies and filthy living conditions commonly observed in fatal neglect/starvation cases

Table 10.1 Characteristics exhibited in pediatric starvation

Standard Growth Charts in the lower third percentile for height and weight
Delayed skeletal maturation
Apathy, lethargy, and withdrawal
Delayed motor, social, and language development
Autoerotic behavior
Growth hormone responsiveness is retained
Physical abuse not evident
Voracious appetite and weight gain during hospitalization

10.4 Findings at Autopsy

The typical autopsy findings of starved infants include obvious signs of cachexia, or wasting syndrome, with dehydration; decreased subcutaneous and visceral fat; muscle atrophy; osteopenia/osteoporosis; osteomalacia; rickets; fractures due to osteoporosis/osteopenia; thin, dry, wrinkled skin and dry brittle hair; decreased organ weights; sunken eyes and cheeks; depressed fontanelles; protruding ribs; vertebrae and iliac crests; empty GI tract; and secondary infections with poor hygiene [5, 6]. The body is usually below the fifth percentile for weight-to-length measures. Other starvation symptoms that have been documented from Nazi concentration camps include loss of hunger, lethargy, weight loss, mental retardation, and reduced resistance to infections [13].

The classification systems that have been developed for the identification of protein-energy malnutrition (PEM) in the developing world can prove to be very useful in diagnosing malnutrition/starvation. In a medicolegal context, an additional benefit of these methods is the simplicity of the various techniques, and the most commonly used systems are presented below.

The equation for PEM using Gomez et al. [14] classification is

$$\text{Weight for Age\%} = \frac{\text{Weight}}{\text{Weight norm}} \times 100 \tag{10.1}$$

The results are then compared to the Boston 50th percentile standard, and a child between the 90th and 110th percentile would be considered normal; a child between 75th and 89th percentile would be considered 1st degree or grade 1, between 60th and 74th percentile 2nd degree or grade 2, and under 60th percentile, 3rd degree or grade 3.

The Waterlow [15] classification is the most commonly utilized method and is based on mid-upper arm circumference and height to determine if the child is wasted and growth stunted. According to this system, stunting is equivalent to growth retardation and indicates chronic malnutrition. Wasting, on the other hand, can be diagnosed as low weight for normal height and indicates a condition of rapid weight loss (Fig. 10.3).

The weight–height ratio to determine the level of wasting is calculated as

$$\text{Weight} - \text{Height} = \frac{\text{Weight}}{\text{Weight of same height}} \times 100 \tag{10.2}$$

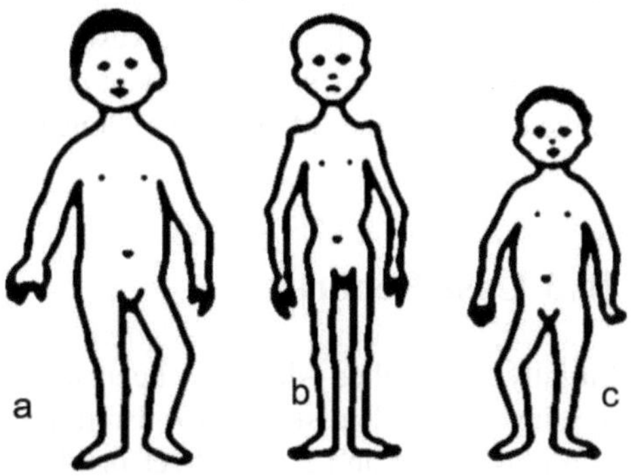

Fig. 10.3 Diagram illustrating the Waterlow guidelines for stunting and wasting; a = normal, b = wasted, and c = stunted (adapted from Waterlow [15])

Table 10.2 Waterlow classification for stunting and wasting [15]

Nutritional status	Stunting Percentage of height/age	Wasting Percentage of weight/height
Normal	>95	>90
Mildly impaired	87.5–95	80–90
Moderately impaired	80–87.5	70–80
Severely impaired	< 80	< 70

The height–age ratio to estimate stunting is calculated as

$$\text{Height} - \text{Age} = \frac{\text{Height}}{\text{Height norm}} \times 100 \quad (10.3)$$

Table 10.2 presents the nutritional status guidelines for stunting and wasting using the Waterlow method.

Nineteen cases of fatal starvation from the literature are summarized in Table 10.3, which also presents the Waterlow [15] classifications for each case. Out of all the cases, 80% fall under the fifth percentiles according to the CDC length-for-age charts clearly illustrating the impact of starvation on growth. Interestingly, eight cases fall within the "mildly impaired," six within the "moderately impaired," and two within the "severely impaired" Waterlow classification for stunting. These results indicate that while the Waterlow classification can be useful, it could underestimate the severity of stunting in fatal neglect homicides due to starvation.

10.4.1 Decomposed and Skeletonized Remains

However, the above autopsy findings are not useful when faced with the remains of a juvenile in an advanced state of decomposition or skeletonization. Oftentimes, the caregiver will attempt to conceal the remains, which may not be discovered for a period of time, significantly hindering the investigation and interpretation of malnutrition and starvation. Because the many indicators that are used to determine starvation such as weight and appearance are not available, it is even more essential to work closely with investigators in a multidisciplinary approach. When confronted with this situation, there are also several skeletal indicators that can aid in the determination of chronic malnutrition/starvation.

10.5 Case Report

Initially, an Amber Alert had been issued in North Carolina for a 11-month-old missing infant. The skeletonized remains of the infant were later found wrapped in a plastic bag and a crib sheet inside a diaper box in the attic of her residence.

Table 10.3 Summary of fatal starvations cases from the literature

Age	Weight (g)	Length (cm)	Percentile for length	Height% of normal height for age	Skeletal changes	Outcome	Reference
6.5 mo	3166	59.5	2.5th	90.5	Harris lines and delayed bone maturation	Mother and father found of food and care deprivation	[16]
14 weeks	3430	57	10th	95.3	No data	No data	[17]
5 weeks	2466	48	<3rd	89.4	No data	Mother convicted of manslaughter and sentenced to 3 years	[17]
3.5 years	No data	98	Ca 50th	99.7	No data	Mother sentenced to 10 years	[17]
19 months	3600	57.5	<3rd	70.4	Bone demineralization	One count child neglect, no jail time	[12]
6 weeks	2394.9	53	0.1th	92.9	No data	Mother serving a life sentence on capital murder	[8]
6 weeks	1770	46	<0.1th	80.7	No data	No data	[9]
5 months	4020	61	<5th	92	No data	No data	[13]
7 weeks	2010	53	5th	91.4	No data	No data	[13]
6.5 months	3400	56	50th	96.5	No data	No data	[13]
3 months	2570	55	<5th	93.2	No data	No data	[13]
7 months	3520	58	<0.1th	82.8	No data	No data	[13]
7 months	2720	59	<0.1th	86.8	No data	No data	[13]
8.5 months	2500	53	<0.1th	75.7	No data	No data	[13]
14 months	4740	68	<0.1th	89.5	No data	No data	[13]
2.4 years	6800	86	25th	97.7	No data	No data	[13]
2.5 years	6510	79	<5th	85.6	No data	No data	[13]
2.5 years	6200	79.5	<5th	86.1	No data	No data	[13]
2.5 years	5450	78	<5th	84.5	No data	No data	[13]

The remains were believed to have been in the attic for 3–5 weeks before being discovered. The investigation of the medical history revealed that the infant was born by scheduled C-section at 38 weeks' gestation on November 15, 2006, but had to remain in the hospital until her release on November 24 because she experienced tachypnea (rapid breathing). This condition, known as transient tachypnea of the newborn, occurs in approximately 1% of newborns and after hospital treatment does not affect growth [17]. The infant was then seen for well-baby visits on November 30 and December 15, 2006, and January 23, 2007, and by the WIC (Women, Infants, and Children) program on January 12, 2007. The infant was typically in the 25th percentile range for height at these visits with her weight in the 10th and 25th percentiles.

Skeletal examination revealed several age-at-death ranges using different hard tissue standards. The deciduous maxillary central (i^1) and lateral (i^2) incisors had erupted or emerged. The mean age of eruption for i^1 is 10 months with a range of 8–12 months and for i^2 is 11 months with a range of 9–13 months [18]. The mandibular incisors were lost postmortem and were not available for examination. Dental development was not possible due to the missing elements. The maximum length of the *pars basilaris* [19] was 19 mm, mid-sagittal length [20] was 15 mm, and the width measured 21 mm. These measures were consistent with an infant between 8 months and 1.1 years of age. Table 10.4 lists the diaphyseal lengths (mm) for all six bones of the decedent along with the mean long bone lengths for female infants at 6, 9, and 12 months of age for comparison. The diaphyseal lengths of all six long bones were consistent with a 6-month-old infant. The upper or proximal extremity (humerus, radius, and ulna) was within the upper bounds of a 6-month-old. However, the lengths of the lower extremities, particularly the femur and tibia, were at or below the 6-month-old mean. Because dental eruption and the *pars basilaris* are less affected by environmental stress such as nutrition and more closely reflects the actual chronological age of the infant, these criteria more accurately reflected the chronological age of the infant between 8 and 12 months of age. There was no evidence of trauma.

Table 10.4 Diaphyseal lengths (mm) for all six long bones of the decedent and mean long bone lengths for female infants at 6, 9, and 12 months of age

	Decedent left	Decedent right	6 mo mean	SD	9 mo mean	SD	12 mo mean	SD
Humerus	89	90	86.8	4.6	n/a	n/a	103.6	4.8
Radius[a]	70	70	66.93	3.42	73.50	4.55	79.52	4.51
Ulna	78	78	75.7	3.8	n/a	n/a	89	4.0
Femur	111	111	111.1	4.6	n/a	n/a	134.6	4.9
Tibia[a]	88	87	97.06	5.01	109.49	17.32	117.08	5.82
Fibula	85	86	84.9	5.2	n/a	n/a	105.0	5.1

[a]From Gindhart [21].
From Scheuer and Black [22].

The proportional discrepancy between the upper and lower extremities as well as the overall length or growth deficit in all long bones is suggestive of chronic malnutrition. The lower extremities are known to show a greater allometric increase than the humerus or radius [23]. Thus, prolonged starvation or severe chronic malnutrition would significantly affect the rate of growth more so in the lower extremities than in the upper limbs as evidenced in this case by the more pronounced growth deficit in femoral and tibial lengths, which measure at or below the 6-month-old mean [23, 24]. Furthermore, it has been well-documented in the literature that growth in long bones is depressed in starvation, protein-caloric deficiency, protein deficiency, and caloric deficiency [24–31]. In addition to the significant physical growth retardation or stunting, abnormal or excessive porosity was observed on the metaphyses of the long bones (Figs. 10.4 and 10.5), which is also indicative of a vitamin and/or mineral deficiency also consistent with malnutrition [32]. In addition, Harris lines of arrested growth were evident on the distal femoral metaphyses and proximal tibial metaphyses.

Normally, when the full body is available, standard body length and weights are taken to assess the severity of nutritional deficit. In this case, the remains were completely skeletonized and these standards could not be applied. However, stature could be predicted from the lower limb bones using the equations developed by Ruff [33] for 1-year-olds. Her stature was calculated as 66 cm using the equations for femoral and tibial lengths placing the infant well below the third percentile for length-for-age using the CDC growth charts for girls from birth to 36 months (see Fig. 10.6).

10.5.1 Bone Mineral Density

Bone mineral density (BMD) increases with age from infancy to adulthood, and boys and girls do not differ significantly in BMD values until the onset of puberty

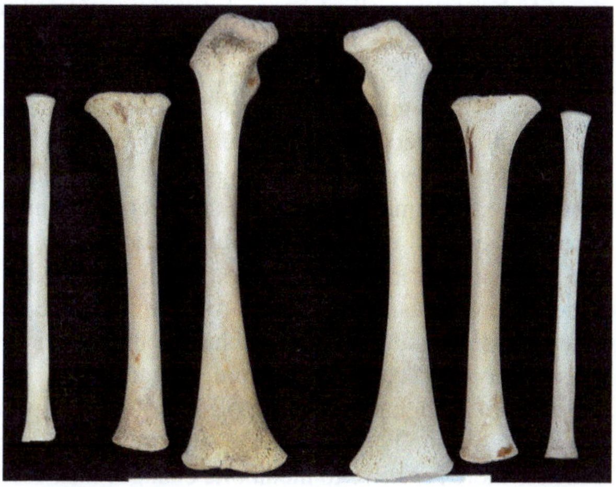

Fig. 10.4 Bones of the lower extremity showing excessive porosity at the cut-back zone

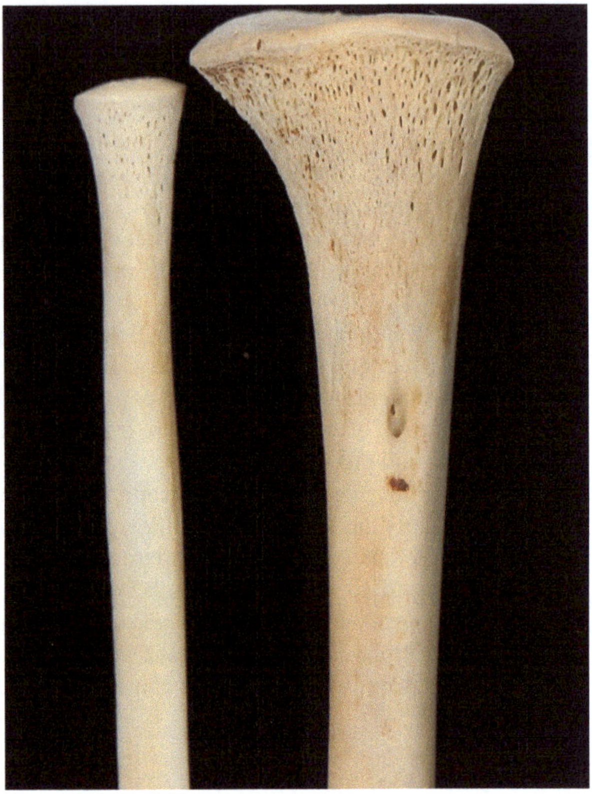

Fig. 10.5 The proximal fibula and tibia illustrating the excess porosity of the cut-back zone

[34, 35]. Dual-energy X-ray absorptiometry (DXA) allows for a noninvasive way to quantify bone mineralization, and it is the preferred method for use in infants and children given their low radiation exposure and shorter time necessary to perform the scan [34, 36-38]. This method has been found to be useful to assess pediatric bone health and nutritional status in developing countries. In addition, BMD is significantly related and correlated to body weight [36, 39].

Because the remains belonging to the 11-month-old infant did not experience a prolonged postmortem interval and were not subjected to extreme taphonomic processes such as exposure to natural elements or burial, the bones were in good condition and did not exhibit evidence of weathering. Therefore, the evaluation of bone mineral density was found to be appropriate and was assessed in the above case as a diagnostic method as chronic malnutrition and starvation are known to cause osteoporosis and bone demineralization.

In infants and small children, vertebral scans, specifically the lumbar vertebrae, are a preferred body area because they are primarily composed of trabecular bone, which is more sensitive to metabolic changes than cortical bone [34] and is the most

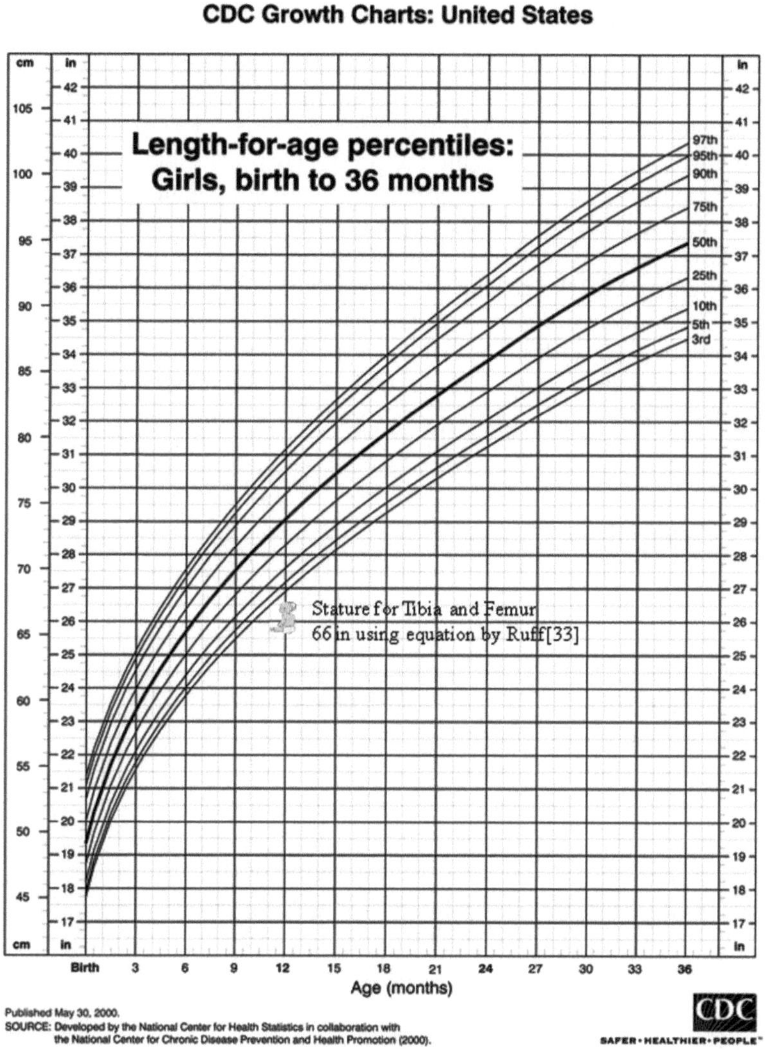

Fig. 10.6 Growth chart illustrating stunting in the infant below the third percentile for her age group

reproducible and accurate skeletal site in juveniles. A *Z*-score, the standard deviation or SD score based on the age-appropriate and population-specific norm, is the appropriate pediatric method to compare a child's BMD to the reference population mean and is calculated as

$$Z - \text{score} = \frac{\text{Measured BMD} - \text{Age matched Mean BMD}}{\text{Population SD}} \tag{10.4}$$

10.5.1.1 Dual-Energy X-ray Absorptiometry (DXA) Results

The DXA scan of the lumbar vertebrae (L1-L4) was performed using a Hologic® scanner. The total BMD (g/cm^2) for L1-L4 for the 11-month-old infant was 0.226. Table 10.5 presents the total BMD and the population BMD norms. The normal BMD values for male newborns (infants at 00) and 1-year-olds (or 01) derived by Hologic instruments were the most appropriate reference population for comparison and were used to calculate the *Z*-scores. As in other aspects of the biological profile, populations vary and population-specific standards should be used when available. The *Z*-score derived for the newborn age group was –3.14 and –4.33 for the 1-year age group. *These scores indicate that the infant had low bone mineral density for chronological age*. According to established pediatric standards, a score less than –2 indicates low bone density. These scores placed the infant well below the 0.1 percentile (Fig. 10.7).

Table 10.5 Measured BMD score for case example and reference population values

	BMD	SD
Case example	0.226	N/A
Hologic 00 age group[a]	0.336	0.035
Hologic 01 age group[a]	0.399	0.040

[a]From Blake et al. [40]

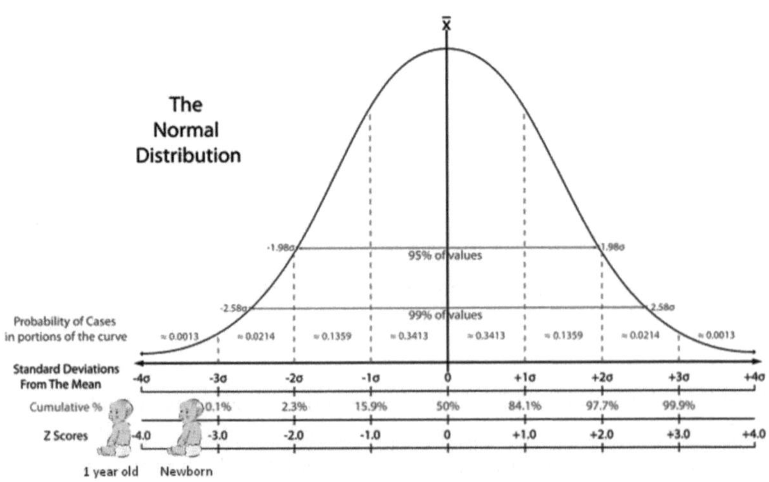

Fig. 10.7 Diagram of normal distribution illustrating that the total bone mineral density for the decedent is well below 0.1 percentile along with *Z*-scores below –2 indicating low bone mineral densities for chronological age

10.5.2 Legal Outcomes

The mother pleaded guilty to second-degree murder and was sentenced to a minimum of 141 months or 11 years and a maximum of 179 months or 15 years. The District Attorney originally sought a capital murder charge, but because the Medical Examiner ruled the cause and manner of death as undetermined, they accepted the second-degree murder plea as it would have been highly contested without a cause of death.

10.6 Recommendations for Investigating Fatal Neglect/Starvation from Skeletal Remains

The determination of malnutrition from the juvenile skeleton has been addressed in Chapter 9 by Cardoso and Magalhães in this volume. In medicolegal cases it is imperative that an interpretation of fatal starvation only be made when there are several lines of evidence including investigative social and medical histories, scene investigation, and biological indicators. In this case, the home and medical backgrounds exhibited clear conditions of neglect. In addition, the interpretation of chronic malnutrition and starvation was made based on numerous biological indicators, which included differential ages obtained from the dentition and *pars basilaris* compared to long bone lengths, clear indicators of stunting or growth deficit as evidenced by the differential long bone lengths between the skeletal elements, evidence of Harris lines, excessive porosity, and osteoporosis. I would caution making an interpretation of fatal starvation if only a single biological indicator is present as any of these could be the result of a different etiology entirely when observed on their own.

References

1. Dolinak D, Matshes E, Lew EO. Forensic Pathology. Principals and Practice. New York, NY: Elsevier Academic Press, 2005.
2. Spitz W. Spitz and Fisher's Medicolegal Investigation of Death. Guidelines for the Application of Pathology to Crime Investigation, 4th Edition. Springfield: CC Thomas, 2006.
3. Reece RM. Child Maltreatment. In: McMillan JA, Feigin RD, DeAngelis CD, Jones MD, editors. Oski's Pediatrics Principles and Practice, 4th Edition. Philadelphia, PA: Lippincott, 2006; 146–64.
4. Johnson CF. Abuse and Neglect of Children. In: Behrman RE, Kliegman RM, Jenson HB, editors. Nelson Textbook of Pediatrics, 16th Edition. Philadelphia, PA: W.B. Saunders, 2000.
5. Knight LD, Collins KA. A 25-year retrospective review of deaths due to pediatric neglect. Am J Foren Med Pathol 2005; 26: 221–8.
6. Collins KA. Intentional Starvation/Malnutrition and Dehydration in Children. In: Griest K, editor. Pediatric Homicide. Medical Investigation. Boca Raton: CRC Press, 2010; 169–85.
7. Block RW, Krebs NF, Committee on Child and Abuse and Neglect and Committee on Nutrition. Failure to thrive as a manifestation of child neglect. Pediatrics 2005; 116: 1234–7.
8. Kellogg ND, Lukefahr JL. Criminally prosecuted cases of child starvation. Pediatrics 2005; 116: 1309–16.

9. Berkowitz CD. Fatal child neglect. Adv Pediatr 2001; 48: 331–61.
10. Child welfare definition of neglect by state http://www.childwelfare.gov/systemwide/laws_policies/statutes/define.pdf.
11. NC Homicide Statues http://www.ncleg.net/EnactedLegislation/Statutes/HTML/BySection/Chapter_14/GS_14-17.html.
12. Davis JH, Rao VJ, Valdes-Dapena M. A forensic science approach to a starved child. J Forensic Sci 1984; 29: 663–9.
13. Madea B. Death as a result of starvation. Diagnostic criteria. Foren Path Rev 2005; 2: 3–26.
14. Gomez F, Galvan RR, Cravioto J, Frenk S. Malnutrition in infancy and childhood with special reference to Kwashiokor. Adv Pediatr 1955; 7: 131–69.
15. Waterlow JC. Classification and definition of protein-caloric malnutrition. Br Med J 1972; 2: 566–9.
16. Piercecchi-Marti MD, Louis-Borrione C, Bartoli C, Sanvoisin A, Panuel M, Plissier-Alicot AL, Leonetti G. Malnutrition, a rare form of child abuse: diagnostic criteria. J Forensic Sci 2006; 51: 670–3.
17. Fieguth A, Günther D, Kleemann WJ, Tröger HD. Lethal child neglect. Forensic Sci Int 2002; 130: 8–12.
18. Lysell L, Magnusson B, Thilande B. Time and order of eruption of primary teeth. A longitudinal study. Odontologisk Revy 1962; 13: 217–34.
19. Redfield A. A new aid to aging immature skeletons: development of the occipital bone. Am J Phys Anthropol 1970; 33: 207–20.
20. Fazekas I, Kósa F. Forensic Fetal Osteology. Budapest: Akadémiai Kiadó, 1978.
21. Gindhart PS. Growth standards for the tibia and radius in children aged one month through eighteen years. Am J Phys Anthropol 1973; 39:41–8.
22. Scheuer L, Black S. Developmental Juvenile Osteology. London: Academic Press, 2000.
23. Buschang PH. Differential long bone growth of children between two months and eleven years of age. Am J Phys Anthropol 1982; 58: 291–5.
24. Fleagle JG, Samonds KW, Hegsted DM. Physical growth of cebus monkeys, Cebus albifrons, during protein or calorie deficiency. Am J Clin Nutr 1975; 28: 246–53.
25. Carlson AJ, Hoelzel F. Growth and longevity of rats fed omnivorous and vegetarian diets. J Nutr 1947; 34: 81–96.
26. Quimby FH, Barteltt RG, Artress JL. Effects of hormone, vitamin and liver supplements on the appetite and growth of the young rat during recovery from chronic starvation. Am J Physiol 1951; 166: 566–71.
27. Outhouse J, Mendel LB. The rate of growth. I. Its influence o the skeletal development of the albino rat. J Exp Zool 1933; 64: 257–85.
28. Dickerson JWT, MacCance RA. Severe undernutrition in growing and adult animals. 8. The dimension and chemistry of the long bones. Br J Nutr 1961;15: 567–76.
29. McCay CM, Crowell MF, Maynard LA. The effect of retarded growth upon the length of life span and upon the ultimate body size. J Nutr 1935; 10: 63–79.
30. Frandsen AM, Nelson MM, Sulon E. Becks H. Evans HM. The effects of various levels of dietary protein on skeletal growth and endochondral ossification in young rats. Anat Rec 1964; 119: 247–61.
31. Himes JH. Bone growth and development in protein-calorie malnutrition. Wld Rev Nutr Diet 1978; 28: 143–87.
32. Ortner DJ, Kimmerle EH, Diez M. Probable evidence of scurvy in subadults from archaeological sites in Peru. Am J Phys Anthropol 1999; 108: 321–31.
33. Ruff C. Body size prediction from juvenile skeletal remains. Am J Phys Anthropol 2007; 133: 698–716.
34. Carrascosa A, Gussinyé M, Yeste D, Audí L, Enrubia M, Vargas D. Skeletal Mineralization During Infancy, Childhood and Adolescence in the Normal Population and in Populations with Nutritional and Hormonal Disorders. Dual X-ray Absorptiometry (DXA) Evaluation. In: Schiinau E, editor. Paediatric Osteology: New Developments in Diagnostics and Therapy. Amsterdam: Elsevier, 1996; 93–102.

35. Yeste D, Del Río L, Gussinyé M, Carrascosa A. Densidad mineral ósea en lactantes y niños (0–4 años) a nivel de columna lumbar. Patrones de normalidad. Anales Españoles de Pediatría 1998;49: 248–252.
36. Lukaski H. Soft tissue composition and bone mineral status: evaluation by dual-energy x-ray absorptiometry. J Nutr 1993;123:438–43.
37. Salle B, Glorieux F. Assessment of bone mineral content in infants: the new age. Acta Paediatr 1993; 82:709–10.
38. Specker B, Schoenau E. Quantitative bone analysis in children: current methods and recommendations. J Pediatr 2005; 146:726–31.
39. Koo W, Bush A. Walters J, Carlson S. Postnatal development of bone mineral status during infancy. J Am Coll Nutr 1998; 17:65–70.
40. Blake G, Wahner H, Folgelman I. The Evaluation of Osteoporosis: Dual Energy X-ray Absorptiometry and Ultrasound in Clinical Practice. London: Martin Dunnitz LTD, 1999; 231.

Chapter 11
Juvenile Stature Estimation: A Chilean Perspective

Rebecca Sutphin and Ann H. Ross

Abstract Limited analysis has been conducted for estimating stature derived from the long bone lengths of juvenile skeletons. Juvenile stature estimation can be particularly useful in the forensic setting, which may have applications for use as a proxy for nutritional health. Stature equations developed by Ruff (Am J Phys Anthropol 133:698–716, 2007) and Smith (J Forensic Sci 52:538–546, 2007) derived from modern European Americans were used to predict juvenile stature from long bones. Significant differences were noted for 13–15 year age range for the femur, tibia, and humerus and for the 16–17 year age range for femur, tibia, and radius between Chilean and European American juvenile long bone lengths and stature. Based on these results, the younger age groups may be used (4–6 and 7–9 years) but not the older ones (13–15 and 16–17 years).

11.1 Introduction

Studies by Fogel [1], Steckel [2], and van Wieringen [3] have noted that a population's general health status and nutritional health can be revealed through mean height analysis. Long periods of marked malnutrition, undernutrition, and chronic physiological stress during adolescence result in permanent stunting of long bone growth [4–8], although if periods of stress are relatively short, catch-up growth may occur [9–10]. Thus, stature can be used as a proxy for nutritional health of present and past skeletal populations [11].

Investigators generally record diaphyseal lengths of juvenile long bones in order to establish age estimates, which may generally be correlated with dental age [12]. Smith [13] and Ruff [14] utilized radiographs from the Denver Study of Child Research Council longitudinal growth to establish regression equations for juvenile stature and body mass estimation, respectively. Smith [13] provides stature regression equations for female, male, and combined sex (if sex cannot be determined) to represent long bone diaphyseal measurements for juveniles aged 3 through 10 the

A.H. Ross (✉)
Department of Sociology and Anthropology, North Carolina State University, Raleigh, NC 27695, USA
e-mail: ann_ross@ncsu.edu

A.H. Ross, S.M. Abel (eds.), *The Juvenile Skeleton in Forensic Abuse Investigations*,
DOI 10.1007/978-1-61779-255-7_11,

femur, tibia, combined femur and tibia, fibula, ulna, radius, and humerus. Ruff [14] provides juvenile stature regression equations for combined sexes, which he applies to the 1–17 age range for the femur, tibia, combined femur and tibia, humerus, radius, and combined humerus and radius. Ruff [14] found that for ages 1–6 the tibia gave a more accurate stature estimate than the femur, while for the adolescent years (except for age 17) the femur was the most accurate. He also gave preference to the lower limb bones for stature estimation with the combined femur and tibia regression, since application of contemporary stature equations of combined femur and tibia has the smallest standard deviation and establishes a more concise proportion of total stature [14]. In addition, he found that the radius better reflected a more accurate stature than the humerus (with the exception of young age groups), but that the combined humerus and radius stature equation was a more ideal stature estimate than single upper arm bones [14]. The maximum diaphyseal lengths were established for ages 1–12 in Ruff's [14] regression equation; for ages 13–17, ratios are provided to convert diaphyseal length to maximum length.

The methods proposed by Smith [13] and Ruff [14] may be integrated into the forensic setting, where juvenile stature could assist in positive identification of skeletal remains.

Stature estimates of modern Chilean juveniles with death dates between 1950 and 1970 from the "Cementerio General," or General Cemetery, housed at the Universidad de Chile will be compared to the modern European American juvenile stature estimates. Such comparison will reveal whether estimated stature for modern European American juveniles may be applied across populations.

11.2 Human Growth and Development

Growth is determined by a complex combination of both genetics and the environment. In a neutral environment with no or very limited stressors, genetics will have a greater impact on growth. In harsh environments, genetics may take a back seat; depending on the sex and age of the child along with the timing, frequency, duration, and strength of the stressors, environmental impact may override genetic predisposition [15]. Environmental stress has a main effect on the endocrine system, specifically altering the release of hormones (growth hormone, IGF-1) from the hypothalamus and pituitary gland [15]. During puberty the endocrine system also influences the gonadal hormones, where estrogen triggers sexual maturation in females and testosterone in males [15]. Cameron [15] defines four growth periods: infancy (with rapid growth), childhood (steady growth), adolescence (rapid growth), and adulthood (slow growth). An individual experiences fluctuating occurrences of saltation and stasis in height, or short intense bursts of growth and no growth [15]. Distinct growth spurts occur during the prenatal period, mid-childhood, and adolescence; the prenatal and mid-childhood spurts occur at approximately the same time for both sexes, but for the adolescent spurt, both timing and magnitude differ between the sexes [15]. Overall height and height-gain magnitude is less for females, who typically experience adolescence 2 years before males [15]. Cameron [15] notes that this marked prolonged childhood for males does not occur in other mammals; he describes this as a uniquely human adaptive response for "developmental plasticity" in response to varied environments. Sexual dimorphism occurs during the adolescent phase: females having marked fat distribution around the gluteo-femoral region and breasts, and males acquiring increased muscle mass [15].

In a study conducted by Cameron et al. [16], height, subischial leg length, tibia, upper arm length, and lower arm length of juveniles (presumed to be of European ancestry) were examined to further determine age at which limb growth spurts occur, the magnitude of the spurts, and the spurt differences between males and females. The Cameron et al. [16] findings revealed that for all components in peak velocities, boys had greater magnitudes. Boys and girls did not differ in the order in which the limb segments displayed their velocity peaks; for both sexes, 0.61 years represented the mean time during, which the peak would occur [16]. However, Cameron et al. [16] did find that within the first year (0.61), the velocity peaks did not result in fixed time intervals; girls displayed more variability in mean time differences than boys.

Within the first year, infants on average grow 25 cm; from the second year until adolescence, mean peak height velocity is 8.5 cm/year for females and 9.5 cm/year for males. Growth hormone regulation in the "growth-hormone dependent phase of growth" controls growth during ages 2–3 [17]. Fat tissue constitutes 14% of the total weight from a new born. By 6 months, 25% of the infant's weight is from body fat. The fat content gradually subsides to 15% of total weight by 5 years. The extra weight seen during the 6-month period is utilized as a nutrient and energy reserve in preparation for the weaning period, when breast milk cannot meet the infant's heightened nutrient requirements [17].

Since infancy is associated with significant growth during the first year, if growth delay occurs during this stage, then it is more likely for final adult stature to be stunted [17]. The growth velocity present during ages 5–10 reaches a plateau with consistent body fat percentages and somatic growth [17]. The juvenile growth spurt or mid-childhood growth spurt for males and females occurs during ages 6–8, and disruption of the plateau can be seen between the ages of 5 and 10 [17].

"Growth has been described as a mirror of the conditions of society [18] and height as a proxy for health [10, 18]." While decreased basal metabolism, reduced physical activity, changed body composition, and morphed mechanical and metabolic efficiency can result from growth retardation, age related decrease in size with continued body size reduction is more common [10]. Displaying growth deficiency as proportional to nutritional deficiency, Lejarraga [17] highlights primary malnutrition as a result of reduced nutritional consumption of proteins and/or calories. Significant protein deficiency results in kwashiorkor, while significant calorie deficiency results in marasmus, conditions that are generally seen in developing countries or in individuals from low socioeconomic settings from developed countries [17] and rarely in cases of fatal starvation. Generally, these deficiencies (which indicate malnutrition) are associated with stunting of height and wasting, or low weight for age [19]. Stunting in height may be the result of such environmental stress, but if the stress is removed or short in duration, catch-up growth can occur [10, 15, 20, 21]; thus a stunted individual may be still able to reach genetic stature.

Out of other age groups from developing countries, infants aged 6–12 months are the group to most often be growth retarded [22, 23]. This growth period, associated with weaning, requires high nutritional demand and high growth velocity [22]. This early age between infancy and childhood is more susceptible to stressors [22]. Stunted children from developing countries, representing 10–50% of the youth, have had reduced height due to PEM or protein-energy malnutrition, the most common nutritional deficiency [22]. While developing countries' growth curves for juveniles aged 2–3 years generally mimic the curves for developed countries [24], Norgan [22] details that not all cases (in differing ecological locations) will reflect Martorell et al.'s [24] conclusion that following the third year, growth-retarded children grow at the same rate as healthy juveniles.

Interestingly, Norgan [22] notes that while catch-up growth can occur for height, it cannot occur in terms of weight or body mass. Also proposed is the potential for genetic population differences in reference to growth potentials for childhood, adolescence, and adulthood [22]. Female height is positively associated with fertility [25]. Malnutrition or undernutrition during or before conception will affect the growth status for the fetus; stunted females will be more likely to birth smaller infants or experience potential issues during birth due to smaller pelvic outlets [22]. Children experiencing undernutrition will have a shift in limb proportions in addition to a reduction in overall size [26].

Stini [27] proposes that delayed puberty and reduced body size and bone length, caused by an adrenocortical function change influencing antibody synthesis and anabolic processes, is an adaptive response in areas where juveniles are likely to experience extended periods of protein deficiency. Reduced body size and less lean muscle mass require less caloric and protein intake of juveniles during growth periods, especially in relation to puberty [27]. Stini [27] also notes that delayed bone growth is more marked in males than in females; he proposes that females are better prepared for nutritional stress in order to maintain the population's reproductive potential.

11.3 Limb Proportions

While juveniles generally display a distal-to-proximal growth gradient for the bones of the limbs, Cameron et al. [16] noted that this may not always be the case. For juveniles who were "late developers," Cameron et al. [16] noted the distal-to-proximal peak velocity trend of forearm to upper-arm growth to be evident in the mean ages of 14.6 and 12.8 for boys and girls, respectively. Conversely, the "early developers" revealed a proximal-to-distal (upper-arm to forearm) peak velocity growth trend, in the mean ages 13.4 and 11.8 years for boys and girls [16]. This year difference in means is statistically significant for males, but not for females [16]. Utilizing the studies of Maresh [28] and Krogman [29], Cameron et al. [16] places the peak velocities for the upper-arm length at 11 years for females (1.5 cm/year) and 13 years for males (1.7 cm/year). For boys of all ages, consistently greater lengths are noted for forearms with peak velocity ages between 12.5 and 14 years with a growth rate of 1.1–1.5 cm/year [16]. Female peak velocity ages fall between 10 and 11.5 years with a growth rate of 1.05–1.3 cm/year [16]. Examining the limb bone relative growth of a multisite Arikara juvenile sample through multivariate analysis (of the femur, tibia, humerus, and radius), Jungers et al. [30] found that faster growth was noted for the long bones of the leg (tibia and femur) than for the arm (radius and humerus) with increasing age. The trend for the proximal limb bone to have a greater increase in growth than the distal limb bone is also noted with the relative growth of the humerus and femur being greater than the radius and tibia, respectively [30]. The forelimb long bones grow at a slower rate than the hindlimb, causing a decrease in the intermembral index (forelimb length/hindlimb length × 100) [30].

Jantz and Owsley [12] investigated size variation of Arikara juveniles and compared size to the variation of limb segment proportions. Notably, they found a trend for the legs to grow more in length than arms during youth, indicating that if an individual is older, they will have longer legs [12]. Jantz and Owsley [12] also noted the pattern of bone growth for proximal bones of the limbs and pointed out that these bones become longer more quickly than distal bones of the limbs [12]. Through allometric scaling (examining regression coefficient variation), Jantz and Owsley [12] revealed that the femur and tibia maintain a negative interaction; with an increase in femoral size, the tibial size will decrease, and conversely, an increase in tibial size will decrease the size of the femur. A negative interaction is also noted with the humerus and radius [12]. Overall, this means that as the length of the distal limb bones increase, the length of the proximal limb bones will decrease. Based on gradients of the distal–proximal long bones, Tanner [31] and Tanner and Whitehouse [32] revealed relative growth as being proportional to adult values [12]. Jantz and Owsley [12] concluded that the distal long bones better represent the individual attaining maturity and adult values.

Meadows-Jantz and Jantz [33] examined secular trends in long bone length, and observed that group differences may not be as significant as sex differences since males are found to be more responsive to environmental alteration [34–38]. Meadows-Jantz and Jantz [33] observed that during 6 months to 3 years, environmental stressors have the largest influence followed by adolescence [39, 40] and possibly again at post adolescence.

11.4 Materials

11.4.1 Sample

Juvenile long bones, including the femur, tibia, humerus, and radius, of 38 individuals were examined from Santiago, Chile's General Cemetery, currently housed by the Universidad de Chile. The age at death was known for the individuals, who had death dates between the 1950s and 1970s.

Due to small sample sizes for 1-year intervals, the age groups were collapsed into groups composed of 3-year intervals (4–6, 7–9, 10–12, and 13–15 years), and the last age category groups only 2 years (16–17 years).

11.4.2 Methods

The maximum lengths in millimeters were measured using an osteometric board for all available juvenile long bones that were intact. Because numerous remains had missing or fragmented long bones, any available long bone belonging to a juvenile individual was measured. Following standard practice, left long bones were used. However, if a left long bone was unavailable or unable to be measured, the right long bone was used.

Age-specified formulae derived by Ruff [14] were used to determine juvenile stature from individuals aged 4–17 years. Ruff provided formulae for the femur, tibia, humerus, and radius for each of the years 4–17 (Table 11.1). Results from the formulae provide Ruff's [14] stature in centimeters, while the long bones were measured in millimeters.

Stature was also estimated using long bone specified equations proposed by Smith [13]. The femur, tibia, humerus, and radius formulae were assessed for ages 3–10. Smith provides sex-specific stature formulae but as sex cannot generally be

Table 11.1 Ruff's [14] Juvenile Stature Regression Equations for ages 4–17

	Femoral length		Tibial length		Humeral length		Radial length	
Age	Slope	Int.	Slope	Int.	Slope	Int.	Slope	Int.
4^d	0.295	37.7	0.327	43.7	0.407	37.7	0.526	39.3
5^d	0.311	34.1	0.322	45.3	0.394	40.6	0.548	37.6
6^d	0.287	40.5	0.330	44.9	0.422	36.8	0.570	36.0
7^d	0.294	39.1	0.325	46.8	0.445	33.2	0.574	36.4
8^d	0.284	42.8	0.304	52.9	0.439	35.3	0.546	41.7
9^d	0.308	35.6	0.324	48.9	0.448	34.3	0.565	39.9
10^d	0.292	40.6	0.321	50.1	0.442	35.6	0.575	38.3
11^d	0.306	36.3	0.331	47.7	0.475	28.6	0.570	39.7
12^d	0.320	31.4	0.333	47.9	0.433	39.3	0.547	44.6
11^t	0.279	36.4	0.296	47.3	0.465	21.6	0.513	43.4
12^t	0.290	31.8	0.309	43.3	0.420	34.3	0.532	40.2
13^t	0.288	33.0	0.321	40.1	0.397	41.6	0.507	45.8
14^t	0.294	31.5	0.307	46.8	0.381	47.7	0.483	51.8
15^t	0.269	43.8	0.273	61.6	0.368	52.1	0.455	59.3
16^t	0.270	43.9	0.274	62.7	0.371	51.6	0.463	57.9
17^t	0.286	37.4	0.281	61.5	0.396	44.3	0.465	58.6

Note: ^{d}using diaphyseal length.
^{t}using total length including epiphyses.
Lengths of long bones are in millimeters.

Table 11.2 Smith's [13] Juvenile Stature Regression Equations for children of unknown sex aged 3–10

Bone	Slope	Int.
Humerus	0.4658	27.053
Radius	0.6229	27.500
Femur	0.2928	36.923
Tibia	0.3519	38.614

determined with juvenile skeletal remains, Smith's unknown sex formulae were used (Table 11.2). Smith's [13] equations required the long bones to be measured in millimeters, while results from the formulae provide stature in centimeters.

T-tests were performed using Windows Excel 2007 for overall and among-age group comparisons.

11.5 Results

Descriptive sample statistics are presented in Table 11.3. Modern European American juveniles from the Denver study and modern Chilean juveniles were examined for overall significant differences and within each age group. No overall statistical significance was observed between Chilean and European American juveniles for the femur ($t=0.19$, $p<1$, d.f. = 24; Ruff stature $t=-0.14$, $p<1$, d.f. = 24; Smith stature $t=1.46$, $p<0.5$, d.f. = 6), tibia ($t=0.11$, $p<1$, d.f. = 24; Ruff stature $t=-0.14$, $p<1$, d.f. = 24; Smith stature $t=1.36$, $p<0.5$, d.f. = 6), humerus ($t=-0.18$, $p<1$, d.f. = 34; Ruff stature $t=0.21$, $p<1$, d.f. = 34; Smith stature $t=1.55$, $p<0.5$, d.f. = 7), and radius ($t=1.17$, $p<0.5$, d.f. = 28; Ruff stature $t=-1.20$, $p<0.5$, d.f. = 27; Smith stature $t=0.72$, $p<0.5$, d.f. = 8). Significance was observed for the humerus for the 7–9 year age group ($t=4.14$, $p<0.05$, d.f. = 3; Ruff stature $t=3.85$, $p<0.05$, d.f. = 3) (Fig. 11.1). The humerus showed a significant difference for length ($t=-2.49$, $p<0.05$, d.f. = 6) but not for stature ($t=2.33$, $p<0.1$, d.f. = 6) in the 13–15 year age group. For the 13–15 year age group, statistical significance was observed for the femur ($t=-4.35$, $p<0.005$, d.f. = 9; Ruff stature $t=3.79$, $p<0.01$, d.f. = 8) and tibia ($t=-4.18$, $p<0.005$, d.f. = 10; Ruff stature $t=3.45$, $p<0.01$, d.f. = 9) (Fig. 11.2). A significant difference was also

Table 11.3 Descriptive statistics for sample

	Humerus			Radius			Femur			Tibia		
Age group	Mean	SD	Range	Mean	SD	Range	Mean	SD	Range	Mean	SD	Range
4–6	166	24	136–176	138	19	110–160	247	35	191–268	194	33	152–233
7–9	179	4	182–176	–	–	–	266	31	240–300	214	20	199–237
10–12	247	29	212–288	182	23	152–210	343	46	273–398	284	49	232–350
13–15	269	21	247–287	205	28	180–249	373	38	324–435	312	37	270–380
16–17	298	21	271–326	216	15	198–230	418	19	393–448	339	19	317–371

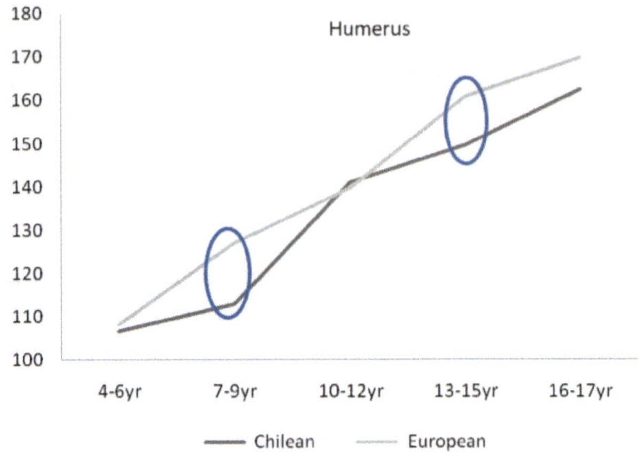

Fig. 11.1 Plot illustrating the humeral stature differences in the 7–9 and 13–15 year age categories

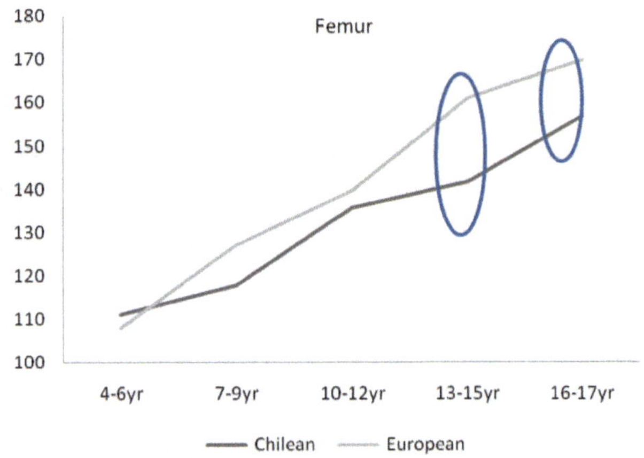

Fig. 11.2 Plot illustrating the femoral stature differences in the 13–15 and 16–17 year age categories

noted for the 16–17 year age range between Chilean and European Americans for the femur ($t = -6.33$, $p < 0.001$, d.f. = 7; Ruff stature $t = 5.79$, $p < 0.001$, d.f. = 7), tibia ($t = -6.84$, $p < 0.0005$, d.f. = 6; Ruff stature $t = 5.88$, $p < 0.001$, d.f. = 7), and radius ($t = -3.69$, $p < 0.05$, d.f. = 4; Ruff stature $t = 3.53$, $p < 0.05$, d.f. = 5) (Fig. 11.2).

11.6 Conclusion

No overall significant differences were found for long bone lengths and stature between modern Chilean and European American juveniles. The humerus showed a significant difference for the 7–9 year age range for length and stature. For the 13–15 year age range, the femur and tibia showed a significant difference for length and stature, while the humerus was only significantly different for length. The femur, tibia, and radius revealed a significant difference for the 16–17 year age range for length and stature. Potentially as a result of nutritional difference or genetic population differences, the Chilean adolescent growth spurt does not appear to follow the same trajectory as European American adolescents. Thus, the older age ranges display the most variation between the two groups. While Ruff's [14] stature formulae may be utilized for overall population comparisons in the younger age groups, caution should be exercised when trying to extrapolate stature in older juveniles who are experiencing puberty or have already experienced puberty.

Acknowledgments We would like to express our appreciation to Dr. Eugenio Aspillaga and Rodrigo Retamal for access and assistance with the collections and to María José Menneschi for assistance with data collection.

References

1. Fogel RW. Second thoughts on the European escape from hunger: famines, chronic malnutrition, and mortality rates. In: Osmani SR, editor. Nutrition and Poverty, New York, NY: Oxford University Press, 1992; 243–86.
2. Steckel RH. Stature and the standards of living. J EconLit 1995; 33:1903–40.
3. van Wieringen JC. Secular growth changes. In: Falkner F, Tanner JM, editors. Human Growth, a Comprehensive Treatise, Vol. 3, Second edition. New York, NY: Plenum Press, 1986; 307–15.
4. Bogin B. 1988. Patterns of Human Growth. New York, NY: Cambridge University Press, 239.
5. Frisancho AR. Nutritional influences on human growth and maturation. Yearb Phys Anthropol 1978; 21:174–91.
6. Gopalan C. Undernutrition: measurement and implications. In: Osmani SR, editor. Nutrition and Poverty. New York, NY: Oxford University Press, 1992; 217–48.
7. Martorell R. Child growth retardation: a discussion of its causes and its relationship to health. In: Blaxter K, Waterlow JC, editors. Nutritional Adaptation in Man. London: John Libbey, 1985; 13–29.
8. Martorell R, Habicht JP. Growth in early childhood in developing countries. In: Falkner F, Tanner JM, editors. Human Growth, a Comprehensive Treatise, Vol. 3, Second edition. New York, NY: Plenum Press, 1986; 241–62.
9. Steckel RH. Growth depression and recovery: the remarkable case of American slaves. Ann Hum Biol 1987; 14:101–32.
10. Tanner JM. Fetus into Man: Physical Growth from Conception to Maturity. Cambridge: Harvard University Press, 1978.
11. Prince JM. The plains paradox: secular trends in stature in 19th century nomadic Plains equestrian Indians. [Dissertation], University of Tennessee, 1998.
12. Jantz RL, Owsley DW. Long bone growth variation among Arikara skeletal populations. Am J Phys Anthropol 1984; 63:13–20.
13. Ruff C. Body size prediction from juvenile skeletal remains. Am J Phys Anthropol 2007; 133:698–716.
14. Smith S. Stature estimation of 3–10 year old children from long bone lengths. J Forensic Sci 2007; 52:538–46.
15. Cameron N. Human growth curve, canalization, and catch-up growth. In: Cameron N, editor. Human Growth and Development. San Diego, CA: Academic, 2006; 1–20.
16. Cameron N, Tanner JM, Whitehouse RH. A longitudinal analysis of the growth of limb segments in adolescence. Ann Hum Biol 1982; 9:211–20.
17. Lejarraga H. Growth in infancy and childhood: a pediatric approach. In: Cameron N, editor. Human Growth and Development. San Diego, CA: Academic, 2006; 21–44.

18. Tanner JM. Growth as a mirror of the conditions of society: secular trends and class distinction. In: Demirjian A, editor. Human Growth: A Multidisciplinary Review. London: Taylor and Francis, 1986; 3–34.
19. Waterlow JC, Buzina R, Keller W, Lane JM, Nichama MZ, Tanner JM. The presentation and use of height and weight data for comparing the nutritional status of groups of children under the age of 10 years. Bull World Health Organ 1977; 55:489–98.
20. Golden M. Is complete catch-up growth possible for stunted malnourished children? Eur J Clin Nutr 1998; 48:58–70.
21. Prader A, Tanner JM, von Harnack GA. Catch-up growth following illness or starvation. An example of developmental canalization in man. J Pediatr 1963; 62:646–59.
22. Norgan NG. Nutrition and growth. In: Cameron N, editor. Human Growth and Development. San Diego, CA: Academic, 2006; 139–64.
23. Karlberg J, Jalil F, Lam B, Low L, Yeung C. Linear growth retardation in relation to the three phases of growth. Eur J Clin Nutr 1994; 48:S25–S44.
24. Martorell R, Khan LK, Schroeder DG. Reversibility of stunting: epidemiological findings in children from developing countries. Eur J Clin Nutr 1994; 48:S45–S57.
25. Eveleth PB. Nutritional implications of differences in adolescent growth and maturation and in adult body size. In: Blaxter K, Waterlow JC, editors. Nutritional Adaptation in Man. London: John Libbey, 1985; 31–43.
26. Bogin B, Smith P, Orden AB, Verela-Silva MI, Loucki J. Rapid change in height and body proportions of Maya American children. Am J Hum Biol 2002; 14:753–61.
27. Stini WA. Adaptive strategies of human populations under nutritional stress. In: Watts ES, Johnston FE, Lasker, GW, editors. Biosocial Interrelations in Population Adaptation. Chicago, IL: Aldine, 1975; 19–41.
28. Maresh MM. Growth of major long bones in healthy children. Am J Disease Child 1946; 66:227–57.
29. Krogman WM. Growth of head, face, trunk and limbs in Philadelphia white and negro children of elementary and high school age. Oxford: Blackwell Publishing, Monographs of the Society for Research in Child Development 1970; 35, paper 3: 80.
30. Jungers WL, Cole TM, Owsley DW. Multivariate analysis of relative growth in the limb bones of Arikara Indians. Growth Dev Aging 1988; 52:103–7.
31. Tanner JM. Growth at Adolescence, Second edition. Oxford: Blackwell Scientific Publications. Springfield: Charles C. Thomas, 1962.
32. Tanner JM, Whitehouse RH. A longitudinal analysis of the growth of limb segments in adolescent. Ann Hum Biol 1982; 9:211–20.
33. Meadows-Jantz L, Jantz RL. Secular change in long bone length and proportion in the United States, 1800–1970. Am J Phys Anthropol 1999; 110:57–67.
34. Greulich WW. Some secular changes in the growth of American-born and native Japanese children. Am J Phys Anthropol 1976; 45:553–68.
35. Wolanski N,Kasprzak E. Stature as a measure of effects of environmental change. Curr Anthropol 1976; 17:548–52.
36. Siniarska A. Sexual dimorphism index (SDI) of body height as an indicator of economic changes in Yucatan, Mexico. Am J Phys Anthropol 1996;[Suppl 22]:215.
37. Stinson S. Sex differences in environmental sensitivity during growth and development. Yearb Phys Anthropol 1985; 28:123–47.
38. Stini WA. Nutritional stress and growth: sex differences in adaptive response. Am J Phys Anthropol 1969; 31:417–8.

39. Martorell R, Rivera J, Kaplowitz H, Pollitt E. Long-term consequences of growth retardation during early childhood. In: Hernandez M, Argente J, editors. Human Growth: Basic and Clinical Aspects. Amsterdam: Elsevier, 1992; 143–9.
40. Tanner JM, Healy MJR, Lockhart RD, MacKenzie JD, Whitehouse RH. Aberdeen growth study: part 1. The prediction of adult body measurements from measurements taken each year from birth to 5 years. Arch Dis Child 1956; 31:372–81.

Chapter 12
Bone Weathering of Juvenile-Sized Remains in the North Carolina Piedmont

Sarah L. Cunningham, Scott A. Kirkland, and Ann H. Ross

Abstract In decomposition studies, soft tissue decay and the effects of the environment on its processes and timing have been the primary focus. Decompositional changes to skeletal material, often called bone weathering, have been observed in far fewer research studies, most notably Behrensmeyer's (Paleobiology 4:150–162, 1978) foundational project that first described the process and time frame for hard tissue decay. While other studies have followed, all have noted that the rate and the process of decay are dependent on the local environmental factors affecting the skeletal material, an issue that is also well known in soft tissue decomposition research. While much of the bone weathering studies are long-term and often use adult elements, this study adds to the literature by focusing on short-term changes occurring within a year to juvenile domestic pigs in the central Piedmont region of North Carolina. In this study, juvenile domestic pigs, *Sus scrofa* ($n = 7$), were used as proxies for human children because of their similarity in size and immaturity of the skeletal elements. Observations took place over an 8-month period; two fleshed pigs ($n = 2$) were placed at the beginning of the observational period, while the other five ($n = 5$) had been in the research field for at least 3 months prior to the beginning of the project. The study found that, while all skeletal elements remained largely intact, specific elements were more affected by different types of weathering. Long, tubular bones, including long bones, metacarpals, metatarsals, and phalanges, were more prone to flaking of the outer layers of cortical bone, while long bones, vertebrae, and ribs were more likely to have loss of bone at the articular facets, leading to exposure of interior trabecular bone. The location of the project, largely underutilized in forensic research, shares similar environmental factors with other large areas of the American South. Consequently, the results could be applied to the broader southeastern United States.

A.H. Ross (✉)
Department of Sociology and Anthropology, North Carolina State University, Raleigh, NC 27695, USA
e-mail: ann_ross@ncsu.edu

A.H. Ross, S.M. Abel (eds.), *The Juvenile Skeleton in Forensic Abuse Investigations*,
DOI 10.1007/978-1-61779-255-7_12,

12.1 Introduction

Forensic research has led to insight into the processes affecting the breakdown of remains after death. The decay of soft tissue has been exhaustively studied, which led to a better understanding of the observable stages and timing of the decay process. While the decomposition process follows a general pattern, researchers have found that the timing of each stage can vary depending on climate and local environmental factors including soil content and acidity, exposure to the elements, and surface versus subsurface deposition [1–4].

Similar to soft tissue decay, skeletal decay occurs in observable stages, but the timing of each stage depends on the local environmental factors acting on the material [5–11]. Skeletal decomposition, or bone weathering, has been defined by one of the original researchers as "... the process by which the original microscopic organic and inorganic components of a bone are separated from each other and destroyed by physical and chemical agents operating on the bone in situ, either on the surface or within the soil zone" [5]. In a study conducted in the diverse local environments of the equatorial climate of Southern Kenya's Amboseli National Park, Behrensmeyer [5] classified the observed decompositional changes into stages (Table 12.1).

The present research study, conducted in the central North Carolina Piedmont, describes the progress of decomposition of both soft and hard tissue remains of juvenile pigs in a semi-wooded environment. Using pigs as proxies for human decomposition has become a common practice due to their availability and similarity to human physiology [12]. Additionally, because of their small size, juvenile pigs have been used as proxies for children in forensic research [13, 14]. This research focus is particularly useful since the many human adult cadaver studies conducted in research fields of the University of Tennessee, Knoxville, and other places may not be appropriate corollaries to child decomposition due to size differences and the immaturity of the skeletal system. The immaturity of the skeletal system, due to the non-fusion of elements during growth, increases the volume of skeletal material present and causes the elements to have an appearance very different from the mature form. Thus, it is necessary to understand how the decompositional processes affect juveniles in an effort to better inform forensic investigators. The purpose of

Table 12.1 Skeletal decomposition according to Behrensmeyer [5]

Stage	Description
0	Fresh, defleshed bone
1	Longitudinal cracking, though some soft tissue may still remain
2 (A)	Topmost layer of bone begins to flake, though some soft tissue may still remain
2 (B)	Topmost layer of bone has almost completely flaked off
3	Topmost layer of bone is gone, compact bone layers (1.0–1.5 mm deep) are fibrous
4	Compact bone continues to appear fibrous and rough, splintering of bone pieces may occur, inner cavity begins to show wear
5	Inner, trabecular bone is exposed, bone itself is falling apart and losing its shape

this project is to establish an approximate timing and description of stages of decay associated with the local environmental factors found in the central Piedmont of North Carolina. This analysis of the effects of the microenvironments is essential if more accurate time-since-death estimations are to be made.

12.2 Background

The North Carolina Piedmont stretches across the state from the Appalachian Mountains in the west to the lowland eastern coastal plain. It is characterized as having a warm temperate climate with fully humid precipitation levels and hot summers [15]. The Lake Wheeler research field is part of land grants connected with North Carolina State University and is located in the center of the Piedmont within the city limits of Raleigh.

The research area is an open agricultural field with partial tree cover bordered by a small stream. Soil samples were collected from two locations where the early fall research subjects were to be placed: one in an open area with no cover and the second located in heavy shade with only minimal sun exposure. Soil analysis was conducted by the North Carolina Department of Agriculture and Consumer Services. The two tests indicate that the research field was composed of mineral class silt or clay loamy soil. While the pH levels varied for the two sampled areas (the shade area measuring at 4.4 and the open area measuring at 5.2), both confirm acidic soil content.

Weather data for the research site was obtained from the State Climate Office of North Carolina and recorded by the Lake Wheeler field lab weather station. The collected data consisted of three environmental measurements: daily average temperature, daily average precipitation, and daily average solar radiation. During the 7 months of field research, spanning the fall through spring season, the average temperature ranged from 77.1°F to 27.5°F, with the lowest temperatures occurring during the winter months (December–February) (Fig. 12.1). Precipitation levels were low during the observation period (7-month average 0.1056 in.), with the

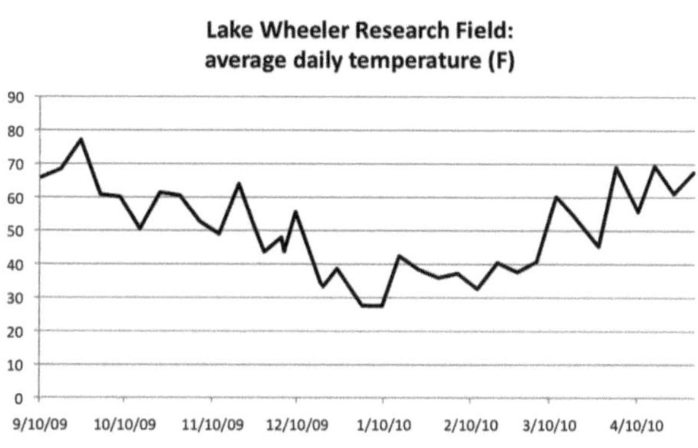

Fig. 12.1 Average Daily Temperature for Lake Wheeler Research Site

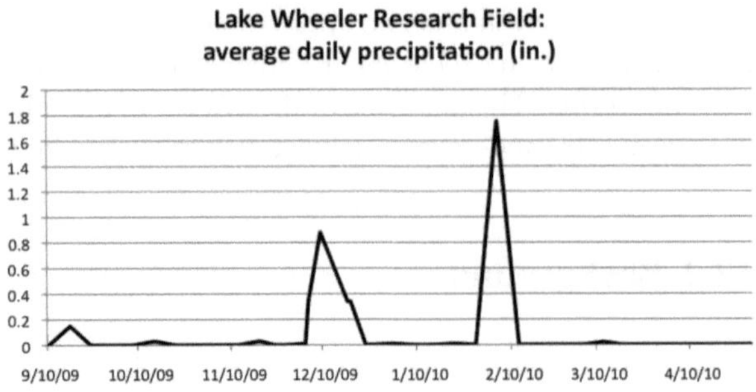

Fig. 12.2 Average Daily Precipitation for Lake Wheeler Research Site

highest levels of accumulation occurring in December (Fig. 12.2). Solar radiation levels were the most variable (averaging 119.467 W/m^2 during the observation period), the lowest occurring between November and early February and the highest occurring from mid-February through the end of April (Fig. 12.3).

Soft tissue decomposition begins to occur soon after death and full skeletonization of remains can be completed within a matter of 2 weeks in a humid, equatorial setting [2]. Skeletal material, however, can remain virtually unchanged long after its initial deposition [7]. Previous decomposition research in warm temperate climate regions, similar to North Carolina, has shown that skeletal remains in warm temperate climate decay at a much slower rate in comparison to equatorial and arid climates [5, 7, 10]. One study, conducted in Somerset, England, found that juvenile cow remains located on the soil surface were largely unchanged for 8 years after death and could be scored only as a 0 on the Behrensmeyer scale [5, 6].

A second study, conducted in Rhulen, Wales, and lasting for approximately 20 years found that after 19 years the surface-deposited large animal remains reached only Behrensmeyer's stage 2 of decomposition. However, after 12 years, remains left in moist, covered environments were found to be more heavily decayed on the epiphyses and articular surfaces [8]. In this same study, small animal bones were found to respond differently to weathering than the large animal remains. While little or no weathering was apparent on large animal bones as late as 12 years after

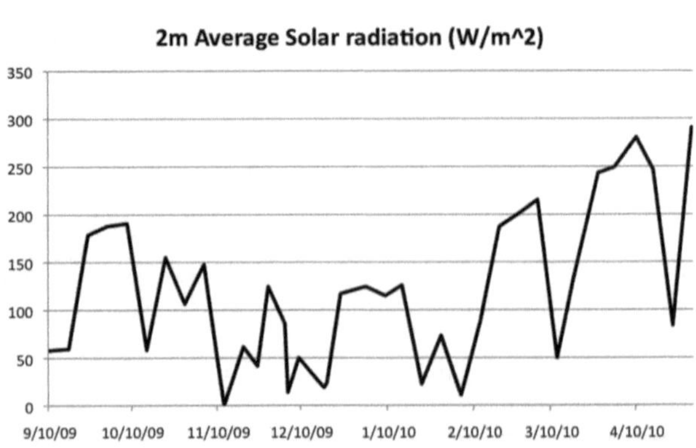

Fig. 12.3 Average Daily Solar Radiation for Lake Wheeler Research Site

death, small animal bones were observed to have more progressive or even complete decay after only 5 years [8]. This differential weathering pattern is likely caused by differences in bone size and density, as it has been found that the greater the density of the bone, the better the preservation [16].

12.3 Methods

Seven juvenile pigs were placed in an open field in staggered phases. Five were placed in early summer, two were placed in early fall, and all, except one, were collected in the late spring/early summer of the following year. The four of the original five pigs were exposed to the elements for 11 months (summer 2009–spring/summer 2010), while the two placed in early fall were exposed for 8 months. One of the pigs placed in late spring/early summer was collected midway through the research period (in early January) and was exposed to the elements for 7 months.

For Behrensmeyer's [5] stages to be applicable, the research subject must be at least 11 lbs (5 kg). Pigs 1 through 5 weighed approximately 35 lbs (15.88 kg), with one reaching 55 lbs (24.95 kg). Pig 6 was 22.5 lbs (11.57 kg) and pig 7 was 23 lbs (10.43 kg). All pigs were juveniles and, based on weight, were approximately between 4 and 10 weeks old. During original placement, all pigs were covered in wired cages to prevent removal by scavengers. Once skeletonized, several of the cages were removed prior to the beginning of the research period (pigs 3 and 5). The subjects were monitored once a week beginning in early September for 34 weeks for a total of 33 observations. One observation was missed in midwinter due to an impassable creek that cut off access to the research field. Pictures taken in the field were with a Nikon Coolpix 4600 point and shoot camera, while those taken during laboratory analysis were with a Canon PowerShot SD750 digital ELPH.

Laboratory analysis included a skeletal inventory of identifiable skeletal elements for a count of bones present. These elements were then analyzed to determine the presence and degree of weathering based on Behrensmeyer's [5] stages.

Because the research subjects were juveniles, no skeletal elements were completely fused, resulting in several components present for each bone. To simplify the count of skeletal material, each whole bone was counted as one element, even if it had several epiphyses present. The epiphyses of long bones were easily identifiable and a special note was made of their condition, but they were not included in the overall bone count. For some major structural elements, the young age of the subjects resulted in some elements remaining in several identifiable pieces. This was especially true for the pelvis. The juvenile pig *os coxae* are made up of three separate bones (the ilium, the ischium, and the pubis) that will later fuse much like the human pelvis. The pubis and ischium were already fused during fetal development. The remaining two elements were easily identified and were each counted as one half of a whole so that each research subject should have two whole innominates (four separate unfused elements from each side) in total.

12.4 Results

During collection, rain, vegetation, and natural soil movement partially buried large portions of several research subjects' skeletal elements. Because of this, collection was performed in two steps: vegetation was cleared and elements that remained on the surface were collected. Then, soil surface was removed and subsurface remains were collected separately. Naturally buried remains were found in proximity to the surface. Roots from surrounding vegetation had grown around and sometimes through many surface and subsurface elements, causing root etching.

The skeletal elements recovered did not show signs of longitudinal cracking or other more advanced weathering forms and were determined to be at stage 0 on the Behrensmeyer [5] scale. However, subtle changes to the bone were present in all study subjects and were categorized as flaking of cortical bone, erosion of articular facets and epiphyseal articulations, pockmarks and erosion of the surface of the elements. Flaking of the cortical bone is characterized by a marbling pattern on the diaphyses of the elements and a series of fine cracks on the outermost layer that had begun to shed parts of itself (Fig. 12.4). This weathering pattern differs from longitudinal cracking in that only the outermost layer is currently affected. Erosion of the articular facets and epiphyseal articulations is characterized as erosion of the outer layer of cortical bone resulting in trabecular bone exposure (Fig. 12.5). Similar to articular facet/epiphyseal erosion, the erosion of the surface of elements, exhibited most often as a circular "pockmark" pattern, due to the wearing away of the cortical bone layer, exposing the underlying trabecular bone (Fig. 12.6). Table 12.2 shows the breakdown of each research pig by the number of elements and weathering percentage. Table 12.3 shows the breakdown of each subject by weathering pattern.

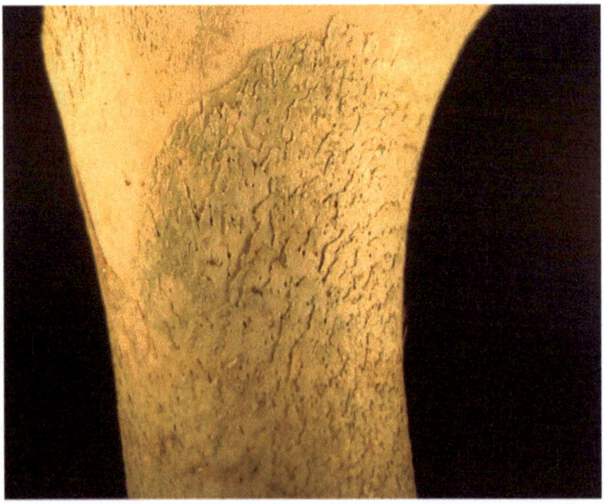

Fig. 12.4 Marbling Pattern on Outer Diaphysis

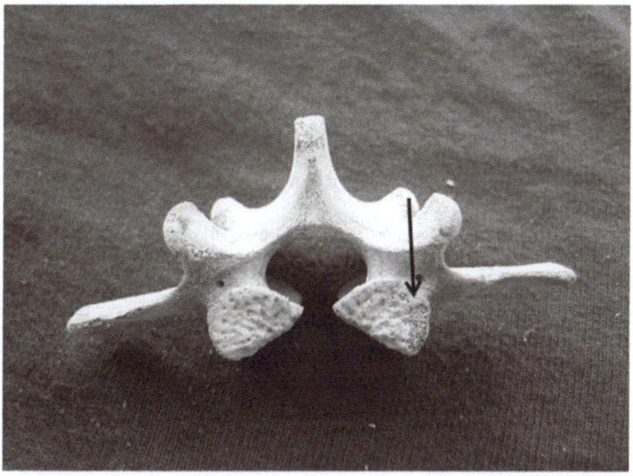

Fig. 12.5 Erosion of Articular Facets

Fig. 12.6 Circular Pockmark Pattern

12.4.1 Pig 1

Pig 1 was the first placed in the field. Vegetative growth was particularly active even during the winter months, and the skeleton was almost completely obscured for a large part of the research period. During the collection phase, 109 elements were recovered. Root activity minimally affected surface elements; however, it was much more pervasive in the subsurface remains. On effected remains, the area surrounding root attachments showed more wear than other parts of the elements (Fig. 12.7).

Of the recovered surface remains present ($n=48.5$), 69% ($n=33.5$) showed some sign of weathering. This was most often seen in the form of erosion of articular facets ($n=23$), which affected ribs and vertebrae most often. Cortical

Table 12.2 Weathering percentage by proxy and deposition level

Proxy	Total elements collected	Surface/subsurface remains collected	Total weathered
Pig 1	109	48.5	33.5 (69%)
		60.5	34 (56%)
Pig 2	118	69	42.5 (61%)
		49	29 (59%)
Pig 3	88	88 (surface only)	75 (85%)
Pig 4	104	74.5	48.5 (65%)
		29.5	8 (27%)
Pig 5	113	113 (deposition not recorded)	74 (65%)
Pig 6	116	91	26.5 (29%)
		25	6 (24%)
Pig 7	126	105	32 (30%)
		21	2 (9%)

flaking was seen only in the long bones ($n=3$). Surface erosion ($n=7.5$) affected several different types of bone, including long bones, but was seen most often in carpals/tarsals. The subsurface remains ($n=60.5$) followed a similar weathering pattern. Articular/epiphyseal facet erosion affected ribs and vertebrae, as well as metacarpas/tarsals and phalanges ($n=32$), while surface erosion accounted for a much smaller element weathering ($n=2$) for a total of 56% ($n=34$) of the subsurface remains presenting some weathering pattern.

Precipitation accumulation was low, though rainfall was recurrent throughout the study period, encouraging the growth of algae on the exposed surfaces of many of the elements (Fig. 12.8). The presence of green algae on the bone was first noticed on the first observations made for pig 1 on September 24, 2009, which persisted throughout the study period.

12.4.2 Pig 2

As with the other research subjects, persistent rainfall and temperatures above freezing caused continued vegetative growth even during the winter months, which resulted in many elements being covered in green algae from the initial observation, September 24, 2009, and persisting throughout the study. The continued vegetative growth caused the skeleton to be completely covered and obscured from view by December 9, 2009. During the collection phase, 118 elements were recovered. Root activity was moderate, and surface remains were largely free of any fibrous roots, while the subsurface remains were more heavily affected. Many, but not all, elements exhibited some sort of fibrous root activity.

Of the 69 elements recovered from the surface, 62% ($n=42.5$) showed some sign of weathering. Erosion of the articular/epiphyseal facets was most prevalent ($n=41.5$) and was found to affect ribs and vertebrae more than other elements. Several elements that were affected by articular facet erosion also presented surface

Table 12.3 Breakdown of weathering by type

Proxy #	Surface/ subsurface elements collected	Total weathered (percentage of total remains)	Weathering type (percentage of total weathered)			
			Cortical bone flaking	Erosion of articular/ epiphyseal facets	Erosion of element surface, "pockmarking"	Multiple patterns in single element (percentage of erosion of articular/ epiphyseal facet count)
Pig 1	48.5	33.5 (69)	3 (9)	23 (69)	7.5 (22)	0 (0.0)
	60.5	34 (56)	0 (0.0)	32 (94)	2 (6)	0 (0.0)
Pig 2	69	42.5 (61)	1 (2)	41.5 (98)	0 (0.0)	5 (12) facet erosion/cortical flaking 5 (12) facet erosion/surface erosion
	49	29 (59)	7 (24)	14 (48)	8 (27)	0 (0.0)
Pig 3	88	75 (85)	3 (4)	70 (93)	2 (3)	9 (13) facet erosion/cortical flaking 3 (4) facet erosion/surface erosion
Pig 4	74.5	48.5 (65)	2 (4)	46.5 (96)	0 (0.0)	2 (4) facet erosion/cortical flaking
	29.5	8 (27)	2 (25)	6 (75)	0 (0.0)	1 (17) facet erosion/cortical flaking
Pig 5	113	74 (65)	0 (0.0)	74 (100)	0 (0.0)	2 (3) facet erosion/surface erosion
Pig 6	91	26.5 (29)	2 (7)	24.5 (92)	0 (0.0)	0 (0.0)
	25	6 (24)	0 (0.0)	6 (100)	0 (0.0)	(0.0)
Pig 7	105	32 (30)	6 (19)	26 (81)	0 (0.0)	5 (19) facet erosion/cortical flaking
	21	2 (9)	0	0	2 (100)	0

Fig. 12.7 Root Activity and Erosion on Epiphysis

Fig. 12.8 Algae Growth on Skull

erosion ($n = 5$), occurring in the carpals/tarsals and sternebrae, and cortical flaking ($n = 5$), which was found more often in long, tubular bones. Only the fibula exhibited just one type of weathering pattern, cortical flaking. Fifty-nine percent ($n = 29$) of the subsurface remains ($n = 49$) were affected by weathering, with articular surface erosion being the most prevalent ($n = 14$). Surface erosion was found only on carpals/tarsals ($n = 8$), and cortical flaking was found on the long bones, phalanges, and the skull ($n = 7$).

12.4.3 Pig 3

Unlike pigs 1 and 2, who were covered by cages for almost the whole observation period, pig 3 was not enclosed. Similarly, while vegetation continued to grow and overtake some of the research subjects, the vegetation from the location of pig 3 only grew enough to partially cover many of the skeletal elements (termed "moderate vegetation growth") by mid-February. This means that pig 3 was completely exposed to environmental factors, particularly the sun, for 4 months. The initial observation (September 10, 2009) found that the bones were bleached white. Rainfall during the week caused many of the bones to become stained with green algae, which slowly faded back to a bleached white/gray color. During the collection phase, 118 elements were recovered. Root interaction was minimal, and fibrous networks attached to elements as seen in pigs 1 and 2 were absent. Pig 3 appears to have been largely unaffected by root activity.

All of the 88 elements were recovered from the surface; no subsurface remains were found. Eighty-five percent ($n = 75$) of the surface remains showed some sign of weathering. Erosion of the articular facets was the most prevalent ($n = 70$) and affected almost every recovered bone. Surface erosion affected 5 elements ($n = 5$), and diaphyseal flaking affected 12 elements ($n = 12$). Several elements that were affected by articular facet erosion also presented surface erosion ($n = 3$) (carpals/tarsals) and cortical flaking ($n = 9$), where long bones were the most represented.

12.4.4 Pig 4

Similar to pigs 1 and 2, pig 4 was enclosed in a cage for the observation period. Root activity was minimal and, similar to pig 3, pig 4 did not have the fibrous root networks attached to elements as seen in pigs 1 and 2. At the beginning of the research period, vegetation was cleared from the cage, revealing elements that were partially buried and several that were green with algae growth. Vegetation within the cage was heavy, though it surrounded the remains, providing some cover from environmental factors, including intensive sunlight, rather than covering the bones. Pig 4 was the closest research subject to the creek that bordered the research field. The creek likely breached its banks in early November as the mid-November observation found sediment deposited in the cage and on the remains, and a cluster of bones had been moved into a pile next to the cage wall. During the collection phase, 104 elements were recovered. No root activity was present.

Sixty-five percent ($n = 48.5$) of the surface remains ($n = 74.5$) presented signs of weathering. Erosion of the articular/epiphyseal facets was most prevalent ($n = 46.5$). Cortical bone flaking was present ($n = 2$) on long, tubular bones such as the femur and metacarpals. Several elements that were affected by articular/epiphyseal facet erosion also presented surface cortical flaking ($n = 2$). Subsurface elements ($n = 29.5$) were affected by weathering patterns at a rate of 27% ($n = 8$). Erosion of articular/epiphyseal facets was the most common type of weathering pattern ($n=6$), while cortical bone flaking was less prevalent ($n=2$). One element ($n=1$), a long bone, was affected by both cortical bone flaking and articular/epiphyseal facet erosion. Surface erosion was notably absent from the remains of pig 4.

12.4.5 Pig 5

Like pig 3, pig 5 was not enclosed in a cage during the observation period. This research subject was collected in early January 2010 (at 7 months exposure) to create a control to understand what weathering patterns took place during longer periods of exposure. Root activity was minimal with only a few elements presenting attached fibrous root networks. During the collection phase, 113 elements were recovered. Depositional levels (surface vs. subsurface), through an oversight on the part of the researcher, were not recorded for this research subject.

Only the erosion of articular/epiphyseal facets and bone surface was present. Sixty-five percent ($n=74$) of the recovered remains ($n=113$) presented signs of weathering effects. All of these remains were affected by articular/epiphyseal facet erosion, while several elements ($n=2$), a carpal/tarsal and ulna, were found to present the additional patterns of surface erosion. No cortical flaking was present.

12.4.6 Pig 6

Set out in the early fall (September 4, 2009), pig 6 was covered by a cage fully exposed to the sun throughout the duration of the research period. Insect activity ceased in mid-October, and the remains appeared to be skeletonized except for the surface-side skin, which persisted. Weather conditions (cool temperatures and sun) caused the remaining skin to mummify. Vegetation growth was slower and root activity was not present. Some elements were stained green with algae.

Of the surface remains collected ($n=91$), 29% ($n=26.5$) presented signs of weathering effects. Erosion of the articular/epiphyseal facets was most prevalent ($n=24.5$). Cortical bone flaking affected two metacarpals/metatarsals ($n=2$). Subsurface elements ($n=25$) were affected only by erosion of articular/epiphyseal facets at a rate of 24% ($n=6$). Surface erosion was notably absent.

12.4.7 Pig 7

Set out at the same time as pig 6, pig 7 was covered by a cage and placed in a corner of the field with complete shade so that only minimal sunlight would reach the subject. Skeletonization and the cessation of insect activity were reached in early October, 2 weeks before the surface skin of pig 6 mummified. Vegetation growth was slower than in other areas, and green plants obscured pig 7 only at the end of March. Leaf litter in the cage due to surrounding trees was more prevalent. Like the other research pigs, the remains were stained green, though not until late November, several weeks after skeletonization was reached. During the collection phase, 126 elements were recovered.

Thirty percent ($n=32$) of the surface remains ($n=105$) presented signs of weathering effects. Erosion of the articular/epiphyseal facets was most prevalent ($n=26$), present in long bones, vertebrae, and ribs, as well as other elements. Cortical bone flaking affected only tubular bones such as long bones and metacarpals ($n=6$). Several elements (humerus, femora, and tibiae) had both types of weathering present ($n=5$). Subsurface elements ($n=21$) were affected only by surface erosion at a rate of 9% ($n=2$) (carpals/tarsals).

12.5 Obstacles

When working with juvenile research subjects in decomposition studies, it is important to remember that the bone was still actively growing and remodeling prior to death. These areas of growth have a coarse and porous appearance that is commonly misidentified as pathological [17]. This problem also occurs in weathering studies where active growth mimics patterns of skeletal decay that expose trabecular bone. One indicator that a roughened, porous area is caused by growth instead of weathering is its location. If the "exposed trabecular bone" is located proximal-posteriorly on the long bones or on the sterno-posterior surface of the ribs, then it is likely growth and not weathering (Fig. 12.9). Another indicator is the timing of these pseudo-weathering marks appear. If the marks have been present since the remains were first skeletonized, it is likely a sign of previous active growth.

Fig. 12.9 Porosity due to growth in the cut-back zone and not related to weathering (proximal long bone)

Within this project, a small bias may artificially inflate the weathering type count. When documenting the different weathering patterns present, it was not indicated if a few elements contained either one or several weathering types. It was unclear if six skeletal elements recovered from pigs 2, 3, and 6 contained a singular or multiple weathering types. For the analysis used in this study, the elements were counted as if they had only one weathering pattern. This is significant because all elements with multiple weathering types contained erosion of the articular/epiphyseal facets and were counted as part of that type's overall occurrence. The percentages of the mixed types were calculated using the second weathering type count divided into the number of articular/epiphyseal facet erosion instances in the depositional layer of the research proxy.

For instance, one of the pigs may have had 14 instances of articular/epiphyseal facet erosion and 5 instances of cortical flaking. It was later found that two of those five elements with cortical flaking also had articular/epiphyseal facet erosion. For the overall count, these two elements would be included in the baseline count for the erosion type, increasing it to 16 counts and decreasing the cortical flaking to 3 occurrences. The mixed-type percentage then is a part of the articular erosion count. The mixed-type element count of 2 is divided into the articular erosion count of 16, to determine a percentage of mixed-type occurrences.

12.6 Discussion

Skeletonization for the two pigs placed in the research field in the fall occurred within a month. Pig 6, placed in the full sun with no tree cover, was expected to reach full skeletonization before the shade-deposited pig 7; however, a combination of mild temperatures, sun exposure, and maggot activity caused the surface-side skin to mummify (approximately 20–27 days since initial deposition), though the rest of the pig decomposed. Bass [18] described this type of mummification as characteristic of maggots leaving more exposed tissue and burrowing deeper into the body to protect themselves from the sun. Pig 7 reached complete skeletonization within 20 days of deposition (September 24, 2009 observation day) according to Galloway's stages of decomposition [3]. While skeletonization timing for the late spring/early summer pigs was not documented, a similar study conducted in the southern coastal area of North Carolina found that pigs set out in the spring seasons (March–April) and weighing 20–40 lbs (9.07–18.14 kg) were skeletonized within 17–18 days. Pigs weighing between 40 and 50 lbs (18.14–22.68 kg) were skeletonized within 20–21 days [19]. A series of pigs of similar size placed in the Raleigh, North Carolina research field the following summer were found to fully decompose within approximately 1 week. While summer is expected to be the fastest decompositional season due to heat and humidity, this project and previous research show that the spring and fall decompositional season rates are largely comparable.

Due to vegetation cover and the cages that separated the researcher from the pigs, it is difficult to determine the exact observation day when weathering patterns first appeared on each research subject. Photographs taken each week, however, have made it possible to determine the approximate timing of some of the weathering types. For others, laboratory analysis established the research period (7 months, 8 months, or 11 months) as the baseline for the appearance of weathering patterns. This was the case for cortical flaking, while some element diaphyses began to take on a marbled appearance, first noticed on pig 1 during the February 2, 2010 observation day, the small, delicate cortical bone flakes were observable only under laboratory conditions when the bones were able to be handled.

For articular/epiphyseal facet erosion, the pattern was first noted on pig 3. Uncaged some time after skeletonization, but before the start of the research study, pig 3 had the first signs of articular/epiphyseal facet erosion from the first observation day (September 10, 2009) when it had lain exposed for approximately 3 months (Fig. 12.10). It is possible that pig 3 was the first to show any kind of bone wear because vegetation cover surrounding it had remained low, exposing the remains to direct sunlight for a longer period of time.

Surface erosion was first noticed on Pig 7 on a carpal/tarsal on January 9, 2010, 4 months after initial deposition and approximately 3 months since skeletonization. This element would later become buried due to natural soil movement and count as one example of only two surface erosion patterns to occur on pig 7 whether the bone remained on the surface or not.

Overall, when compared to one another, the bone weathering pattern percentages (Table 12.3) indicate that the erosion of articular/epiphyseal facets is the most pervasive weathering pattern in both depositional levels followed by cortical bone flaking and surface erosion. While the weathering patterns can occur in any type of bone, they appear to occur in certain elements more often than in others. The articular/epiphyseal facet erosion tends to occur most often in ribs and vertebrae, likely due to their fragile and less dense structure, particularly in juveniles. Surface

Fig. 12.10 Early Erosion Depicted on Facet and Algae Growth

erosion, or "pockmarking", was most prevalent in carpal/tarsal bones, though it was also seen on long bones, long bone epiphyses, and phalanges, showing a tendency to occur more often in denser element types. Cortical flaking occurred most often on long bone, metacarpal/tarsal, and phalange diaphyses, preferring long, tubular bone elements.

Deposition within the soil layer has been found to drastically slow the decay process [1, 4]; in fact, Rodriguez and Bass [1] found that soft tissue decayed at a rate eight times as slow as surface depositions. This delay does not appear to have been actively at work on the elements found in the soil layer at the time of excavation. This is likely due to the method of burial. Rather than placed immediately at depth, all pigs were deposited on the surface, and some elements were only buried due to natural soil, wind, and water action over time.

12.7 Conclusion

Three types of weathering patterns were noted during the 11-month research period: erosion of articular/epiphyseal facets, surface erosion of elements, and cortical flaking. In her research, Behrensmeyer [5] describes the appearance of cortical flaking on some of her research subjects in Africa, though it was not categorized within the stages of skeletal decomposition and it was unclear when it developed. Other research in colder climates found that pig long bones developed longitudinal cracking between 6 and 9.5 months of exposure, though this was attributed to the freezing and thawing action common in southern Ontario [11].

In the current study, cortical flaking was found in all research proxies, except pig 5, which had been collected at 7 months of exposure. Pig 2 (cumulative 13 elements affected), Pig 3 (12 elements), and Pig 7 (11 elements) had the most amount of cortical flaking. Pigs 2 and 7 maintained a majority of cover for much of the research period, while pig 3 was largely exposed for its duration. Sun exposure, therefore, may not play an intense part in cortical flaking. Articular/epiphyseal erosion was present in all remains and was first noted on pig 3 during the September 10, 2009 observation day, 3 months after deposition. Surface erosion was noted on pig 7 in early January 2010, 4 months after deposition. A preliminary postmortem interval can then be constructed from this information (Table 12.4).

Table 12.4 Postmortem interval (PMI) based on weathering pattern

Weathering pattern	Postmortem interval	Description
Erosion of articular/epiphyseal facets	3–5 months	Erosion facets and bone ends
Surface erosion	4–7 months	Erosion of circular sections of bone; "pockmarking"
Cortical flaking	8–11 months	Marbling of diaphyses, flaking of small pieces of outer layer of cortical bone

In the Piedmont of North Carolina, soft tissue remains can be expected to decompose within approximately 7 days during the summer and within a month during the early fall. While mummification does occur, researchers should be aware that complete decomposition and skeletonization may likely have occurred and only the non-soil side of the remains persisted as a "cover" for maggot activity. While variability is still a possibility, bone weathering patterns will likely appear at approximately 3–5 months with articular/epiphyseal erosion of the less dense bones the first to occur. Between 4 and 7 months, surface erosion will begin to affect more dense elements. Between 8 and 11 months, marbling of diaphyses and cortical flaking will begin to appear on elements, particularly tubular bones.

These weathering patterns are best applied to decomposition cycles that start in the summer and fall. Winter decomposition cycles in the mild temperatures of central North Carolina have not been attempted, but would be expected to have a faster time between deposition and skeletonization in comparison to colder, northern climes. When working with juveniles, the pattern of weathering must be categorized without confusing normal areas of growth. The primary active growth areas are located on the proximal-posterior section of long bones underneath the section of epiphyseal attachment and the posterior portion of the sternal rib ends.

This study provides a baseline for the weathering patterns that investigators will likely encounter. Further, it highlights issues related to bone appearance and growth that are specific to juveniles, whether pig or human. These identified patterns could, with more research, prove to be more variable than they are now understood to be. However, the current patterns are a foundation upon which further knowledge can be expanded and are a reliable basis to estimate the postmortem interval of juvenile remains in central North Carolina and similar environments.

Acknowledgments Climate information was provided by the State Climate Office of North Carolina; phone 919-515-3056, http://www.nc-climate.ncsu.edu/, Suite 100, Research III Building 1005 Capability Drive, Centennial Campus, Box 7236, NC State University, Raleigh, NC 27695-7236. USA. Soil information was provided by the North Carolina Department of Agriculture and Consumer Services; phone 919-733-2655, http://www.ncagr.gov/agronomi/, 1040 Mail Service Center, Raleigh, NC 27699-1040, USA.

References

1. Rodriguez W, Bass W. Decomposition of buried bodies and methods that may aid in their location. J Forensic Sci 1985; 30: 836–852.
2. Ubelaker DH. Taphonomic applications in forensic anthropology. In: Haglund W, Sorg M, editors. Forensic Taphonomy: The Post-mortem Fate of Human Remains. New York, NY: CRC Press, 1997; 77–90.
3. Galloway A. The process of decomposition: A model from the Arizona-Sonoran Desert. In: Haglund W, Sorg M, editors. Forensic Taphonomy: The Post-mortem Fate of Human Remains. New York, NY: CRC Press, 1997; 139–150.
4. Janaway RC, Wilson AS, Diaz GC, Guillen S. Taphonomic changes to the buried body in arid environments: An experimental case study in Peru. In: Ritz K, Dawson L, Miller D, editors. Criminal and Environmental Soil Forensics. London: Springer Science, 2009; 341–356.

5. Behrensmeyer, AK. Taphonomic and ecologic information from bone weathering. Paleobiology 1978; 4: 150–162.
6. Andrews P, Cook J. Natural modifications to bones in a temperate setting. Man 1985; 20: 675–691.
7. Tappen, M. Bone weathering in the tropical rain forest. J Archaeol Sci 1994; 21: 667–673.
8. Andrews, P. Experiments in taphonomy. J Archaeol Sci 1995; 22: 147–153.
9. Bell LS, Skinner MF, Jones SJ. The speed of post mortem change to the human skeleton and its taphonomic significance. Forensic Sci Int 1996; 82: 129–140.
10. Andrews P, Whybrow P. Taphonomic observations on a camel skeleton in a desert environment in Abu Dhabi. Palaeontol Electron 2005; 8: 1–17.
11. Janjua MA, Tracy LR. Bone weathering patterns of metatarsal v. femur and the postmortem interval in Southern Ontario. Forensic Sci Int 2008; 178: 16–23.
12. Miller ER, Ullrey DE. The pig as a model for human nutrition. A Rev Nutr 1987; 7: 361–382.
13. Morton RJ, Lord WD. Taphonomy of child-sized remains: a study of scattering and scavenging in Virginia, USA. J Forensic Sci 2006; 51: 475–479.
14. Enwere PI. Taphonomy of Child-sized Remains in Shallow Grave and Surface Deposit Scenarios. 2008. Theses and Dissertations-Anthropology. Paper 12. http://ecommons.txstate.edu/anthroptad/12.
15. Kottek M, Grieser J, Beck C, Rudolf B, Rubel F. World map of the Köppen-Geiger climate classification updated. Meteorol Z 2006; 15: 259–263.
16. Willey P, Galloway A, Snyder L. Bone mineral density and survival of elements and element portions in the bones of the crow creek massacre victims. Am J Phys Anthropol 1997; 104: 513–528.
17. Buikstra J, Ubelaker D. Paleopathology. In: Buikstra J, Ubelaker D, editors. Standards for Data Collection from Human Skeletal Remains: Proceedings of a Seminar at the Field Museum of Natural History. Fayetteville, NC: Arkansas Archaeological Survey, 1994; 107–159.
18. Bass, WM. Outdoor decomposition rates in Tennessee. In: Haglund WD, Sorg M, editors. Forensic Taphonomy: The Postmortem Fate of Human Remains. New York, NY: CRC Press, 1997; 181–186.
19. Albert M, Tomberlin J, Johnson C, Karp T. Observations of decomposition in southern coastal North Carolina. Proc Am Acad Forensic Sci 2006; 12: 309.

Index

Note: The letters 'b', 'f' and 't' following the locators refer to boxes, figures and tables cited in the text.

A.H. Ross, S.M. Abel (eds.), *The Juvenile Skeleton in Forensic Abuse Investigations*, DOI 10.1007/978-1-61779-255-7,

MIX
Papier aus verantwortungsvollen Quellen
Paper from responsible sources
FSC® C105338

If you have any concerns about our products,
you can contact us on
ProductSafety@springernature.com

In case Publisher is established outside the EU,
the EU authorized representative is:
Springer Nature Customer Service Center GmbH
Europaplatz 3, 69115 Heidelberg, Germany

Printed by Libri Plureos GmbH
in Hamburg, Germany